**PRACTICAL TOOLS
FOR NOT-FOR-PROFIT LEADERS**

CREATING SOCIAL IMPACT

ACHIEVING FINANCIAL SUSTANABILITY

and

DRIVING POLICY CHANGE

**NICHOLAS TORRES
TINE HANSEN-TURTON**

Copyright 2018 by Social Innovations Partners
All rights reserved

No part of this publication may be reproduced, stored in a retrieval system, or transmitted in any form or by any means, electronic, mechanical, photocopying, recording, or otherwise, without the prior permission of Social Innovations Journal Publishing Company.

Social Innovations Publishing Company
970 Sproul Road
Bryn Mawr, PA 19010

ACKNOWLEDGEMENTS

Our promise to you is that there is nothing more fulfilling in life than working for a mission driven not-for-profit that serves people in need. We both established roots in the not-for-profit sector early on and became executive directors in our late twenties. While we were both passionate about our organization's missions, the reality is that neither of us, initially, was adequately prepared to lead a not-for-profit. Contrary to popular belief, not-for-profits are not easy to manage or lead, they are highly complex organizations that are often highly regulated. Not-for-profits are essentially the "middle-child" of government and the private sector. They serve as agents of government and guards against the profit driven private sector, which often do not take the social needs of people in mind when they make decisions. For that reason, not-for-profit leaders have to understand politics just as much as they have to understand managing an organization that has good outcomes and is sustainable.

We wrote this book to help everyone who wants to or works in the not-for-profit sector to have practical tools and strategies available to them to lead a high performing not-for-profit. It is essentially our "brain-dump" with "to dos" and "not to dos" when working in or leading a not-for-profit.

Now, we fully recognize that no one becomes an expert without the support of many people on our journey who we worked for or who mentored us along the way. For the past 25 years we have been fortunate to have people in our lives who shaped who we are as leaders and taught us a lot about leadership. These people have come from all sectors, such as government, the private and nonprofit sectors, as well as community leaders.

Thank you to all of you. We would not be here today without your support and guidance. Special thanks to Alescia Dingle for editing the book.

Michael Ayotte
Dominique Bernardo
Aaron Binder
David Castro
Pat DeLeon
Julie Cousler Emig
Cynthia Figueroa
Diane Gass
Web Golinkin
Nilsa Gonzales
Jeff Gordon
William Green
Dan Hawkins
Dr. Frances Hughes

David Hunter
The late Trellie Johnakin
Steve Kaplan
Tom Knox
Alba Martinez
Wanda Mial
Wanda Novales
Pedro Ramos
Hal Rosenbluth
Sandra Ryan
Teresa Sarmina
Susan Sherman
Laura Shubilla
Kenneth Trujillo
The late Virginia Wilks
John F. White, Jr.
Kelly Woodland

Congreso Board of Directors and colleagues
Convenient Care Association Board of Directors and colleagues
Fels Institute of Government Current and Past Leadership: University of Pennsylvania
National Nursing Centers Consortium Board of Directors and colleagues
Philadelphia Housing Authority colleagues
PHMC leadership, Board of Directors and colleagues
Woods Services Board of Directors and colleagues and colleagues
The late Fred DiBona (formerly Independence Blue Cross)
The late Andrew Swinney (formerly Philadelphia Foundation)

Our Friends and Family

AUTHORS' NOTE

PRACTICAL TOOLS FOR NOT-FOR-PROFIT LEADERS is designed for Board Members and Not-for-profit Managers and Leaders who are relatively new in their roles and have a practitioner's interest in the development, leadership, and management of not-for-profit organizations and their intersection with the private sector and government. Giving not-for-profit leaders practical tools to be successful provides readers with the essential competencies, tools, and ready-to-use materials to manage, lead, and conduct in-depth analysis of a not-for-profit's effectiveness, ultimately leading to social impact, financial sustainability, and systems and policy impact. Giving not-for-profit leaders practical tools to be successful also addresses contemporary challenges related to organizational ethics, accountability, emerging legal frameworks, and public policy.

Readers are provided with "best practice" templates that include articles of incorporation, bylaws, governance roles, strategic business plans, organizational scorecards, three-year budget projections, development plans, and public policy strategies that can be applied to the governance, leadership, strategic and/or business model, financial sustainability, social impact, marketing and communications, and public policy of their own organization to influence best practices.

PRACTICAL TOOLS FOR NOT-FOR-PROFIT LEADERS is the result of more than 50 years of combined experience of founding and leading small, large, regional, and national service and policy organizations in health, education, human services, and social enterprise sectors; interviewing and collaborating with hundreds of not-for-profit intermediaries and 10 years of teaching the course, Leading Nonprofits, at the University of Pennsylvania. This Playbook is composed of our validation of much of the current literature in not-for-profit leadership and many of our own practices leading to socially impactful and financially sustainable not-for-profits. Throughout the Playbook, you will find useful templates that can be used for any not-for-profit organization or anyone interested in starting one.

The intention of this playbook is to give not-for-profit leaders the knowledge and a practical toolbox to successfully lead in the evolving social sector.

PRACTICAL TOOLS FOR NOT-FOR-PROFIT LEADERS

SOCIAL IMPACT
FINANCIAL SUSTAINABILITY
POLICY PLAYBOOK

AUTHORS
NICHOLAS TORRES, MEd
TINE HANSEN-TURTON, MGA, JD, FCPP, FANN

CASE STUDY AUTHORS
Lauren Buckheit
Katie Chisholm
Jennifer Chu
David Griffith
Justin Harlem
Frances Hughes
Alyssa Kaminski
Sam Margolius
Denise Mount
Megan Osvath
Jacqueline Omorogbe
Callie Perrone
Brian Valdez
Allison Wortley

CONTENTS

Introduction ... 1

Chapter 1: Incorporation Strategy, Organizational Policies, and Key Decisions ... 3

Chapter 2: Social Impact Leadership and Governance ... 9
- Theory of Change Related to Strategic Action Plans
- Scorecards for Effective Governance

Chapter 3: Financial Sustainability and Building Profits in Your Not-for-Profit ... 15
- Internal Financial Controls
- Fiscal Agent Considerations
- Building Three-Year Financial Projections
- Building Profits in Your Not-for-Profit
- Forms 990 and Audit Considerations

Case Studies
Education Plus Health by Megan Osvath ... 21
Greensgrow by Katie Chisholm ... 23

Chapter 4: Branding, Marketing, and Raising Money ... 25
- For Profit vs. Not-for-Profit Considerations
- Not-for-Profit Funding Models
- Donor Prospectus
- Case Statements and Investment Plans

Case Studies
Common Market by Alyssa Kaminski ... 33
Philly Basketball by Jennifer Chu ... 35
WOMAN'S WAY by Lauren Buckheit, Denise Mount, and Allison Wortley ... 39

Chapter 5: Leadership; Performance Management; Professional Development, and Culture of Innovation ... 43
- Culture of Innovation
- Leadership Considerations
- Organizational Culture/Context Considerations
- Rethinking Performance Evaluations
- Rethinking Professional Development
- Employee Manual Considerations

Case Studies
Food Trust by Callie Perrone and Jacqueline Omorogbe　　51
Starfinder Foundation by Sam Margolius　　55

Chapter 6: Creating and Leading Systems and Policy Change　　59
- Players and Power Map
- Process and Collaborations
- Written and Oral Public Testimony
- Legislation

Case Studies
Muddy Books by David Griffith　　69
Principles for Changing Policy with Limited
Resources: Nurse-Led Care by Brian Valdez　　77
Providing Nursing Leadership in a Community
Residential Mental Health Setting -- Case Study in
New Zealand by Frances Hughes　　89
Border Action Network Case Study: Advocating
Policy Change to Elected Officials by Justin Harlem　　101

About the Authors　　109
Endnotes　　229

APPENDICES
Appendix A: IRS CODE　　117
Appendix B: Governance/Bylaws Template　　121
Appendix C: Budget Projection Template　　161
Appendix D: Internal Control Manual Template　　163
Appendix E: Fiscal Sponsor Template　　171
Appendix F: Case Statement Template　　175
Appendix G: Marketing and Communications Strategies　　177
Appendix H: Organizational Health Assessment　　185
Appendix I: Human Resources Categories　　187
Appendix J: Policy Brief Instruction and Examples　　191
Appendix K: Policy Brief and Testimony Templates　　195
Appendix L: Policy Fact Sheet Examples　　219
Appendix M: Sample Legislation　　223

INTRODUCTION

Over the past two decades, inequality and poverty have become more pervasive in the United States. Economic data shows that the divide in the United States between the haves and the have-nots is growing. High levels of inequality are more prevalent across all types of counties today than two decades ago[i]. As an example, according to Elizabeth Bradley, Yale Global Health Leadership Institute, there is a direct correlation between health outcomes and a country's investment in the social supportive web of education, social mobility, housing, transportation, and safety. Yet, we find that the United States invests only half of what other developed countries do in social services.

This reality represents a failure of our policies and institutions that are responsible for providing and paying for public services. If we use economic inequality as a measure, we can conclude that the United States' federal and state policies and their implementation have caused more harm than good over the last two decades.

In our combined 50+ years of experience working on social sector system change, we have observed that very little disruption occurs in the social sector, unlike in the private sector, which thrives on market-driven consumer feedback and behavior. This is primarily because our social sector institutions including government, foundations, and not-for-profits, typically fund and serve the consumers of public services, exist in a closed system. In this system, the funder (i.e., government, quasi-government, and foundations) and service providers make the decisions on behalf, sometimes with passive input, of the recipient consumer. In many cases, this results in the recipient consumer being left with substandard services or products because the provider has not been "forced" to evolve through consumer-driven feedback or choice. These substandard services are amplified as funding decisions exist in silos (e.g. HUD, HHS, Environment, Education, Labor) that don't connect, resulting in inconsistent and often harmful policies that are in conflict with one another. As a result, well-intentioned social sector change agents reach high levels of frustration and feelings of helplessness when they want to develop new models to address significant social issues or influence system change.

More recently, and potentially more relevantly, actors in the Social Innovation and Enterprise Sector are concluding that they need to engage the world of public policy and systems change if their solutions are going to have large-scale impact. Large-scale change can only be achieved through national, state, and local system and policy changes that truly embrace innovation and the new social sector models. It is our belief that not-for-profits and social enterprises need to be these Social Capital/Policy Agents, as they are motivated by the desire to have an impact on the social good through fostering policy change, and they are there for the long-term.

Currently, the Typical Not-for-profit/NGO Landscape includes a high degree of complex programs, services, and customers, but often doesn't have a business or sustainability plan beyond grant funding. The daily life of the typical not-for-profit executive includes questions such as: How much money do we need? Where can we find the money? Why isn't there more of it? Meanwhile, philanthropists are struggling to understand the impact of their donations.

As mentioned above, part of the underlying problem in the not for profit sector is that the customer or beneficiary is not the payer but is the recipient of the value provided by a third-party payer often leading to perceived vs. real value of a service or product. The Typical For-Profit Landscape, on the other hand, has a high degree of clarity on financial issues and whose principles of business models are widely known and accepted. There might not be uniformity, but there is general agreement among investors and business leaders about what is important and how to measure success. The daily life of the typical for-profit executive includes asking questions such as: Are we selling? Where can we find investments? Who are our customers and where is the market place? Funders/Investors are close to the business leaders and communicate succinctly about investments and investment strategies. In for-profits, customers are the source of revenue and pay for value.

Over the years, we've come to understand a few key realities for the not-for-profit sector. First, the best way to understand a not-for-profit is not necessarily from their website or marketing materials, but from their financials. Understand a not-for-profit's financials and you will gain a better understanding of the not-for-profit's priorities. Second, despite being independent entities, many not-for-profits do not operate as independent "thinkers," but rather adapt their behavior to the interests of funders. One of the largest challenges a not-for-profit leader has to grapple with is dealing with funders who have strong opinions on their investments. We explore this challenge in depth in Chapter 4.

Returning to the idea that financials tell the real story of any not-for-profit, in 2009, William Landes Foster, Peter Kim, & Barbara Christiansen published an article[ii] in *Stanford Social Innovations Review* identifying 10 distinct funding models. We continue to reference this article in our writings and teachings because it represents the reality of how our not-for-profit industry has evolved over time and leaders, in order to be successful, need to understand this evolution in the reality of operating a not-for-profit. The first three models (Heartfelt Connector, Beneficiary Builder, and Member Motivator) are funded largely by many individual donations. One model (Big Bettor) is funded largely by a single person or by a few individuals or foundations. Three models (Public Provider, Policy Innovator, and Beneficiary Broker) are funded largely by the government. One model (Resource Recycler) is supported largely by corporate funding. And two models (Market Maker and Local Nationalizer) have a mix of funders.

We conclude that examining a not-for-profit funding strategy is critical to understanding its success and to position the organization within a funding sphere.

CHAPTER 1: INCORPORATION STRATEGY, ORGANIZATIONAL POLICIES, AND KEY DECISIONS

This chapter provides a general overview of the essential steps and documents you will need for starting a not-for-profit corporation. More important than the steps themselves is answering critical questions about your not-for-profit and defining how the not-for-profit will be governed and managed. Not-for-profits are governed by multiple individuals requiring, oftentimes, long hours of discussion to reach critical decisions before a not-for-profit can be incorporated.

Let's start with an overview of what is a not-for-profit. A not-for-profit is a type of corporation that is founded for public benefit to accomplish a mission, isn't operated for the financial benefit of individuals, has individuals who organize and speak together for a common mission, and provides collective action for the public good. Not-for-profits are formal, private, self-governing corporations that do not distribute profits and, instead, return excess revenue to the organization's mission. Not-for-profits generally have voluntary, non-compensated, boards. The term not-for-profit combines two meanings: that of a <u>state</u> not-for-profit corporation and <u>federal</u> tax exemption status: 501(c)(3).

Not-for-profits serve the community in many ways and include, among the most commonly known of the charitable organizations 501(c)(3), the organization types below:

- Schools, education, and job skills training
- Arts and culture
- Environmental protection and awareness
- Religion
- Human services
- Health care
- Social and economic justice
- Training and technical assistance
- Research
- Philanthropy
- Recreation
- Consumer protection
- Job skills development

Not-for-profits make contributions to society and are the "glue that holds communities together." They are viewed as the social capital of a civil society. Every type of belief, artistic endeavor, democratic practice, and individual right is played out in the not-for-profit sector and not-for-profits play important social, economic, and political roles. Most major social changes in American history came from the not-for-profit sector.

Economically, according to the National Center for Charitable Statistics (NCCS), more than 1.5 million not-for-profit organizations are registered in the U.S. This number includes public charities, private foundations, and other types of not-for-profit organizations, including chambers of commerce, fraternal organizations, and civic leagues. This represents 9.2 percent of all wages paid out in the United States. Public charities, in 2013, reported more than $1.74 trillion in total revenues and $1.63 trillion in total expenses.

The first question, before you incorporate as a not-for-profit, is to ask yourself whether not-for-profit is the right legal status you need to accomplish your social mission.

Consider the following realities:
- There isn't any real advantage to being a not-for-profit except to secure tax exemption status. If you are operating within the framework of a social enterprise (contractual, earned income, et al) you might achieve your goals through operating like a for-profit.
- Competition for contributions and grants is greater than ever and there is potential redundancy in the sector. With limited funds, competition does not always equate to better services, as often, redundancy signifies no entity has sufficient funds to operate effectively.
- You might be able to achieve your social goals through utilizing another not-for-profit as a Fiscal Agent/Not-for-profit Intermediary.
- The direction and purpose of your social mission, by incorporating as a not-for-profit, will now be determined by a board of directors and/or members, limiting your authority and autonomy.
- Not-for-profits are heavily regulated, requiring much paperwork and oversight including but not limited to: Articles of incorporation, by-laws, tax exemption application to federal and state tax bodies.
- A tremendous amount of time and energy, that could be used to advance a social mission, is used toward maintaining a board, corporate records, running programs, and membership maintenance.
- Not-for-profits restrict political activity.

Ultimately, you will need to analyze the above limitations and may determine it is better to incorporate as a for-profit. To further guide you, we recommend that you do not incorporate as a not-for-profit if: you are time-limited, you need to support an individual in need, you think a lot of grant money will be available, you have something you want to sell below cost and get a tax exemption, you need a career change or more meaningful work, you want to be free of bureaucracy, or you want to share important knowledge or perspectives.

Assuming you still want to incorporate as a not-for-profit, below are many of the advantages that include:

- Not-for-profit corporations are able to access foundation grants and often have advantages in receiving government contracts.
- Not-for-profits as corporations have limited liability that generally means that members are **not** held personally liable for the debts and obligations of the company.
- Not-for-profits can enjoy a perpetual existence. Even if you stop operations, you always have the option to re-start operations when funding becomes available.
- The most common not-for-profit, a 501(c)(3) tax exemption, can grant you state and federal income tax exemption, tax deductible donations, eligibility for public funds, lower rates on postal and other services, and estate tax benefits

---

Not-for-Profit Preparations
Before you prepare the forms for incorporation you will need to have the following information to complete the necessary forms:
1. A name that is not misleading and not currently in existence
2. An office location and address
3. A clear vision and mission that is somewhat broad in scope and benefits public good
4. A program and evaluation plan
5. An execution strategy that includes budget revenues and expense projections: The organization must receive most of its money from broad public sources (donations, fundraisers, foundations) or government, no more than one-third from one single private source, and no more than two-thirds from fees for service.
6. A list of convening board members and supporters: Board Members should be selected based upon Passion / Interest / Commitment; Expertise; Connections / Resources; Diversity; and Potential Customers.
7. A selected Executive Director/CEO/President

Before you incorporate, you will need to determine the type of not-for-profit your organization should be from the IRS Code listed in **APPENDIX A.** Keep in mind that the most popular not-for-profit is a 501(c)3. Appendix A provides you with a list of types of not-for-profits the IRS recognizes.

Not-for-Profit Powers
Before you incorporate you should understand the powers of a not-for-profit corporation. These include:
- To use a corporate seal
- To alter bylaws
- To operate in other states and countries
- To deal in, and with, its own bonds, notes, debt securities, etc.
- To have members

- To establish fringe benefits and indemnification plans
- To levy dues, assessments, and admission fees
- To make donations to other institutions
- To borrow money
- To do business jointly with other people and entities
- To act as a trustee
- To engage in for-profit activity (as long as board members do not receive profits; money must be turned back to services)
- To do just about anything -- all the powers of a natural person

Not-for-Profit Governance Documents
Before you incorporate you will need to write the organization's governance or bylaws **(APPENDIX B).** Bylaws are rules made by a company or society to control the actions of its members. The Bylaw Provisions include:
- Purpose: "As stated in the Articles of Incorporation."
- Number of Directors: You must have one. We recommend at least five. You will need to determine if you will only have a Directorship in which the not-for-profit is self-governed by the directors or a Membership and Directorship in which members appoint directors to govern on their behalf.
- Term for Directors: It must be at least one year. We recommend at least two years and staggered terms.
- Board Meetings: They must be at least annual. We recommend monthly meetings during the first year.
- Board Committees: Executive; Finance; Audit; Governance; and Development.
- Officers: You must have a President, Secretary, and Treasurer. We recommend a Vice-President as well.
- Quorum:
    - Must have at least a majority when Board is fewer than seven
    - Must have at least one-third when Board is more than seven
    - Recommend majority
- Dedication of assets: providing for distribution of assets upon dissolution.

Not-for-Profit Forms
Form 1023: Organizations file the 1023 form to apply for recognition of exemption from federal income tax under section 501(c)(3). You may be eligible to file Form 1023-EZ, a streamlined version of the application for recognition of tax exemption. This form determines your tax-exempt status.
- Requires a budget and fundraising plan.
- Federal application determines whether your organization meets the "public support test."
- You will receive an "initial letter of determination," good for three to five years, then you will need to apply for permanent status.

IRS Form 1023 exceptions include:
- Churches and related associations/schools

- Branch of national exempt organization
- Organizations with gross receipts under $5,000 annually.

Form SS-4: This form is used to apply for an employer identification number (EIN). An EIN is a nine-digit number (for example, 12-3456789) assigned to employers, sole proprietors, corporations, partnerships, estates, trusts, certain individuals, and other entities for tax filing and reporting purposes.

Other Registrations to Consider
- Charitable Trust (Attorney General)
- Charitable solicitation registration (Dept. of Attorney General)
- Lobbying registration (Dept. of State)
- State and local withholding (Dept. of Treasury)
- Sales Tax (Dept. of Treasury)
- Property Tax (local assessor)
- Not-for-profit postage rates (U.S. Post Office)

Ongoing Operations
- Annual filings
- Insurance
- Financials & audits
- Employment administration

Many estimate the incorporation process for a not-for-profit to take approximately 70 hours of preparation and the answering of critical questions. As not-for-profits are governed by a board, more important than the answers to the critical questions are the board and leadership process that builds the desired governance and leadership culture.

The preparation time and costs can be significantly reduced by using pre-existing templates. We'd strongly advocate for a final legal review and filing once critical decisions are made.

CHAPTER 2: SOCIAL IMPACT LEADERSHIP AND GOVERNANCE

Most individuals or groups who want to form a not-for-profit start with their mission and vision statements. In our opinion, if a not-for-profit wants to be effectively governed and led, new and existing not-for-profit boards and leadership teams need to take a different approach.

Instead of starting and oftentimes getting stuck on mission and vision statements, we advocate for starting with a solid theory of change and, in concrete terms, defining what social impacts one's efforts hope to achieve. Both a good theory of change and concrete expected social impacts will not only inform a not-for-profit's vision and mission but will also provide the not-for-profit with the tools and structure leading to effective governance and leadership. Before you can develop your not-for-profit, you must develop a theory of change. A theory of change drives your not-for-profit's purpose by identifying the population targeted for service and the outcomes of your program's actions. An effective theory of change has meaning for stakeholders, clearly states how the program will be delivered, and can be measured or tracked over time.

This chapter will help you understand the importance of an organizational theory of change and its relation to strategic action plans and impact measures, and their relation to effective governance/management; social return on investment (SROI); and scorecards with the purpose of using data to drive and adapt service models.

Why Join a Not-for-Profit Board?

Most individuals join a not-for-profit board because they want to contribute to society, to meet/network with new people to gain new skills, because they believe in the mission of the organization, for personal growth or fulfillment, and/or for professional development. Yet, many forget that joining a not-for-profit board comes with legal and financial responsibilities and risks.

The primary responsibilities of a not-for-profit board member are governance and legal as outlined below. Some board members confuse governance with operations. It is advised to define clearly the governance (board of directors) versus leadership roles (executive director) in order to avoid conflicts.

Governance Responsibilities

1. Determine the organization's mission and purpose
2. Select the Chief Executive
3. Support the Chief Executive and assess performance
4. Ensure effective organizational planning
5. Ensure adequate resources
6. Manage resources effectively
7. Determine, monitor and strengthen the organization's programs and services
8. Enhance the organization's public standing
9. Ensure legal and ethical integrity and maintain accountability
10. Recruit and orient new board members and assess board performance

Legal Responsibilities
Many board members do not realize their legal duties and accountability when joining a not-for-profit board. All board members have the duties of care, loyalty, and obedience as defined by case law and this includes legal standards against which all actions taken by board members are held.

Accountability is demonstrated through the effective discharge of Duty of Care; Duty of Loyalty; and Duty of Obedience. Board members should fully understand the significance behind each of these.

- Duty of Care includes being reasonably informed about the organization's activities, participating in good-faith decision-making, and exercising care of an ordinarily prudent person.
- Duty of Loyalty includes exercising power in the best interest of the organization and avoiding self-interest and affirming conflicts of interest. This includes adherence to policy, full disclosure, and abstaining from discussion and voting when conflicts arise.
- Duty of Obedience includes compliance with applicable federal, state, and local laws, adhering to the organization's bylaws, and being a guardian of the organizational mission.

Financial Responsibilities
Fiscal Responsibility starts with the understanding of financial data, managing risks, and, ultimately, ensuring the organization's financial stability.

- Understanding Financial Data includes ensuring the proper preparation of, and approving of, a realistic budget, reading and understanding financial reports, requesting clarification for any not understood or questionable financial data, and ongoing and close monitoring.
- Ensuring Financial Stability includes determining current revenue sources, actively seeking to identify new sources of revenue, supporting the organization monetarily, and, when appropriate, enhancing earned revenue activities.
- Managing Risk includes assessing potential exposure and maintaining appropriate insurance coverage (i.e. Director and Officers; Exclusions; Riders; Special Policies).

Operational Responsibilities
Effective governance starts with quality board management which can be achieved with clearly defined and communicated time commitments that include governance, committee meetings, and events; meeting schedules/dates set annually to ensure a quorum; and clear objectives for committee meetings.

Managing board meetings for optimum productivity includes establishing committee structures; planning for effective use of time (i.e., a consent agenda is a board meeting practice that groups routine business and reports into one agenda item where many items can be approved of in one action, rather than filing motions on each item separately); predetermining if a board item is classified as Information, Discussion, or Decision; and ensuring good information flows through integrated technology (email, web site, teleconferencing, etc.).

To effectively govern, we remind not-for-profit boards that they need both a good theory of change and concrete expected social impacts that will provide the not-for-profit with the tools and structure for effective governance.

Let's explore this concept further. A common practice for boards is strategy planning. We argue that before any type of strategic planning can occur, a board has to have a clear theory of change and clear impact measures defining what they hope to socially achieve. Once a theory of change and social outcomes are defined, strategic planning is focused on how to achieve the theory and social outcomes.

Much has been written about a not-for-profit Theory of Change. We've chosen to highlight the Hunter approach as it is concerned with the macro organization strategy and not programs. The Hunter approach defines a theory of change as the systematic linkages that align an organization's daily operations (the things front-line staff do) with the organization's overarching strategy. A Theory of Change ties together an organization's motivating thoughts with the actual, hard facts of its performance -- and provides a blueprint for getting performance to match intentions. According to Hunter, a Theory of Change must be:

- Meaningful -- It describes the whole organization accurately in ways the Board of Directors, executive leaders, managers, and staff acknowledge is accurate and persuasive. Furthermore, it is designed to accomplish something of value, recognizable as such by all interested parties ("stakeholders" both internal and external).
- Plausible -- If the efforts it describes can be implemented, they are likely to achieve intended goals, objectives, and outcomes.
- Doable -- It is realistic, taking into account the organization's capacities in relation to its resources, context, or environment. In other words, it describes something that really can be achieved within existing constraints.
- Measurable -- It is made real by measuring key areas of performance, including outcomes and other indicators of success.
- Monitorable -- The theory of change provides a useful framework for an organization to monitor and manage organizational performance and to improve and maintain the quality and effectiveness of its programming in an ongoing and sustainable manner.

In simplistic terms, we define a theory of change as the organization's hypothesis or theory about what impact they will have if they provide a particular type of service or intervention.

Once a not-for-profit board has a good theory of change it can move to defining what social impacts it wants to achieve. We again point the reader to Hunter's thinking as a way to put an organization's social impact objectives into concrete terms. We recommend Hunter's thinking, despite not being directly applicable to advocacy, intermediaries, or system change organizations, because, ultimately, we are attempting to socially impact people.

As we think about social impact on individuals, Hunter states that "generally one acquires knowledge before improving skills, improves skills before changing attitudes, changes attitudes before adjusting behavior, adjusts behavior before improving achievements, achieves new things before attaining new heights, and attains new heights before changing life status." Below is a list of types of outcomes an organization can adapt. Key to selection for organizational outcomes is ensuring the outcomes can be MEASURED and the organization will be held ACCOUTABLE to them.

Hunter Social Outcomes:
- Change in Knowledge (e.g., acquisition of information about sound parenting practices, nutrition, technology, effective communication)
- Change in Skills (e.g., improved reading and math skills, work readiness skills, parenting skills, conflict management skills)
- Change in Attitude (e.g., commitment to the importance of success in education, success at work, reading to one's children, treating young people with respect, eating healthy foods and exercising)
- Change in Behavior (e.g., eating nutritious food and exercising, attending school regularly, completing homework, avoiding "trigger" situations that lead to high-risk behavior, maintaining employment)
- Change in Achievement (e.g., better report card grades, improved standardized test scores, better work performance, bringing an unstable medical condition under control)
- Change in Attainment (e.g., graduating high school, completing post-secondary education, having self-sustaining employment, having achieved a new and sustainable level of functioning)
- Change in Status (e.g., being healthy; being a student, a dropout, or a graduate; being employed or unemployed; having a supportive social network)

Once an organization has a good theory of change and concrete social impact measures, the organization has the tools to insert these into an organizational scorecard. We argue that an organization's scorecard is ESSENTIAL for effective governance as the board is provided with social metrics to confirm its organizational vision and mission are being achieved. More importantly than the scorecard itself, is that it provides board members with social sector data and the ability to use this data to drive an organizational strategy or service model. Below is an example of an organizational scorecard. We would recommend the inclusion of a baseline expected outcome in the below example that Nicholas Torres and his team developed at Congreso de Latinos Unidos in 2018. Done right a scorecard will withstand the test of time.

Education Outcomes

Indicator Name	Outcome	
Increased numeracy and/or literacy skills in alternative education (TABE Score)	49% increased	46 clients
Increased numeracy skills in traditional education (Math Grade)	94% increased	1164 clients
Increased literacy skills in traditional education (English Grade)	93% increased	1081 clients
Proficient or Advanced in Reading (Pan American PSSA Results)	31% increased	130 clients
Proficient or Advanced in Math (Pan American PSSA Results)	11% increased	46 clients
Attended school regularly (80% attendance rate or better)	97% attended regularly	930 clients
Promoted to the next grade (Edison, Norristown and Kensington H.S. afterschool)	90% promoted	85 clients
Obtained a GED	Obtained GED	14 clients
Obtained an Associate's Degree	Obtained an Associates Degree	38 clients

Employment Outcomes

Indicator Name	Outcome	
Obtained industry-recognized certification	91% certified	42 clients
Placed in a job	95% placed	35 clients
Reached 6 months of job retention	89% retained	33 clients

Supportive Services: Economic Stability

Indicator Name	Outcome	
Applied for public benefits	applied	676 clients
Returned tax dollars to community members	$ 948,823 dollars returned	515 clients
Increased financial management knowledge	53% increased	39 clients
Purchased a home	purchased	7 clients
Prevented foreclosures	prevented	202 clients

Supportive Services: Client Health & Safe Living Outcomes

Indicator Name	Outcome	
Increased knowledge of nutrition and disease	63% increased	217 clients
Increased knowledge of domestic violence	73% increased	217 clients
Increased parenting knowledge	55% increased	44 clients
Developed safety plan (DV survivors)	81% planned	83 clients
Achieved good adherence to HIV treatment	80% succeed	164 clients

Primary Client Model (PCM™) Outcomes

Indicator Name	Outcome	
Clients Addressing at least one Issue Area identified on Progress check	82% addressed issues	942 clients

Source: http://www.congreso.net/impact/impact-metricsdata/

Measuring outcomes is a necessary step to achieve effective social impact governance and, though it can pose considerable challenges, it is not as difficult as many might suggest. The primary difficulty lies in determining which data are needed, and establishing an efficient, accurate system for collecting them over time. To quantify and confirm impact, outcomes must be directly attributable to an organization's program or service.

Strategic Action Planning
As there has been much written about strategic planning we will not provide an elaborate recommended process in this playbook. However, we will refer you to the chapter in our book, *Social Innovation and Impact in Nonprofit Leadership* titled The Death of Planning -- the Birth of Strategic Action Plans, that emphasizes the broader business of planning process that focuses on identifying market-based, sustainable, and value-added solutions.

The best planning processes for today's environment are those that meet organizations where they are, create a framework for dealing with change, and build structures through which decision makers are able to access information to measure impact and respond to evolving realities. Most important in any strategic planning process is to remember the value of strategic planning is not necessarily the plan itself but the process and its effectiveness in engaging and building "buy-in" with key stakeholders.

Conclusion
Most not-for-profit boards have financial management competencies but are not provided with the data and metrics for effective social impact governance. We argue that a not-for-profit cannot be effectively governed or effectively develop strategic action plans if it doesn't have a well-developed theory of change; or concrete social sector metrics framed within a governance scorecard. Most importantly, the discipline of a theory of change and tracking social outcomes provides the organization with data to inform an organizational strategy and/or adapt service models.

CHAPTER 3: FINANCIAL SUSTAINABILITY AND BUILDING PROFITS IN YOUR NOT-FOR-PROFIT

Many funding streams for not-for-profits that serve many of the most vulnerable come from government and philanthropy sources. Given the restrictive nature of these grants and contracts, not-for-profits often find themselves in a position where they cannot generate enough administration support to cover their costs or plan for end of the year surpluses. With these restrictions, most not-for-profits find it impossible to build reserves leading to healthy cash flow and assets. This chapter, in addition to touching upon building financial projections and creating internal financial controls, provides insight to financial strategies to create annual surpluses, thereby, moving not-for-profits to a position of being financially healthy.

This chapter will help you understand, from a governance and leadership perspective, strategies for building multiple year financial projections, setting up internal financial controls, building profits in your not-for-profit through conservative budgeting, and managing your 990 and Audit process.

Establishing Your Budget and Projections
Given the advancement of accounting software programs, boards and leadership have increasingly relied upon the financial staff and accountants to provide them with a real time budget that includes revenues and expenses. However, accounting software programs and financial staff are limited to providing one- to three-year budget projections, as many of a not-for-profit's key revenue inputs are based upon one-year grants or contract and industry trends resulting in projections based upon assumptions and not reality.

Given the reality that most not-for-profits have to piece together different funding sources to fully cover the costs of initiatives and operations, organizational leadership and development teams often submit for multiple grants outlining program budgets and then compile the organizational budget pieces together to achieve an organizational budget. At best, with this strategy an organization receives all grant and contract revenues and finds itself with additional revenue, as many line items might have been submitted in different budgets. At worst, an organization finds itself at a deficit as fewer projected proposals were funded, thus creating a deficit for administration and organizational costs. These complexities put boards and leadership at a disadvantage to fulfill their financial duties.

An additional challenge for not-for-profit organizations is where and how to allocate EXPENSES across multiple funding sources with different classifications, restrictions, and funding dates. This is especially challenging when the external environment is constantly changing and with inconsistent policies (i.e. allowable administration rates, acceptable expenditures) among different funding sources. This often leaves the leadership and boards "throwing up their hands" and fulfilling their fiduciary responsibility through financial reports that only measure revenues against expenses, BUT do not help in planning or making good projections.

What we recommend, based upon our combined 50+ years managing not-for-profit organizational budgets, in this chapter is to use our excel spreadsheet template that allows the leadership and board, when appropriate, to project, understand, and manage organizational budgets and, therefore, fulfill their fiduciary responsibility. We've outlined three essential steps and a process that allows for boards and leadership to understand and, therefore, plan for their organization's financial health. We've supplied a template in **APPENDIX C** to illustrate the planning document outlined in the following steps.

Step 1: Allocating Staff Salaries Across Revenue Sources
As in any budgeting, **REVENUES** should be classified in the top row with the AMOUNT, TYPE (governmental or foundational grant or contract, restricted or non-restricted, earned revenue), STATUS (confirmed, probability), and DATES. Simply summing the cells will give the not-for-profit leadership and governance a projected annual budget. **EXPENSES** should be classified in the first column and be listed by staff salaries, staff benefits (full-time and part-time), contractors, operational expenses, and administration costs.

Step 2: Changing Agency Fringe, Administration, and FTE Rates
Before EXPENSES can be allocated across REVENUES the organization needs to have a good enough understanding of three key agency line expense items. These include: 1) administration costs that determine an organization's ADMINISTATION RATE; 2) FRINGE BENEFITS; and 3) NUMBER OF FULL TIME EQUIVALENT STAFF (FTE) that are allocated across organizational operational expenses. If the organization budgets conservatively along these three line items, it can successfully strategize and project end of the year surpluses for its organization.

How to Determine an Organization's Administration Rate
The first step is to determine what expenses an organization will include in the administration rate. At the very minimum, the organization should include the administration staff salaries, but there is a question of which administration staff salaries should be included. We recommend that at least fiscal, human resources, development, technology, marketing and communications, and data and evaluation staff are included. What most organizations debate is whether or not to include a percentage of the Executive Director or other administrative management staff salaries. As you can imagine, the higher the number of people included, the higher the organizational administration rate will be. The resulting number divided by the total agency budget will give the organization a conservative administration rate to write into grants and contracts.

Many leaders in the not-for-profit sector would say that determining one's administration rate is a pointless effort as most of the funding streams dictate what level of administration fees they will or will not allow. What we learned is that an organization needs to know and start with their highest (most conservative) administration rate because organizational survival depends upon some funding sources subsidizing those funding sources that are most restrictive.

Surpluses can sometimes be realized across multiple funding sources when administration costs are kept low (budgeted against the lowest projected administration fees collected) and do not exceed the total amount allocated/permitted across all funding sources.

How to Determine an Organization's Fringe Rate
The first step is to determine what costs will be included in an organization's fringe rate. At the very minimum, organizations should include employment taxes, unemployment insurance, health and dental costs, retirement allocations, and/or any additional staff benefit that will have to be paid for by the organization. As most not-for-profit leaders have realized, these costs constantly fluctuate based upon number of employees (weekly/monthly), health and dental insurance increases (annually), and unemployment rates (annually) making it impossible to budget with 100 percent accuracy.

Therefore, we recommend first getting the actual costs per person (health, dental, retirement contribution) and then multiplying it by the **highest** number of full time equivalent employees (conservative budgeting). The resulting number divided by the total agency budget will give the organization a conservative fringe rate to write into grants and contracts.

Surpluses can sometimes be realized across multiple funding sources when more revenues are collected from funding sources than costs expended due to staff fluctuations. These fluctuations are from vacancies and/or savings due to reduced rates.

How to Determine an Organization's Operational Full Time Equivalent Rate
The first step is to determine what hard costs (non-staff) an organization has that need to be allocated across multiple funding sources. These often include real estate (i.e. rent), utilities, technology, marketing/communication, leadership training, and office supplies. By understanding the full amount an organization expects to spend, it can allocate them equitably across all funding sources. In order to do this, the organization needs to determine a FTE rate per category, which is simply the total costs, divided by the total number of employees. However, as most not-for-profit leaders have realized, organizations have unexpected costs and the number of employees fluctuate based upon what grants are obtained or lost.

Therefore, we recommend first getting as close as possible to the actual amount an organization expects to spend on operational costs (real estate, rents, technology, utilities, marketing, training, supplies) and then multiplying it by the **lowest** number of full time equivalent employees. The lowest number will give the organization a higher FTE rate (conservative budgeting). The resulting number divided by the total agency budget will give the organization a conservative FTE rate per organizational category to write into grants and contracts. Surpluses can sometimes be realized when more staff end up being budgeted into contracts then projected as costs are generally fixed while increased staff equals increased revenues.

Step 3: Assigning EXPENSES across multiple REVENUES sources.
The **first step** is to allocate staff salaries across revenue sources with the purpose of ensuring 100 percent of the staff salaries are covered. Direct program staff is the easiest to allocate as they generally only need to be charged to one funding source. Managers and executive staff are a little more challenging because they often need to be charged at different amounts based upon what a funding source can afford. A best practice is that people should be charged according to their time allocation, but the reality is that budgeting occurs based upon what funding source allows for coverage that ensures all staff are covered 100 percent. Along this process, we recommend allocating staff **last** to non-restricted revenue sources as the non-restricted revenue sources are oftentimes the only remedy to cover restricted foundations and governmental grants who do not cover their "fair" share of the organizational costs.

The **second step** is charging agency fringe, administration, and FTE rates across all revenue streams based upon the number of FTE equivalents allocated to the revenue stream.
The **third step** is charging any program specific costs the remaining amounts in a budget.

Once all the expense inputs (salaries, agency fringe, administration, and FTE rates, and program expenses) are entered into the appropriate cells under revenue sources, one is able to determine the following key information: 1) Does each revenue source project a surplus or a deficit?; 2) Are current salaries covered?; and 3) What percentage of the total organizational fixed and variable administration costs are covered? With this information, one is able to reallocate expenses across revenue sources to ensure all expenses are covered, add or remove expenses (salary positions or operational costs) based upon financial results, and set different scenarios if tentative revenue sources become realized. Ultimately, it's important to realize that, because of conservative budgeting along the lines of administration rates, FTE rates, and fringe rates, an organization should, minus a disaster, result in end of the year surpluses adding to a healthy cash flow.

Managing Finances
Once your budget is set, the governance and leadership of a not-for-profit need to understand how to effectively manage and control finances. Although this is the responsibility of the organizational staff, it is the board and leadership's responsibility to ensure the appropriate policies and controls are in place to meet their fiduciary responsibility.

The two primary controls the board and leadership want within their organizational are: 1) ensure that staff are not expending more money than a budget allows and/or that they are not expending it in inappropriate or not permitted ways; and 2) ensure that staff or others are not "stealing" financial resources from the organization.

To accomplish this, unfortunately, one has to think like a "thief" as only by thinking like a thief can an organization build in adequate controls. In the process of thinking like a thief, we discovered that the most prominent and high-risk ways, primarily in large organizations, an individual can "steal" resources from an organization are:

1. Fake positions or enhanced salaries: Payroll is processed by very few people (human resources and fiscal) resulting in payroll becoming an easy target to add or enhance a person's salary. It is the responsibility of the leadership to approve payroll, but when there are a large number of staff members working at an organization it is impossible to recognize everyone's name and do calculations on their salary. The question becomes: What controls and what parties will an organization put in place to prevent this?
2. Fake or enhanced contracts: Another way to "steal" money from an organization is to create "fake" contracts. Often "fake" contracts can go to outside organizations or individuals who work on behalf of the organization. However, as many of the contracts work for programmatic staff, there is the question of whether the work was actually accomplished or if a work contract was created to "steal" money from the organization. Generally, the fiscal staff requires staff signatures to ensure the work was done, but they do not have any context or controls to determine if the work was actually done. The question becomes: What controls and what parties will an organization put in place to prevent this?
3. Influx of Checks and Identical Bank Accounts: Generally, checks are received by a receptionist and delivered to the fiscal staff. A person can easily intercept checks and then deposit them into a bank (different than the bank that the organization banks with) that has the same or a similar name. The question becomes: What controls and what parties will an organization put in place to prevent this?

4. Check Replication: When an organization is processing lots of checks, it becomes difficult to determine if a check was copied, replicated, and cashed. This is especially easy for a staff member to take advantage of when the person who replicates the check knows the order of the check. Oftentimes, a bank will catch the replication, but not before money is lost and, often, unrecoverable. The question becomes: What controls and what parties will an organization put in place to prevent this?
5. Gift Cards or other cash valued assets: When an organization gives out gift cards or other cash valued assets (i.e. transportation tokens) there are not great controls to ensure they are going to the appropriate parties. Generally, a signature is required, but signatures are easily obtained. The question becomes: What controls and what parties will an organization put in place to prevent this?
6. Credit Cards and Fake Receipts: When credit cards are authorized, it means charges that are either not appropriate or approved can be processed. The question becomes: What controls and what parties will an organization put in place to prevent this?
7. Cash Revenues: When cash is taken in, it is very easy for an individual(s) to keep a percentage of the cash. The question becomes: What controls and what parties will an organization put in place to prevent this?

We've provided the start of an Internal Controls Manual Template in **APPENDIX D**, but each organization should add their own policies and procedures to the Internal Control Manual to protect against the above.

Serving as a Fiscal Sponsor
Often, a not-for-profit might be asked to serve as a fiscal sponsor. As a reminder, we encourage people to consider seeking a fiscal sponsor for a program rather than incorporating a new not-for-profit. The general considerations needed are that the work has to be aligned with their mission as stated in the articles of incorporation and that one is assuming fiscal responsibility for an independent group. A fiscal agent template agreement is provided in **APPENDIX E.**

We've provided two case studies, to elaborate on the above points, representing a social enterprise, not-for-profit selling products direct to consumers; a mid/large size not-for-profit receiving contracts, grants, or earned income primarily from governmental sources; and a not-for-profit that is based upon governmental earned income, education, and health reimbursements.

Education Plus Health Case Study
by Megan Osvath

Education Plus Health is a not-for-profit that advocates for school-based health centers (SBHCs) as critical sources of healthcare for underserved students. They provide in-school health services to children of all ages through school nursing and primary care, serving more than 7,000 students in more than two dozen Philadelphia-based SBHCs. By removing barriers to healthcare facing children in underserved communities, Education Plus Health aims to increase both access to healthcare and academic performance. Over the past several years, their organization has helped to reduce emergency department visits, overall Medicaid costs, and absenteeism among asthmatic students by 64 percent.

By nature, Education Plus Health operates under a fee-for-service funding model, gathering approximately 75 percent of annual revenue through Medicare reimbursements. Both public and charter schools pay for their healthcare partnerships with Education Plus Health, which contributes to their earned revenue as well. Thus, this funding model is heavily reliant upon the community of schools participating in their services, which is at times variable as charter schools are required to be re-approved each year. To provide a safeguard against an unforeseen drop in school partnerships, Education Plus Health garners about five percent of their revenue in flexible philanthropic dollars, allowing them to react to these situations more nimbly. Over the next two years, the organization intends to increase their fundraising to 10 percent of revenue to allow for more flexibility and growth as Education Plus Health continues to mature.

Ultimately, peer organizations have only succeeded when their efforts were recognized by the state government, eventually receiving state funding as a significant and stable portion of their revenues. Education Plus Health is no different and will eventually require state support for its financial sustainability over time. Historically, no other school-based health centers have survived indefinitely on a fee-for-service funding model. The key to obtaining this state support is a combination of impact and advocacy: Education Plus Health is working to identify impact indicators for their programs and use those outcome measures to advocate for state support. Recently, the organization performed an external review with the help of a foundation grant, enabling extensive data collection and the creation of outcome metrics for absenteeism and decreased hospital and emergency department visits. Education Plus Health is also leading a coalition of Pennsylvania school-based health centers, uniting their voices in support of the impact they are making in cities across the state. They believe that together, they can produce enough crucial impact measures to convince state legislators that their work is improving both academic achievement and the population's health, particularly in underserved communities.

Unlike a funding model reliant on individual donors, Education Plus Health uses taxpayer dollars to offer services, and can easily be the subject of debate or criticism if found to be non-transparent or untrustworthy. As described in this chapter, it is important to the health of a not-for-profit to ensure that finances are protected, monitored, and reported frequently. Education Plus Health protects against oversight and fraud in many ways, but first and foremost with a comprehensive internal controls manual. The organization outlines all financial procedures in a handbook and reviews it regularly with organization and board leadership to ensure fidelity. Some of the specific controls they maintain include requiring multiple staff signatures on checks and insisting on collecting multiple bids when contracting work. The organization also requires all board members to disclose any potential conflicts of interest, and treat those relationships with caution, when appropriate. In the not-for-profit sector, particularly when providing community services with community dollars, public perception can become reality -- public trust can take years to build but only a matter of days to destroy. Even the perception or hint of impropriety can send a vulnerable organization into a messaging battle with the press and the public. In addition to their extensive internal controls, Education Plus Health also undergoes regular internal reviews and audits, which helps to build trust with the public by displaying clean audits consistently. The organization is able to prove to the public that the financial controls they have in place are not only protecting the not-for-profit from harm, but also setting it up for success with careful budgeting, reasonable spending, and continuous checks and balances to ensure long-term financial health. Because Education Plus Health operates on such a thin margin with little flexible fundraising revenue, this public trust is invaluable to current community success and future success advocating for state support.

In closing, Education Plus Health provides an exceptional example of a healthy not-for-profit organization operating on fees and reimbursements over several years. They have harnessed outcome measurements to show the social impact the organization is making in its community and have spent time planning for future financial sustainability as part of their annual reviews. They are an excellent model for using the tools available at their disposal in the not-for-profit sector to maximize impact on those who need it most.

Greensgrow Case Study
by Katie Chisholm

Since the transition of leadership in 2016 at Greensgrow from Mary Seton Corbo to Ryan Kuck, the organization has undergone an overhaul of organizational finances; implementing formal checks and balances, processes and procedures. A not-for-profit finance expert was hired to dive into the financial structures of the $2 million+ organization to mitigate risk and assess the fiscal health of Greensgrow. Visibility into the financial structures of the organization is essential for sustainability and to identify the effectiveness of the business units that operate under the umbrella of Greensgrow.

Greensgrow generates the majority of its income from the sale of goods and services at several locations throughout the city of Philadelphia. Over an eight-week window of time in the spring, Greensgrow earns 85 percent of its sales revenue. This income is essential for the organization to sustain itself and yet it is completely weather dependent. If the weather does not cooperate for the planting season, they operate with a deficit. Millions of dollars pass through this organization annually, specifically during the spring season, and often as cash transactions. Without formal checks and balances and procedures, there is an increased risk of fraud and exposure of the organization.

The interdependence of the seven unique business units within Greensgrow presents challenges when evaluating their financial solvency. Gaining insight into which business units are profitable versus which business units are strictly a draw on resources will allow for the organization and the board to make informed decisions about their priority areas and the ways in which they can have the greatest impact. As Greensgrow is going through a formal process of developing a consistent mission, vision, and value statement, establishing their priority programming is essential to their identity.

Annually Greensgrow struggles to bridge a 15 percent gap between income and expenses. Due to the nature of their work, selling goods and services, foundation support and grant funding are a challenge to secure. Individual donors are also difficult to identify due to the fact that their individual constituents perceive the purchasing of Greensgrow's produce as supporting the organization in and of itself.

Many organizations want to partner with Greensgrow due to their brand recognition and captive audience; however, this does not often come with financial backing or support. Greengrow's partnership with Subaru is a prime example of this challenge. For years Subaru has partnered with Greensgrow through their marketing and public relations arm, not through their corporate social responsibility arm. Subaru leverages their partnership by co-branding cars and other paraphernalia, however they do not supply operational income support.

Additionally, Greensgrow's main facilities are all located outside without covering. This limits their year to a 10-month cycle versus a 12-month cycle. They are unable to generate income over the first two months of the year due to the weather and as a result they cannot carry all of their employees for a full 12 months. Initiating a capital campaign to build reserves for creating their own indoor structure would allow for them to make money year-round and minimize the funds they have to cultivate through other channels.

Greensgrow is open to exploring alternative business structures depending on the outcome of the financial evaluation of the organization. There is a possibility they could incorporate as a for-profit, they could move into a cooperative model, they could create a for-profit structure within the not-for-profit or they may just strictly remain as a traditional not-for-profit. They are also exploring partnerships with other organizations that will result in financial support. Ryan is charged with moving Greensgrow into the next stage of its legacy, while remaining true to Mary's founding principles.

The upward potential of Greensgrow is limitless, anticipating they can create the right budgetary structure to operate in the black.

CHAPTER 4: BRANDING, MARKETING, AND RAISING CAPITAL

This chapter provides a general overview of strategy that leads to obtaining financial resources to carry out the mission of the not-for-profit. This chapter reminds the reader to first determine if a not-for-profit status is necessary to carry out the social mission. Assuming that the answer is yes, this chapter has the reader analyze the primary 10 not-for-profit funding models and create a development strategy around the one, or combination of funding sources, that best fits their not-for-profit. This chapter concludes with tools and templates related to brand, marketing, and ultimately leveraging investments into the organization.

For-Profit or Not-for-Profit?
Most not-for-profits depend upon philanthropic grants and/or donations and therefore, in our view, may never prove their value-added proposition as a third party is paying for a service and demonstrating social impact in the social sector is extremely complicated. Some not-for profits operate more like for-profit entities, as their financial business model doesn't depend upon philanthropic grants and, yet, they are still creating social good and, often, social impact. Social Enterprise not-for-profits are often contracted by government, quasi-government, and not-for-profits and/or have direct sales to consumers. Many argue that this type of organization is a better business model as the value-added proposition is proven when entities or individuals "purchase" the product or service.

The key consideration to whether a not-for-profit needs to be established is whether or not the entity can exist without philanthropic charitable donations or grants. If it can, there are a few reasons we would suggest that a for-profit entity should be considered, and/or a for-profit/not-for-profit strategic partnership be established.

1. It is likely that the not-for-profit may have to pay taxes on the earned revenue portion of its business and, therefore, obtaining a tax-exempt status is moot.
2. Not-for-profits are heavily regulated (in comparison to for-profits), costing the not-for-profit additional financial resources on governance, compliance, audits, and accounting.
3. Operating with a for-profit mindset keeps the importance of financial revenues on an equal balance with the social impact measures. In the not-for-profit space, often, the individuals are only concerned with the social impact as the revenues were "granted" by a third party only requiring a report on outputs and efforts.
4. For-profit entities can attract social impact investors who will invest in scaling and expansion, thereby increasing the likelihood that the social impact will extend beyond the foundation and charitable support.

Many individuals, despite having an earned revenue business model, may still select to incorporate as a not-for-profit for some of the following reasons.

1. They may need to leverage tax-exempt foundations and other philanthropic support during the start-up phase and/or the earned revenue only covers a portion of the true costs resulting in the need for philanthropic subsidies.
2. Often, governmental or quasi-governmental agencies prefer to contract with not-for-profits instead of for-profits with the knowledge that the public dollars will be required to pass an independent audit verifying the funds were used for intended charitable purposes.
3. For social-political reasons, a not-for-profit might be required to provide needed social impact products or services so as to not be shadowed by the perception that for-profits put margin over mission.

Understanding Not-For-Profit Business Models
Many not-for-profits believe that diversification is the strategy for growth. However, despite diversification being a good idea, in practice, Foster & Gail (2007)[iii], in testing this theory, concluded that most of the organizations that have gotten really big did so by concentrating on one type of funding source, not by diversifying across several sources of funding.

This leads us to conclude that the not-for-profit should develop a strategy based upon the behavior of proven and existing not-for-profits and their investors. In 2009, Foster, Kim, & Christiansen (2009)[iv] categorized 10 primary not-for-profit funding models based upon the source of funds, the types of decision makers, and the motivations of the decision makers.

What is relevant in this chapter is that, before a development, marketing, or branding strategy can be developed, the organization should be informed about these funding models as the not-for-profit will need to leverage investments from one or more of the funding sources.

Key within marketing, branding, or a development strategy should be full knowledge on where the funding will be obtained. According to the study, the types of social sector funds include individual donations, few individuals or foundations, government, corporations, or mixed. The motivations for the investors to provide these funds include: personal impact on self, friends, or family and/or societal benefits.

The 10 Funding Models include:
1. Heartfelt Connector Model (e.g. Komen Foundation) whose descriptors include: individual funding source/s, multiple decision makers, altruism funding motivation, mission has broad appeal, benefits touch lives of funders, and has tactical tools including: special events, corp. sponsorship, direct appeal
2. Beneficiary Builder (e.g. universities) whose descriptors include: individual funding source/s, multiple decision makers, self-interest followed by altruism funding motivation, mission creates strong individual connection and prestige, tactical tools including: Fees, major gifts

3. Member Motivator (e.g. National Public Radio) whose descriptors include: individual funding source/s, multitude of decision makers, collective interest funding motivation, benefits belong to collective community, tactical tools including: membership, fees, special events, major gifts, etc.
4. Big Bettor (e.g. Medical Research) whose descriptors include: individual funding source/s, few individuals are decision makers, altruism funding motivation, mission fulfilled within a few decades, builds majority of support from small number of individuals and foundations, tactical tools including: major gifts
5. Public Provider (Human Services Organization) whose descriptors include: government funding, administrators are decision maker, collective interest funding motivation, provides services that are core gov't responsibility, clear definition of services and process, tactical tools including: government and, sometimes, fees
6. Policy Innovator (e.g. Policy or Advocacy Organization) whose descriptors include: government funding, policymakers are decision makers, collective interest funding motivation, secures funding for new problem-solving approach, addresses problems not currently considered government responsibility, champion is required at gov't level, succeeds with time and pressure, tactical tools including: earmarks, pilot projects, studies
7. Beneficiary Broker (e.g. local Community Development Corporation) whose descriptors include: government funding, multitude of individuals funding decision makers, self-interest funding motivation, individual beneficiaries decide how to spend government benefits, multiple gov't decision makers must be influenced for eligibility and compliance with reimbursement requirements, tactical tools including: government reimbursement
8. Resource Recycler (e.g. Foodbanks, Volunteer orgs, Pharma assistance) whose descriptors include: corporate funding, few individual funding decision makers, self-interest funding motivation, not-for-profits use excess goods produced in the market like pharmaceuticals, textiles, food, etc., tactical tools including: in-kind giving
9. Market Maker (e.g. Environment, conservation, etc.) whose descriptors include: mixed funding, individuals/masses, can be both altruism or self-interest funding motivation, not-for-profit with ability to pay for a good or an individual donating good, tactical tools including: fees and corporate or individual major gifts (land)
10. Local Nationalizer (e.g. Teach for America, Big Brothers, Boys and Girls Clubs) whose descriptors include: mixed funding, few individual funding decision makers, altruism funding motivation, issues critical at the local level and yet common nationally, funding usually limited to areas, tactical tools including: major gifts, special events

The study concludes that it is a mistake for not-for-profit leaders to seek money wherever they can find it. Rather, the not-for-profit leader should be disciplined about a funding strategy and develop it according to the motivations and decision criteria of the individual, foundation, or government source.

We also note that a whole new type of investor has emerged that weighs investments by both financial and social impact returns. This new type of investor may shift the current 10 not-for-profit funding models or, at a minimum, add a new type of not-for-profit funding model that is a blend between the traditional funding models and the private sector.

With full knowledge about the reasoning for choosing a not-for-profit model and determining what funding model and related funder motivations and tactics can be deployed, the not-for-profit board and leader are ready to develop a branding, marketing, and development plan.

The first thing the not-for-profit board and leader should consider is the brand and how they want the not-for-profit to be perceived by investors and consumers. Brand often determines who and what type of investments a not-for-profit can leverage. A strategy to expand upon one's brand and attract funders is a not-for-profit's marketing strategy. Finally, an initial development plan should be based upon relationships with potential investors.

Branding
To start, the not-for-profit should consider its brand. Social investors are usually risk-averse resulting in them not investing or contracting with not-for-profits that have a tainted brand. A tainted brand can include any negative media attention, questionable leadership, audit management letters, negative end of year fiscal balances/declining net assets, and perceived conflicts of interest. Regarding perceived conflicts of interest, the government may not have any issues with conflicts, but foundations and donors often don't want to provide grants/donations to organizations who hire or contract with family members related to the board and/or staff leadership. There is always extra risk that the organization mission might come into conflict.

Marketing
A marketing plan, at its center, should pick the target donor and/or investor and then develop strategies around the target donor. At this stage, we go back to the type of funding model the not-for-profit is using and pick from some of the tactical tools. Different tactics need to be applied if one is requesting funds from a multitude of individuals, fewer but larger individual donors, family foundations (i.e. driven by family members), institutional foundations (i.e. driven by hired staff), and/or corporations (motivated by bottom line and city, state, and federal policies or regulations effecting products). If the target is governmental grants, then a marketing strategy needs to be focused on reaching local, regional, state, and national governmental agencies and might be focused more on writing competitive proposals. To write competitive proposals often requires hiring or working with grant writers who have served on review panels and understand how grants are rated. Our experience tells us that the more local a governmental agency is, the more funding might depend upon an organization's brand. The more federal a governmental agency is, the more funding might depend upon the quality of the grant proposal and ability for the organization (e.g. only large not-for-profits need apply) to manage large projects and have sufficient cash flow.

Development: When constructing developmental plans for individuals/foundations, one needs to consider the two primary factors of passion/purpose and access via relationships. The first step is to prospect what foundations fund the organizational mission. The easiest way to obtain a list of foundations (within search criteria such as geographic location) is to obtain it from the Foundation Directory Online Professional that can often be accessed via the Public Library system. This directory will list the foundation, its geographic focus, focus areas and funding interests, size of grants, assets, grant recipients, and, sometimes, contact information. The easiest way to get a list is by buying a list of individuals who donated to charity. Keep in mind that the data (e.g. contact information) purchased might have very limited value as it is not based upon a relationship. Once the not-for-profit has mapped its organization mission against the funding interests of the foundation and/or individual, it should then create a list of all primary stakeholders (e.g. board members; leadership; partnerships; current donors) of the not-for-profit. This way it can determine if any of the stakeholders have relationships with any of the foundations. This strategy will narrow the list of potential investors significantly to a workable number for setting up meetings. Most important to remember is that most philanthropic investments come from a combination of matching passion/purpose with a personal relationship.

Regarding obtaining donations from individuals, we suggest applying a three-part strategy: 1) Obtain donations from yourself, friends/families, and board members; 2) Crowdsource for additional funds that provide friends and family and board members an easy tool to ask for matching donations; and 3) Conduct blind marketing campaigns through purchased lists.

Investor Generational Motivations

Before you go out and implement a developmental plan, you should also understand the individual's motivational differences and leadership styles. Different generations were influenced by different factors. These differences often play themselves out within the investment priorities.

Chart 1: An overview of the working generations

Characteristics	Maturists (pre-1945)	Baby Boomers (1945-1960)	Generation X (1961-1980)	Generation Y (1981-1995)	Generation Z (Born after 1995)
Formative experiences	Second World War, Rationing, Fixed-gender roles, Rock 'n' Roll, Nuclear families, Defined gender roles — particularly for women	Cold War, Post-War boom, "Swinging Sixties", Apollo Moon landings, Youth culture, Woodstock, Family-orientated, Rise of the teenager	End of Cold War, Fall of Berlin Wall, Reagan / Gorbachev, Thatcherism, Live Aid, Introduction of first PC, Early mobile technology, Latch-key kids, rising levels of divorce	9/11 terrorist attacks, PlayStation, Social media, Invasion of Iraq, Reality TV, Google Earth, Glastonbury	Economic downturn, Global warming, Global focus, Mobile devices, Energy crisis, Arab Spring, Produce own media, Cloud computing, Wiki-leaks
Percentage in U.K. workforce*	3%	33%	35%	29%	Currently employed in either part-time jobs or new apprenticeships
Aspiration	Home ownership	Job security	Work-life balance	Freedom and flexibility	Security and stability
Attitude toward technology	Largely disengaged	Early information technology (IT) adaptors	Digital Immigrants	Digital Natives	"Technoholics" – entirely dependent on IT; limited grasp of alternatives
Attitude toward career	Jobs are for life	Organisational — careers are defined by employers	Early "portfolio" careers — loyal to profession, not necessarily to employer	Digital entrepreneurs — work "with" organisations not "for"	Career multitaskers — will move seamlessly between organisations and "pop-up" businesses
Signature product	Automobile	Television	Personal Computer	Tablet/Smart Phone	Google glass, graphene, nano-computing, 3-D printing, driverless cars
Communication media	Formal letter	Telephone	E-mail and text message	Text or social media	Hand-held (or integrated into clothing) communication devices
Communication preference	Face-to-face	Face-to-face ideally, but telephone or e-mail if required	Text messaging or e-mail	Online and mobile (text messaging)	Facetime
Preference when making financial decisions	Face-to-face meetings	Face-to-face ideally, but increasingly will go online	Online — would prefer face-to-face if time permitting	Face-to-face	Solutions will be digitally crowd-sourced

*Percentages are approximate at the time of publication.

Investor Giving Trends by Personality

Before meeting with potential investors, you need to understand their giving behaviors and leadership style. If you do not adapt your request to the giving behavior and/or style, your not-for-profit can lose out on essential investment opportunities. People can be classified in four leadership styles that also predict what motivates them. In simple terms we have individuals who are quick decision makers and motivated by results (i.e. social and financial impact); individuals who are quick decision makers motivated by passion, causes, and stories and are socially oriented; individuals who are slow decision makers and motivated by relationships (i.e. others will tell them it's a good investment); and individuals who are slow decision makers who are motivated by data and details.

The key for the not-for-profit leader who is soliciting donations is to make the request not in their own leadership style, but in the style of the individuals who determine how the funds will be deployed. In order to do this, he/she first needs to understand his/her relationship strategies strengths and weaknesses and learn to adapt them to the person(s) from whom they are seeking funds.

To do this, we recommend that each not-for-profit leader determines his/her behavioral style and, more importantly, understands the other three behavioral styles in order to categorize investors and adapt any materials to their style. Keep in mind that, often, not-for-profit leaders are presenting to a multitude of people and therefore need to ensure materials potentially target all four behavioral styles.

Marketing Materials
It should go without saying that before a not-for-profit solicits charitable investment funds it should have polished marketing materials that include a polished website; case statement outlining the purpose, development goals and use of funds; and, potentially, an investment fund that includes a Social Return on Investment calculation.

To provide you with some guidance, we provided you a case statement template in **APPENDIX F.** In addition, to provide you with some guidance as the way to structure a case statement, we provide you with marketing and communication strategies adapted from field experts in **APPENDIX G.**

This chapter provided you with a general overview of strategy that leads to obtaining financial resources to carry out the mission of the not-for-profit. We encourage you to remember the following key questions as you develop your not-for-profit development plan.

Key Questions to Remember
1) Which legal structure best allows you to accomplish your social mission? a) Not-for-Profit; b) For-Profit; c) Not-for-Profit/For-Profit Legal/Financial Partnership.
2) What is your rationalization for creating the legal structure?
3) What not-for-profit funding model best categorizes your not-for-profit? What are the top potential investment individual, foundation, and/or governmental targets for your not-for-profit?
4) What brand/image do you want associated with your not-for-profit?
5) What individual, foundation, and/or governmental connections do you or your board have to start the process of attracting investors?
6) What marketing strategies will you need to implement to strengthen your brand and attract funders with whom you do not have an existing relationship?
7) What is you and your team's leadership relationship strategy? Who is best positioned to solicit funds from investors?
8) Do you need to adapt your plan based upon the investor's generation?

Finally, to provide concrete examples of not-for-profits with great brands, marketing strategies, and successful development plans we've provided three case examples below.

Case Study: Common Market by Alyssa Kaminski

The Common Market's mission is to connect communities with good food from sustainable family farms. They achieve this goal by distributing sustainably grown, local food to institutions, community organizations, corporate cafeterias, and more. When the Common Market was its initial stage of conception, its founders were impartial to what their business model would look like. During an extensive three-year planning period, they looked into for-profit, not-for-profit, and cooperatives as potential business models for their organization. In the end, they decided to incorporate as a not-for-profit for two distinct reasons: the motivations of the people at the table and the feasibility of initial investment.

During the planning phase, Haile Johnston and Tatiana Garcia Granados, co-founders, gathered a working group of individuals looking to find solutions to specific challenges in their communities. Some were looking for answers to disease disparity, supporting small farm viability, and increasing nutritional education. Others were interested in land conservation through agriculture and solutions for meeting increased demand for locally sourced food. Everyone with a seat at the table was there to contribute solutions to the problems that faced their communities and the needs of their customers. Nobody was looking for an answer in which they could make a personal financial gain. This was the primary reason Common Market chose to incorporate as a not-for-profit organization. The underlying mission was community driven with priority placed on reinvesting in the community and resolving complex problems in food-systems.

The secondary reason for this type of incorporation was the organization's need for initial capital. At inception, few organizations were similarly structured and regional food systems were not an area of interest for potential investors. It would have been challenging for the founders of the Common Market to prove they could be financially viable and provide investors a significant return on investment. Furthermore, the investor-model did not fit within the group's motivation for the financial viability of its famers, nor the financial viability of its funders. Instead, the Common Market chose to seek initial funding through individual donors and foundations. Foundations and donors could provide the initial investment needed to operate and cover projected loses within the first few years.

Five years later, Common Market Mid-Atlantic reached break-even operations and discovered new aspirations for growth. They realized they had a model that could work in cities with similar issues of healthy food access and small farm sustainability. By expanding their model to new regions, the Common Market could share some of the overhead costs while establishing new locally-focused iterations of their initial model. They started in Atlanta, a city similar in size, demographics, and problems with disease disparity.

The Common Market found much of their Mid-Atlantic success by partnering with established health-focused institutions and Atlanta had a similar institutional landscape. They worked with an individual from Atlanta, who came to them looking to create a hybrid of both the Common Market's and her vision. By working with someone established in Atlanta, the Common Market was able to engage local stakeholders in Atlanta's food system, formulate a regional board of directors, and employ members of the community.

Today, 75 percent of the Common Market's budget comes from earned income and 25 percent from traditional philanthropy. They are the sole member of two regional branches: The Common Market Georgia and The Common Market Texas. The organization continues to trend towards becoming a Local Nationalizer as they seek the funding for more regional branches. Their total operation has consistently been defined by the financial structure of a for-profit and the moral ambition of a not-for-profit. With aspirations of more regional networks, they will certainly become a national force in enhancing the viability of local family farmers and providing healthy food access to local communities.

Philadelphia Youth Basketball (PYB) Case Study by Jennifer Chu

Philadelphia Youth Basketball (PYB), is a sports-based-youth-development (SBYD) nonprofit that serves as an example of successful branding, marketing, and development strategies. PYB's mission is to create opportunities for young people to reach their potential as students, athletes, and positive leaders (Philadelphia Youth Basketball [PYB], n.d.). PYB chose to incorporate as a nonprofit in 2015 for several key reasons. President and CEO, Kenny Holdsman stated that PYB needed to subsidize its potential for earned revenue with donations from private donors and grant funding (personal communication June 12, 2018). In 2014, he met with potential stakeholders and made a "soft pitch" for seed money. Holdsman and PYB could leverage a nonprofit status to justify donations of startup dollars from several private investors, which substantiated the need for immediate incorporation in 2015.

With its 501(c)(3) status, PYB was ready to move into the next stages of branding, marketing, and development. The nonprofit status is part of PYB's brand as it emphasizes the importance of social impact and precludes a perception that PYB would prioritize revenue over mission. This factor is especially important given PYB's plan to build a state of the art basketball and education center in Philadelphia's Logan Triangle. Once the center is built, PYB can potentially rent out the space to basketball and other sports teams as a source of revenue. They could also form an LLC within the nonprofit as a source of earned revenue. The 501(c)(3) status protects PYB's reputation as a social impact driven enterprise.

At its launch, PYB garnered media attention and created excitement around its concept and brand. On December 3, 2015, PYB hosted a press conference to announce its kickoff. Key attendees included: Mayor-elect Jim Kenney; Dawn Staley, former WNBA player, Olympic gold medalist and Philadelphia native; Aaron McKie, former NBA player; Fran Dunphy, Temple University head basketball coach; Steve Donahue, University of Pennsylvania head basketball coach; and Phil Martelli, St. Joseph's University head basketball coach. The head coaches hail from Philadelphia Big 5, an informal association of Philadelphia's oldest and most successful men's basketball teams (Dougherty, 2015). Assembling city officials, local basketball celebrities, and storied head coaches was a strategic branding and marketing move to demonstrate support of PYB and its mission.

In addition to branding and marketing, PYB's key development strategy includes a campaign to raise $25 million to build a basketball and education center in Logan Triangle, an area in Northeast Philadelphia with a fraught history. In the 1950's residents noticed that houses were beginning to sink into the coal and ash that sat atop a buried creek. By the 1980's the city spent $38 million to cover demolition and resident relocation costs.

In 2015, the Triangle was an overgrown area used as a dump site, contributing to the urban blight of the area (Gammage, 2015). Holdsman has partnered with Philadelphia Redevelopment (PRA) and Goldenberg Group to redevelop Logan Triangle (Bray, 2015). Through key partnerships, PYB demonstrates that it has corporate and city support to build the center and carry out its mission which in turn can attract more funders.

In 2015, after publicly announcing its launch and incorporating, PYB boldly decided to jump immediately into program implementation rather than wait to build the center. PYB currently operates three core areas of programming: HoopHers, a girls' basketball league and empowerment program; Middle School Partnership Program, a school-based basketball and academic enrichment afterschool activity; and Collegiate Summer Camp Series, which hosts week long basketball camps at local colleges. By initiating programming prior to building the center, PYB has created a unique fundraising challenge in which it must simultaneously raise operating funds and run a capital campaign for $25 million.

PYB's development strategy can attract different types of funders: those who may want to invest in real estate with a social impact return and those who want to directly support basketball programming targeted towards at risk youth. PYB can adapt its marketing materials to both types of funders and once a funder is engaged, pitch for donations for the other initiative. Holdsman explained that if a donor is already supporting operational costs and wants to donate to the capital campaign, the capital donation must be in *addition to* funds directed towards operations. Holdsman prioritizes funding that ensures programming continues to run over funding for the center ensuring that donors cannot "switch out" their donations (personal communication June 12, 2018).

PYB's marketing materials must be catered to a donor's interest and passions and identify if the donor is primarily interested in supporting the capital campaign, existing programming or both. Holdsman notes that as a startup PYB does not have generations of grateful donor roots in the way that universities and hospitals do, and as a SBYD lacks wealthy grateful alumni who could serve as donors (personal communication June 12, 2018). Applying Foster, Kim, & Christiansen's (2009) fundraising model, PYB does not fit into beneficiary builder like a university in which grateful alumni donate out of self-interest to promote the prestige and success associated with their alma mater. In contrast, PYB must use the heartfelt connector model to "grow large by focusing on causes that resonate with the existing concerns of large numbers of people at all income levels, and by creating a structured way for these people to connect where none had previously existed."

Beginning direct service for underserved Philadelphia youth in 2015 was a risk. However, the programing provides a "proof of concept" which can be an effective marketing strategy for the capital campaign. By facilitating successful after school programs, summer camps, and basketball tournaments, many hosted at well-known colleges and universities, PYB can generate press coverage, photo-ops with college coaches and players, and demonstrate social impact prior to the building of the center. Certainly, the decision to immediately provide sports and academic enrichment opportunities to at risk youth was motivated by altruistic factors including filling a need, supporting youth and their families, and positively impacting the Philadelphia community. However, the same decision is also a smart tactic in PYB's branding, marketing, and development strategies.

CEO and President Kenny Holdsman as a founder has been the driving force behind PYB's marketing, development, and fundraising strategies. As former President/CEO of Legacy Youth Tennis and Education (formerly Arthur Ashe) and cofounder of Philadelphia Youth Sports Collaborative (PYSC) (PYB, n.d.),

Holdsman brings an extensive network of connections. Through networking among the Philadelphia basketball community, he brought in the initial seed money to start the organization and galvanized support from prestigious universities with storied basketball histories. He also leveraged partnerships with PRA and Goldenberg Group to support real estate in Logan Triangle, the proposed site for the basketball and education center. In its initial startup phase, Holdsman, serves as the face of the PYB brand. He brings connections and networks to PYB both for funding and partnership resources and board leadership. He has worked tirelessly to promote PYB and galvanize support for the organization. As PYB enters its fourth year of existence, it remains to be seen if the organization can grow and become sustainable beyond Holdsman's influence. Yet, for now as the case study demonstrates, Holdsman's leadership has created successful marketing branding and development strategies and campaigns.

Case Study References

Bray, J. (2015, September 30). *Goldenberg Group Selected to Redevelop Logan Triangle*. Retrieved from http://planphilly.com/articles/2015/09/30/goldenberg-group-selected-to-redevelop-logan-triangle.

Dougherty, M. (2015, December 3*). Philadelphia Youth Basketball Launches Citywide Development Initiative.* Retrieved from https://philadelphia.cbslocal.com/2015/12/03/philadelphia-youth-basketball/.

Foster, W., Kim, P., & Christiansen, B. (2009). Ten Nonprofit Funding Models. *Stanford Social Innovation Review.* Retrieved from https://ssir.org/articles/entry/ten_nonprofit_funding_models.

Gammage, J. (2015, December 3). Center Could Bring New Life to Logan. *Philadelphia Inquirer,* pp. B1, B4.

Philadelphia Youth Basketball. (n.d.). Philadelphia Youth Basketball mission statement. Retrieved from https://phillyyouthbasketball.org/about/our-mission/.

Women's Way Case Study
by Lauren Buckheit, Denise Mount, and Allison Wortley

Women's Way is a grant-making and advocacy organization focusing on the issues facing women and girls within the greater Philadelphia area. Their mission is "to inspire and mobilize the community to invest in organizations and leaders that will advance the rights of opportunities for women and girls, to achieve gender equality for all." Founded in 1977, Women's Way began as an umbrella organization for struggling women-centered nonprofits in the Philadelphia area who decided to pool resources to create a stronger impact. The organization focuses on four areas -- economic security, leadership, healthcare, and safety -- putting more than $23 million to work in the region, valuing community, opportunity, intersectionality, innovation, and accountability. Women's Way hopes to become the thought leader on the issues of women, girls, and gender equity.

The social issues that Women's Way supports are important and resonate with all women. The organization allows a structured way for women to connect and address issues that are applicable both locally as well as nationally. Yet local, state, and national governments have been unable to successfully address or resolve the problems, leaving Women's Way to rely heavily upon individual donors and fundraising events. The organization aligns with the Heartfelt Connector Funding Model as it rallies a cross-section of women together, all passionate about the cause of equality.

Women's Way also meets the criteria for the Local Nationalizer Funding Model. Most of their money is raised with proper buy-in from each community and Women's Way could scale as the advancement of women, girls, and gender equity is relevant nationwide. Both models support the organization's current revenue sources which consist of 65 percent individual donations and 35 percent corporate sponsorships.

Women's Way adopted a new strategic plan "to re-establish Women's Way as a powerful catalyst for achieving gender equality and justice." There are four strategic goals; the first is to cultivate high impact philanthropy through an engaged network of individuals dedicated to supporting the organization through significant donations. The second priority is to help create the opportunities and supportive conditions for leaders in organizations to pursue innovative and strategic work. The next priority is to build the Women's Way community, which includes their donors, volunteers, funded organizations, and activities. Their final goal is to invest in the growth and sustainability of the organization. As of 2017, the impact of the plan can be measured with an improved financial position and a 25 percent increase in donor contributions.

In addition to introducing a new strategic plan for their work, Women's Way recently went under a complete rebranding as well as change in leadership. Women's Way recently hired Diane Cornman-Levy as their new Executive Director. Cornman-Levy has more than 30 years of experience leading nonprofit organizations and has been an advocate for gender equality throughout her career. During her first year at Women's Way she has worked to better the relationships with the board as well as improve the organization's relationships with their donor base.

Traditional philanthropic models stand in contradiction with the mission and strategic plan of Women's Way. Historically, the disbursement of funds has been top-down, especially in terms of grant funding. Nonprofit organizations submit written proposals to funding entities who then select a recipient. Grantors typically decide how much of the funding can be used for overhead costs versus the mission of the nonprofit and expect to see results in a specific, short term, period of time. If a nonprofit fails to produce suitable deliverables, it will lose funding.
Though well intended, the problems here are numerous. First, the current model rewards nonprofits with the best grant writers, not those who are doing the best work. Second, those deciding how much money each nonprofit should receive and how those funds should be spent are often lacking expertise in the mission of the nonprofit and the financial realities faced by not-for-profit organizations. Thirdly, it creates a short-term timetable as opposed to a sustainable relationship between donors and nonprofits. Diane Cornman-Levy has a vision to change this.

The new philanthropic model, collective initiative, is designed based off principles of collaboration, sustainability, and the intent to be high impact. Starting with the application process, the way Women's Way issues grants to organizations will now be in line with its model. No longer will grants be awarded to the best grant writers, for strong writers are not necessarily the strongest advocates or changemakers in a community. As opposed to written proposals, grant applications will now be in the format of a presentation allowing nonprofits to demonstrate their impact. This will make funding from Women's Way more accessible to everyone in the Philadelphia community.

Arguably, the biggest change will be bringing more seats to the table. Beyond diversifying her board, Cornman-Levy wants to bring the community to the funding table eliminating the top down style of grant funding. Members of the community who will be receiving and benefiting from grants from Women's Way will be present during philanthropic conversations. Able to share their expertise and engage in active conversations with the board, this collaboration will allow Women's Way to connect donors with organizations building a united network. In turn, such conversations will promote greater transparency; Cornman-Levy believes that Women's Way should be transparent about what funds it has to give and where it is going. Transparency will build trust within the community and continue to ameliorate the relationship between Women's Way and its donor.

Women's Way's commitment to long-term, collective initiative-driven funding will not only strengthen their network of donors and organizations, but also it will build sustainability within the greater Philadelphia community. Even those not directly involved with the funded nonprofits or Women's Way will benefit from its successful programming. Furthermore, if the collective initiative philanthropic model pioneered by Women's Way is successful, it could be replicated by similar nonprofit organizations furthering Cornman-Levy's goal of making Women's Way the thought leader on issues of women, girls, and gender equity.

Case Study References
Landes, W. F., Kim, P., & Christiansen, B. (Spring 2009). Ten Nonprofit Funding Models. Stanford Social Innovation Review, 32-39. Retrieved June 23, 2018.
Scout, M. C. (2016, August 31). Women's Way 2016 Tax Form 990. Retrieved from Guidestar.com: https://www.guidestar.org/FinDocuments/2016/231/989/2016-231989161-0dd4711e-9.pdf.
Scout, M. C. (2017, August 31). Women's Way 2017 Form 990. Retrieved from Guidestar.org: https://www.guidestar.org/FinDocuments/2017/231/989/2017-231989161-0edcdc80-9.pdf.

CHAPTER 5: LEADERSHIP; PERFORMANCE MANAGEMENT; PROFESSIONAL DEVELOPMENT; CULTURE OF INNOVATION

"In the years ahead, America's nonprofits will become even more important. As government retrenches, Americans will look increasingly to the nonprofits to tackle the problems of a fast-changing society. These challenges will demand innovation -- in services, and in nonprofit management." Peter Drucker

This chapter provides a structure for an emerging or existing not-for-profit leader to examine his/her beliefs and motivations. The most important factor in great leadership is understanding one's own belief structure and values that influence organizational decisions and being able to articulate these beliefs and values to both internal and external audiences.

What Are Your Leadership Beliefs and Motivations?
We've provided the essential steps and process to understand your beliefs and motivations so as to be able to communicate them to both internal and external organization audiences.

Step 1: We all have ingrained experiences that have influenced our leadership. However, if we do not know what these are or if we are not able to articulate these to our teams and organization then we only create ripples of frustration among the people who we are supposed to lead.

The best strategy to understand what drives us and our motivations is to write a "This I Believe Essay" as it can be a powerful tool for self-reflection. Your motivations that drive your professional behavior and decisions are ingrained in these beliefs and in drawing them out you have a foundation for owning your leadership style. Below are guidelines taken from WHYY (https://thisibelieve.org/guidelines/).

1. **Tell a story about you**: Be specific. Take your belief out of the ether and ground it in the events that have shaped your core values. Consider moments when belief was formed or tested or changed. Think of your own experience, work, and family, and tell of the things you know that no one else does. Your story need not be heart-warming or gut-wrenching -- it can even be funny -- but it should be *real*. Make sure your story ties to the essence of your daily life philosophy and the shaping of your beliefs.
2. **Be brief**: Your statement should be between 500 and 600 words. That's about three minutes when read aloud at your natural pace.
3. **Name your belief**: If you can't name it in a sentence or two, your essay might not be about belief. Also, rather than writing a list, consider focusing on one core belief.
4. **Be positive**: Write about what you do believe, not what you don't believe. Avoid statements of religious dogma, preaching, or editorializing.

5. **Be personal**: Make your essay about you; speak in the first person. Avoid speaking in the editorial "we." Tell a story from your own life; this is not an opinion piece about social ideals. Write in words and phrases that are comfortable for you to speak. We recommend you read your essay aloud to yourself several times, and each time edit it and simplify it until you find the words, tone, and story that truly echo your belief and the way you speak.

This essay should be one of the hardest essays you ever write, but it should be easily translated to professional statements to inform organizational teams and constituents.

Step 2: After understanding your motivations, we ask leaders to compare themselves with other leader characteristics as defined in the book *Good to Great and the Social Sectors*. At the very least, comparing oneself to other leaders is a reminder regarding what we all strive for, but often times forget to be as leaders.

The Good to Great monograph frames leaders into executive, effective, competent, contributing, and capable. We all play different roles at different times in our leadership journey. Nevertheless, we should all strive to evolve to the executive level and their related characteristics including setting up successors (i.e., what is in the best interest of the organization) for even greater success, being modest and attributing success to others, being fanatically driven to produce sustainable results, being more of a plow horse than show horse, and taking full responsibility for poor decisions.

When emphasizing some of the successful behaviors of successful leaders, notice that great leaders always consider the "who" before the "what;" confront the brutal facts; focus on the right balance between passion, economics, and talent; apply discipline; and use technology (working smarter and not harder) whenever possible.

What Different Skills are Needed for Management vs. Leadership?
When we move from leadership to management, we want to emphasize the functions of management that are different from leadership. Based upon a particular role or function, individuals often switch between leadership and management roles. Essentially, a manager wants to be both efficient, which is a measure of how well or how productively resources are used to achieve a goal, and effective, which is a measure of the appropriateness of the goals an organization is pursuing and the degree to which they are achieved.

Managers essentially plan, organize, project lead, and measure plans. Planning is the identification and selection of appropriate organizational goals and courses of action. Organizing is creating a structure of working relationships among staff that allow organizational members to interact and cooperate to achieve organizational goals. Effective organization and project leadership implies both working in hierarchical and functional structures. This means managers can no longer lead because they are in a position of authority but must lead with competencies of bringing essential people and teams together to work collaboratively to accomplish the organizational goals. Keep in mind that the level of the manager shifts the time spent on planning, organizing, leading, or measuring. The highest level spends the most time on planning and the least time on measuring and the lowest manager (coordinator) spends more time on project leading and measuring.

How to Create a Positive Work Culture
Now that the primary values and functions are outlined, a not-for-profit leader needs to set up strategies and systems to ensure a positive and effective work environment.

We frame the two essential strategies for effective management within a not-for-profit as instituting a robust performance evaluation and professional development system. This section of the chapter discusses the traditional behavior and systems of the traditional not-for-profit and then outlines how not-for-profit systems structures are shifting.

What is Your Performance Management Strategy?
Let's begin with the behavior of most not-for-profits, which usually includes writing a job description that, in theory, leads to a performance system that holds the employee accountable or at best motivates him/her to improve performance. From a philosophical perspective, a job description (JD) is linked to a performance evaluation. Each employee has two components of measurement which are: 1) Actual job performance and any related interpersonal behaviors that facilitate job performance; and 2) Interpersonal skills and behaviors that relate to being "a good corporate citizen" (i.e., a non-toxic employee who contributes favorably to a positive organizational culture). As such, both components should be included in a performance evaluation.

The most common measurement scale levels (i.e., Unsatisfactory, Basic, Proficient, and Distinguished) of the traditional evaluation tools need significant clarification. The truth is that anyone rated at the "Unsatisfactory" level should have been fired long before ever receiving an annual evaluation, which really just leaves us with three performance measures. To us, the word "Basic" is a bit insulting and inflammatory, especially to a professional. "Basic" is similar to "average" in a performance evaluation and nobody wants to be rated as "average." What usually results, with the exception of poor performers, is that most people end up with a proficient or distinguished rating on their performance evaluation which defeats the purpose of improving organizational effectiveness through professional feedback.

The simple truth about performance is that I, as a staff person, must perform to my superior's expectations. If my supervisor considers *"simplicity and beauty"* to be posters, charts, and material that cover every square inch of wall space in an office, then I need to meet that expectation. If a new supervisor gets hired who has the exact opposite view, then I need to change to meet that superior's expectations. Regardless of the "shifting sands" here, the point is to clearly articulate the expectations and hold people accountable for those expectations.

When discussing performance evaluations, the issue of goals is an important discussion. Aubrey Daniels states, "The purpose of a goal is to give a manager another opportunity to recognize an employee." Attainable goals allow for this recognition, while stretch goals almost always result in an employee having to explain why the goal wasn't achieved -- the opposite of "pat on the back" recognition. We don't recommend that managers reward people for achieving goals since goals are simply part of the expectations of doing a good job and part of everyone's responsibility. In other words, people should be setting goals as a routine part of their responsibilities for professional development. Additionally, management may set a few of these goals for an employee in the event that the employee is not aware of the hard skills he/she needs to develop or the soft-skills he/she needs to improve.

Cappelli and Tavis (2016)[v] write, in the *Performance Management Revolution*, that companies are shifting away from traditional performance management systems because they "heavily emphasize financial rewards and punishments and their end-of-year structure, they hold people accountable for past behavior at the expense of improving current performance and grooming talent for the future…"

Effective Performance Management
The initial intention of performance evaluations is to reinforce desired behaviors and manage performance. Cappelli and Tavis, in their analysis, conclude that companies are adapting performance management systems that are more aligned with the natural cycle of work that includes people development, the need for agility, and the centrality of teamwork.

Much of what the research says is more easily said than done, which brings us the question of how to apply these lessons to a not-for-profit organization. Before considering the application of these concepts to a not-for-profit, a leader has to reflect upon the organizational structure, as this sets the tone and establishes an organizational culture.

Most not-for-profits think in hierarchical structures for reasons of simplicity and organizing. However, hierarchical structures serve to create silos within organizations, undermining efforts toward teamwork and creating a need for additional "bandages" for cross organizational communication. An alternative is to set up a functional organizational structure in which an employee has multiple inputs from team members according to the function of his/her job. This type of organizational structure puts teamwork (inputs and support from multiple people) at the center of any performance management system. The direct supervisor is still responsible for creating and aligning the employee goals with the organizational goals, but it demonstrates that the employee is also accountable to other functions within the organization and encourages him/her to increase communication and seek support across these functions in order to achieve organizational goals.

Steps to Set-up an Evaluation System in a Not-for-Profit
Step 1: As a first step, the organization has to have clear organizational impact measurements as discussed in Chapter 2. Without clear organizational measures, it becomes impossible to align company goals with individual performance.
Step 2: These organization impact goals then need to be incorporated into employee job descriptions. Employee job descriptions will have additional goals, but they should all be aligned with the organization macro impact goals. Following this step also communicates to the employee how they and their work fits into the organizational mission/structure.
Step 3: We recommend writing quarterly objectives/work plans rather than job descriptions. Job descriptions generally are descriptors of responsibilities but don't provide direction or concrete goals, tasks, or measurements. By shifting to quarterly objectives/work plans, it ensures the job description is a living document that evolves/adapts according to the lessons and evolving direction of the organization. Quarterly objectives/work plans also provide a framework that shifts discussion with supervisors and teams from accountability to brainstorming on strategies to improve performance.
Step 4: Define the process and expectations for supervisors and employees. It's important to remember that the purpose of performance evaluations is to shift from accountability to learning. With this said, a process should encourage frequent discussions between supervisors, employees, and team, to review goals and challenges and brainstorm solutions. Much of what is captured in traditional performance evaluations can now be captured in reviews of goals and progress toward these goals.
Step 5: Research and use technology tools to give feedback, document conversations, allow for feedback from multiple sources, and track progress. This also provides a platform for leadership to get a sense on organizational culture and efforts toward organizational goals.

What is Your Professional Development Strategy?
The second essential function for effective management in setting up a robust not-for-profit system is setting up a professional development system that gives employees the knowledge and tools they need to be successful in the organization.

Beer, Finnstrom, and Schrader (Harvard Business Review, 2016) write that despite spending $160 billion in the United States and close to $356 billion globally (2015 statistics) the traditional type of learning doesn't lead to better organizational performance, because people soon revert to their old habits. They go on to state that there are six common managerial organizational barriers that prevent people from applying what they've learned that include: 1) unclear direction on strategy and values leading to conflicting priorities; 2) senior executives who don't work as a team or continue with old habits/behaviors; 3) a top-down or laissez-faire style by the leader preventing honest conversations; 4) poor coordination across business functions; 5) inadequate time and attention given to talent development; and 6) employees' fears of repercussions.

Keeping in mind the organizational obstacles listed, a not-for-profit can only have a robust professional development system if it has assembled many of the ingredients previously mentioned that include:

1) A leader with clear and articulated values and beliefs, which is why we believe each leader needs to write their own personal essay.
2) Clear organizational outcomes that provide a clear strategy from the board to staff.
3) A functional chart that displaces poor coordination across business functions.

Once the not-for-profit assembles the above ingredients it can set-up a robust professional development strategy.

Step 1: Outline the primary job functions for the primary positions within the organization and list desired job competencies and skills. This exercise will give the organization a sense of the primary skills and competencies staff need to be successful at their jobs.

Step 2: Determine mandatory organizational content that all employees must know, such as the organizational mission, values, and goals.

Step 3: Set-up an internal training/professional development institute that provides professional development sessions on the primary desired job competencies and skills by position and mandatory organizational content. In this process, track employee participation and knowledge accumulation.

Step 4: Set-up a policy, including allocating time and financial resources, allowing for employees falling outside of the primary positions within the organization to seek professional development opportunities related to their professional industry.

Step 5: Finally, to address the final barrier of employees' fears of repercussions, we recommend a process allowing for ideas to emerge from the bottom to the top. We refer the reader to our *Social Innovator's Playbook* where they can find a process to develop great products, services, dedicated employees, and great teams. This process is "A Company's Guide to Creating Innovation from the Bottom-Up." The process simply reverses the normal communication within organizations where the top has all the ideas and then "sells" these to staff to a process where the staff is given a place to design their ideas and "sell" them to the top. Generally, this creates better services/products and opens-up communication. Most importantly, employees lose their fear and feel heard leading to company "buy-in."

Ultimately, a not-for-profit needs a robust performance management and professional development system and strategy because: 1) Employees with more positive experiences at work are half as likely to leave their organization compared to those with less positive experiences (21 percent vs. 44 percent) (IBM Smarter Workforce Institute's 2016 The Employee Experience Index survey); and 2) Companies that heavily invest in culture, technology, and work space: have four times the profit and two times the revenue of other companies studied and were nearly 25 percent smaller, indicating higher levels of productivity and innovation (*The Harvard Business Review* article "Why the Millions We Spend on Employee Engagement Buy Us So Little").

The truth is, your culture is the foundation of your organization because it determines your team's collective understanding of how your nonprofit operates. Beyond that, it can also impact donor satisfaction, and the excitement and commitment with which your team will do its work.

Organizational Health Assessment
A not-for-profit can get a general sense of the organizational health and readiness for a robust performance management system and professional development strategy through issuing the organizational health assessment found in **APPENDEX H** to staff.

Employee Manual Considerations
Outside of setting up robust performance management and professional development systems to achieve organizational effectiveness, a not-for-profit leader and board need to consider many policies that determine the "rules" from which the not-for-profit operate. These are often a mixture between organizational policies and operations. As a guide for what policies and operations a not-for-profit need to consider, we've provided the table of contents for a not-for-profit employee manual **in APPENDIX I** that lists more than 100 potential policies an organization needs to adopt. Any employee manual should be reviewed by legal to ensure they are in compliance with federal, state, and local law.

Remember, to lead or manage a person first needs to examine and understand his/her beliefs and motivations as these influence organizational decisions. Being able to articulate these beliefs and values to both internal and external audiences is essential to leading

To conclude this Chapter, we provide you with two case studies of not-for-profits that, through leadership, have created positive and effective work cultures.

The Food Trust Case Study by Callie Perrone and Jacqueline Omorogbe

The Food Trust is a leading Philadelphia-based nonprofit dedicated to food access and nutrition education. Since the organization's inception in 1992, its mission has been to "ensure that everyone has access to nutritious, affordable food and information to make healthy decisions" (The Food Trust, n.d.). The Food Trust carries out its mission through an intentional blend of policy change, research, and community-based programming. Following the departure of The Food Trust's founder Duane Perry, Yael Lehmann became President and CEO in 2006. Since then, The Food Trust has become nationally recognized for its high-impact work. The Food Trust's efforts and accomplishments have been praised by the Obama Administration, replicated nationally and internationally, and given various awards including America's #2 "High Impact Nonprofit" in children's health and nutrition. Under Lehmann's leadership, The Food Trust has expanded from a 30- to more than 130-person operation, a $3 to $10 million budget, and a local to national organization (Philanthropedia, 2013; Warnshius, 2014).

Leadership Beliefs and Motivations
Aligned with the core values of The Food Trust, Lehmann believes that everyone deserves access to healthy, affordable food. She believes that public health and social justice must intersect. She believes that an integrated approach of direct service, policy work, and research are crucial for meaningful, lasting social change. In what could have easily been a "This I Believe" essay, Lehmann shared the events that shaped her core beliefs and motivations: amidst the trauma and fear of the HIV/AIDS crisis in the 1990s, she was inspired by the successful political organizing that she witnessed and participated in -- which merged policy and direct service, public health, and social justice. She found those same core beliefs at the heart of The Food Trust's mission, leading her to join the team in 2001. These core beliefs have guided The Food Trust's work from its founding under Perry and have continued to do so under Lehmann's leadership as The Food Trust has grown in size, scope, and impact. Perry and Lehmann's intentional emphasis on core beliefs and values, rather than on themselves as individuals, contributed to a successful leadership transition that has enabled the mission to remain central to the work.

Leadership Style and Organizational Culture
Lehmann has a hands-on approach to management and stays in constant communication with her staff to ensure that the needs of the organization are being met. She has an open-door policy and encourages her staff members to reach out with questions and concerns at any time. Lehmann puts the mission ahead of herself, especially when it comes to making tough decisions and having difficult conversations. She has long ago accepted that making the right decision for The Food Trust inevitably means that not everybody is going to like her. "What is best for our organization?" is always at the forefront of her decision making (Y. Lehman, personal communication, June 18, 2018).

One of Lehmann's proudest accomplishments is the organizational culture she has helped to create (Y. Lehman, personal communication, June 18, 2018). The organization's staff is diverse, representing various socioeconomic, racial, and professional backgrounds. It is inclusive and adheres to the commitment of providing equal opportunity (The Food Trust, n.d.). The work environment is fun-filled, high-energy, and informal. Staff appreciation events and parties occur frequently, and staff members regularly celebrate each other's achievements. Even though the office environment is informal, staff members are hardworking, highly dedicated, and passionate about the work of the organization -- which Lehmann says is a must. Because of the heavy workload, Lehmann stresses the importance of self-care to her staff and encourages work-life balance to prevent burnout. Staff members highly value the organization's culture, as Lehmann notes that some choose to work there because of the culture even when they know they could make more money elsewhere (The Food Trust, n.d.).

Professional Development
Under Lehmann's mission-driven leadership, professional development plays a key role in advancing the capacity and impact of The Food Trust. Just like the organization as a whole, Lehmann asserts that individuals at all levels of the organization should be "constantly growing, adapting, and learning" (Y. Lehman, personal communication, June 18, 2018). The value of professional development is recognized by leadership and staff alike. According to Lehmann, professional development is her staff's number one request. In order to meet the professional needs of staff and forward the organization's mission, The Food Trust allocates a set amount of funds to each department for their employees to spend on professional development as they see fit. The only requirements are that it has to relate to the mission, and it has to benefit the organization. In addition to these off-site opportunities that employees can pursue, The Food Trust provides all staff members with on-site opportunities through an ongoing guest speaker series. Recognizing the strengths and skills that staff members have to offer one another as a valuable resource, The Food Trust also gives employees have a platform to share their expertise through staff-led presentations and workshops.

Professional development additionally encompasses on-the-job experiences that enable employees to excel at their current position and advance their career. Through an explicit delineation of roles and expectations, Lehmann's staff has a clear understanding of what skills and experiences they need in order to excel and advance, and, due to the emphasis on professional development, the opportunity to gain them. At the Food Trust, this is achieved by providing staff with opportunities to shadow, collaborate, and challenge themselves on the job.
For example, if a managerial role requires experience supervising staff, employees will have an opportunity to supervise interns in order to become competent and eligible for a promotion.

Throughout the Food Trust's mission-driven opportunities for professional development, all staff members are given the agency to set their own objectives and trajectories, and the ability to collaborate and share their skills. This display of trust, equity, and bottom-up decision-making contributes to a culture of goodwill and positivity, increased employee "buy-in," and organizational capacity-building and impact. The value placed upon a robust professional development system undoubtedly contributes to The Food Trust's healthy and effective work environment.

Performance Management and Evaluation
Performance management helps employers build effective feedback, develop goals, and optimize performance within an organization. Performance evaluations are designed to promote ongoing communication between an employer and staff regarding performance, expectations, and goal setting. Though the Food Trust conducts performance evaluations on an annual basis, Lehmann believes in constant feedback throughout the year to encourage ongoing communication among supervisors and staff. She believes in constant communication and feedback whether positive or negative, and in the importance of celebrating accomplishments. Lehmann also believes that nothing should be discussed during annual performance education that has not been already been discussed. She asserts that supervisors should address issues as they arise and resolve them in a timely manner.

The Food Trust's success and impact can be attributed in part to Lehmann's mission-driven, compassionate leadership. Exhibiting personal humility and professional will, Lehmann harnesses core beliefs and values, fosters a positive organizational culture, and emphasizes ongoing performance evaluation and professional development. Together these aspects contribute to The Food Trust's positive, effective, and innovative work environment, and offer valuable insights for emerging and existing nonprofit leaders.

Case Study References
Lehmann, Y. (2018, June 18). Personal interview by phone with C. Perrone and J. Omorogbe.
Philanthropedia. (2013). "Ranked Nonprofits: National Childhood Nutrition/Health." Retrieved
from: http://www.myphilanthropedia.org/top-nonprofits/national/childhood-nutrition-health/2013.
The Food Trust. (n.d.). "Our Mission." Retrieved from:
http://thefoodtrust.org/about/mission.
Warnshius, C. (2014). "Meet Yael Lehmann, Executive Director of The Food Trust." Rad Girls.
Retrieved from: http://www.rad-girls.com/blog/meet-yael-lehman'.
The Food Trust. (2012). "Staff Members". Retrieved June 29, 2018, from:
http://thefoodtrust.org/about/staff.

Starfinder Foundation Case Study by Sam Margolius

Heidi Warren brings more than 20 years of experience in the public sector to her leadership at Starfinder Foundation. She joined Starfinder Foundation in 2002 as the Chief Operating Officer and has since served as Deputy Director for four years and assumed the role of Executive Director in 2013. Outside of Starfinder, Heidi has also served in leadership roles for 10 years at Village of Arts & Humanities in Philadelphia and as an Independent consultant helping Philadelphia nonprofits develop and implement practices that promote clarity of purpose, institutional integrity, shared vision, and responsible action. Her leadership at Starfinder Foundation exemplifies many of the highlighted lessons in the previous chapter.

This case study highlights first and foremost the necessity for a leader to understand their core beliefs and values. Although she had not previously written a "This I Believe" essay, when asked in an interview, "Why do you do what you do?" Ms. Warren did not hesitate. Rather, she replied with a cohesive statement that touched on each of the component parts of a well written "This I Believe" essay: she told a story, kept it brief, named a positive belief, and kept it personal. Warren began by sharing her belief in peoples' fundamental shared humanity, that everyone has talent and aspirations for themselves, and that, "some of us have an awful lot more support to reach those aspirations than others."

She also shared a personal story in which a woman she met early in her career told her, "'I can't solve peoples' problems, but I'm an artist and I have this thing I can bring to the table and can invite people to join me.'" Warren shared, "for me, that's the idea of having a flame, inviting others to bring theirs, and suddenly having a bonfire." Warren offered this frame for her work as contrary to the historical top-down patriarchal notions of nonprofit administration and rather a bottom-up leadership approach that emphasizes humility and collectivism toward a shared mission.

Humility and consensus building are clearly key ingredients to Ms. Warren's leadership style. As Executive Director, Warren describes her role as that of a facilitator. Oftentimes, organizational managers and leaders may fear that too much of a focus on consensus building or process rather than product can limit an agency's efficiency and effectiveness. Although Ms. Warren acknowledges the need for decisiveness within her role, she also emphasizes that Starfinder's success is grounded in the open spaces it provides for voices and expertise of youth participants, staff, and the leadership team to shape the organization's work. With one of the primary goals of the organization being the leadership development of high school students, it is no coincidence that high schoolers have a great deal of voice and choice in the programming Starfinder Foundation offers.

This involvement at many organizational levels distributes a certain degree of power traditionally held by executives in more hierarchical organizational structures. It is the shift to a functional structure described previously in the chapter that breeds sharing expertise across departments and minimizes the hierarchical structure's consequence of silos. Warren emphasizes that this is critical to facilitating an organizational culture that models mutual respect and trust at many levels. For Warren, this is the definition of a healthy organization stating that, "Starfinder has its biggest breakthroughs when we can have honest dialogue with each other and that only happens with trust."

Ms. Warren also brings into her executive role many years of experience from operational perspectives in organizational dynamics. It's perhaps these experiences that have contributed to her nuanced understanding of organizational cultures that thrive. One example of this is Warren's approach to performance management. As described above, a nonprofit leader's responsibility is, "to set up strategies and systems to ensure a positive and effective work environment" (pg. 53). Warren has shifted Starfinder's approach to performance management in many ways to focus on optimizing learning rather than accountability and on safety rather than fear. For example, rather than annualized performance reviews with arbitrary metrics, Starfinder Foundation has implemented a quarterly review system. During the first and third quarters, staff meet with their supervisors informally for a check in. Oftentimes this takes place off-site over coffee, without any formal documentation, and without explicit review of job responsibilities from a job description. Warren describes these check-ins as opportunities for staff to share things they are struggling with, collectively problem solve, and as spaces for open feedback that does not go into a personnel file. During the second and fourth quarter check ins, the supervisors bring the list of mutually agreed upon personal and professional goals of that employee. These meetings are more formalized and documented but continue to emphasize problem solving.

Warren highlights that part of the challenge in promoting learning is the inherent imbalance of power between employees and supervisors. She states that a central component to facilitating employee learning is building a sense that mistakes are okay and won't be met with judgment or blame. Ms. Warren describes this power imbalance as a constant threat to healthy personnel feedback and effective learning. As Starfinder's leader, Warren employs three primary strategies to address this challenge. First is the process of identifying and operationalizing of organizational impact metrics connected to a theory of change.

These impact measures provide supervisors and employees with a mutually understood frame to discuss performance. Similarly, Warren highlights the centrality of clarity in an organization's mission in providing language to discuss the mutually agreed upon goals of each staff person in their shared work. With the foundation of mission and metrics, Warren believes it is possible for both parties to more openly express feedback that is direct, empathetic, and promotes the organizational goals. She also notes that, at a minimum, this structure for performance management provides no fewer than four touch points for supervisors to establish trust and dialogue with staff.

Warren's leadership style exemplifies critical components of the Executive Level of leadership offered in the Good to Great framework. It is clear when you meet her that she exudes commitment to the work and mission. She is diligent and intentional about the need to invest in alumni and program staff so that they assume the agency's leadership roles and she consistently attribute the program's impact to the work of the collective effort rather than herself. Additionally, she is rarely center stage and embodies the role of a plow horse rather than a show horse. Finally, and above all else, it seems Ms. Warren's humility, empathy, and self-reflective efforts to detach personal ego from her work are the engine that promotes Starfinder Foundation's organizational health, collective effort, and authentic social impact.

CHAPTER 6: CREATING AND LEADING POLICY AND SYSTEMS CHANGE

There are generally two types of not-for-profit organizations: service organizations that provide services and education and advocacy organizations whose purpose is to raise awareness, ensure accountability, and influence provider and consumer systems and policies.
Our work and experience have concluded that service organizations cannot exist in isolation and their service bubbles. They need engage in direct service with policy and systems change to influence often unintended consequences of existing policy that may harm the consumers they serve. We find that most not-for-profits don't engage in the political or policy and education process, but if we take lessons from the high impact not-for-profits, as argued in *Forces for Good: The Six Practices of High Impact Nonprofits*, we can bridge the divide between service and advocacy for policy change at the local, state, and/or national level. We understand that all not-for-profits need service organizations to learn how to engage in systems and policy change.

Most not-for-profit service organizations don't lead systems and policy change for a variety of reasons. This includes not wanting to "upset" the governmental funding sources that pay for the services. Although these are valid reasons, we argue that most not-for-profits don't engage in systems and policy change simply because they have not done so in the past and have not developed the skills and tools to effectively lead or engage in the process.

This chapter provides a framework, case-studies, and tools on how to create and frame a systems and policy strategy and how to organize partner organizations around this strategy. All not-for-profits need a system and policy strategy in addition to focusing on social impact, for the simple reason that most not-for-profits will not scale, even though they have the potential to scale their social impact if they have a parallel scaling impact strategy. Ironically, not-for-profits who engage in systems and policy change may not yield short-term direct benefits for their own organization, but in the long-term, they both advance the larger cause and see different but direct benefits.

Players in the Public Policy Process

"Many writers have imagined for themselves republics and principalities that have never been seen nor known to exist in reality; for there is such a gap between how one lives and how one ought to live that anyone who abandons what is done for what ought to be done learns his ruin rather than his preservation…" THE PRINCE by Nicolai Machiavelli

What we take from Machiavelli is that we need not-for-profits to protect against human beings who essentially are selfish beings. In spite of society's belief that policy and system brokers are essentially good people, we need to understand and therefore construct counterbalances knowing that power is an essential part of human nature and good people often stop working for the greater good when compromised by their own need to acquire, keep, and use power. Simply, not-for-profits must engage in policy and systems changes because, as Machiavelli states, "there is such a gap between how one lives and how one ought to live…" With not-for-profits engaged in systems and policy change, we ensure policy and system's key actors do not fall into the trap of acquiring, keeping, and using power for selfish reasons.

Nonprofits should be key players in the public policy process for the reason that they are often closer to the consumer and understand how social policies can be harmful. Not-for-profit service providers, because they serve end consumers, have a deeper and real-time understanding of their evolving needs and circumstances, putting them in the position to educate and advocate for systems and policy changes.

The government provides goods universally. However, the government is not always in contact with end consumers and does not focus on the particular needs of people. Government is also limited because it usually responds to majority rule; government officials are elected for the short-term, motivating them to focus on short-term goals, and government bureaucrats' primary role is to regulate and not to challenge the status quo.

Not-for-Profits, historically and currently, are Social Capital Agents as they are motivated by social good and are there for the long-term and they foster, formulate, perform, and evaluate society's policies that are in the furtherance of public good. The not-for-profit role is generally, for good or bad, to step in when free markets fail. Not-for-profits need to act as Social Capital Asset Agents because: the not-for-profit tax-exempt status licenses require and obligate it to be accountable to the public; they are usually owned by a collective group, and their assets come from investments from the community, donations, funders, etc. Not-for-profits are best positioned for systems and policy change because they often have direct consumer data based on their roles of 1) Assisting Consumers; 2) Assisting Workers with training and coaching; 3) Assisting Producers by conducting research and helping in development of firms and coalitions; 4) Assisting Savers by providing credit counseling and credit unions, pensions, etc.; 5) Assisting Investors by providing information and advocacy information; 6) Assisting in the Improvement of an Industry and Economic Environment by promoting fair business practice, provide info, educate, etc.; and 7) Assisting Employers through training, counseling, certification, and screening.

Not-for-Profits need to create and lead policy and systems change together, requiring them to meet regularly, build capacity, and build coalitions and membership organizations which can represent the group interests.

Public Policy and Systems Change Process
First and foremost, remember that **Systems Change is a Collective Responsibility.**

The first step in creating and leading a policy and systems strategy is to clearly define the problem, understand the policy instruments, and understand and outline the cast of characters.

Problem Definition: Clearly define the issue, the current knowledge base, and conditions, and determine if it is a federal or state issue. From this problem statement, one can build the rationalization for action and determine the plausibility on whether it stands a chance to influence the key system or policy actors.

Policy Instruments
Clearly define the means or options to influence the system or policy actors that include:
- Legal: State and Federal Courts.
- Administrative: Issue regulatory orders with the assumption that the authority exists.
- Legislative: Change in the law.
- Negotiation: Bring all the parties to the table to reach an agreement.
- Political: Create buy-in and an alliance with the key actor who has decision making authority.
- Media: Feed the press, social media, or other venues with consumable science.
- Inertia: Do nothing and let the process go forward on its own momentum.

Cast of Characters
Clearly understand the cast of characters on both sides of the issue; their motivations; and how any systems or policy change may positively or negatively personally influence them in ways that include money, power, and public perception.

The cast of characters includes:
- Stakeholders/Consumers/Voters/Constituency
- Decision makers which can include legislative members
- Influence Brokers which can include the President, Governor, Secretary, Commissioner, and Industry leaders

To effectively define the cast of characters, you will need to create a Policy Power Map, as focus drives success. Keep in mind that the definition of lobby (as a verb) is: to try to influence public officials for or against a specific cause. So, in order to identify key stakeholders to influence that will ultimately lead to policy or legislative change, you create a Power Map. You ask: 1) Who votes or influences this issue?; 2) When do they vote?; 3) What motivates these individuals or what influences their positions?; 4) For policymakers, what is their voting history?; and 5) Who influences these policymakers or individuals in influential positions?.

Creating the Power Map
1. Identify the issue in context. E.g., here, you put the issue "poor teacher training and preparation" in the center.
2. Identify key decision-making institutions or associations that are related to this issue. Write in a ring around the issue. E.g., go through a process from local to county to state to national, identifying departments and individuals that set or influence policies and practices related to teacher training.
3. Map people & their associations. Think about people who are connected to these key individuals or who influence them (for example, supervisors, constituency groups, spouses, not-for-profit or other organizations, companies, etc.). Essentially, you want to map how these key decision-makers are influenced and by whom. The purpose of this step is to help identify ways to access the individuals or institutions that could address the issue (in other words, the "dominoes"). At this step, also note any relationships that members of the group have with the people/entities listed and any information you have about them.
4. Target priority relationships. Ask 1) Does this person vote or influence this issue? How?; 2) When do they vote?; 3) What motivates this individual or what influences their position?; 4) What is this person's voting history?; and 5) Who influences this official/policy maker?

The second step in creating and leading a policy and systems strategy is to clearly lay out the steps, define a tactical plan, and enter or create negotiations/regulation/and legislative conversations.

Defining Steps: Define your constituency and clearly outline the impediments; define your strategy that includes attacking the industry and a coherent policy position on actions required by the industry (get them down and then kick them while they are down). Key to success is operating as though your agency has the authority and the resources to enforce policy/systems change that forces opponents onto your playing field.

Defining a Tactical Plan: Define a required response by the industry you are attacking and ensure that their actions can be monitored and can be enforced within the resource base (or expected resource base) of the Agency. In addition, put into a place a system to provide information to the media and structures to inform/influence/sway influence brokers. These might include:

1. Sending a mass postcard, email, or letter (use full address and target the district where you live)
2. Hand-written or personalized letters
3. Telephoning the office of the legislator
4. Getting community and issue opinion leaders to telephone the office of the legislator

5. Conversing over the telephone with a Congressional Aide or public official's key advisor
6. Getting an article published in a state/district newspaper
7. Meeting with a Congressional Aide or public official's key advisor or visiting the official's offices
8. Meeting with the legislator (Congressional Representative at federal or state level) or official in his or her home district
9. Meeting with the legislator (Congressional Representative at federal or state level) or official in the State Capitol or Washington DC
10. Working with a lobby or coalition to apply a variety of approaches

Negotiation/Legislation/Regulation: Negotiate toward the most acceptable position with industry; Legislation that includes writing/assisting in writing any required change in laws; Regulation that includes writing/assisting in writing the rules to be implemented and be certain that they are enforceable.

The third step in creating and leading a policy and systems strategy is preparing your written policy brief and oral testimony.

Written Strategies for Advocacy
Legislators and legislative staffers are busy people and they are expected to be knowledgeable about a wide range of issues. Just within the healthcare field, this could mean that the typical staffer must have superficial knowledge of everything from Medicaid enrollment procedures and hospice care, to opioid addiction and renal disease, and that does not take into account the whole host of additional domestic and foreign policy issues that come before legislative officials. Legislative offices are constantly being bombarded by requests and they cannot possibly read everything they are given. This means that unless the legislator has a special connection to an issue, the position he or she will take depends upon which side makes the most noise. In some cases, it is a simple numbers game. Legislators will literally add up the number of visits, telephone calls, letters, emails, and social media posts they have received for or against a particular position and make their decision based on volume.

Obliviously, money also plays a part. Reelection is always a big concern, especially for representatives who serve for only two years. It is no secret that politicians tend to support the positions favored by organizations and individuals that donate to their campaigns. Nonprofits, especially those serving vulnerable communities, typically do not have a lot of money to influence elections, which can put them at a disadvantage. This disadvantage, however, can be overcome through massive grassroots mobilization.

Grassroots mobilization may seem like an expensive and time-consuming strategy, but it doesn't have to be. As an example, there was an instance where our team was trying to influence Pennsylvania state representatives to vote for legislation that would recognize nurse practitioners as primary care providers in managed care organizations. The organizations opposing the legislation were bigger and more well-resourced. The supporters of the legislation choose to counteract this by mobilizing nurse practitioner patients. We contributed to this campaign by asking each patient visiting a nurse-run clinic to fill out a postcard with one quick sentence explaining why they choose to visit a nurse practitioner and what would happen to them if the clinic had to close. These post cards were collected and mailed to legislators by clinic staff, so that all the patient had to do was take a few minutes to complete the card and leave. Over time, we collected hundreds of cards, which all arrived in the state capitol shortly before a crucial vote on the nurse practitioner legislation. Needless to say, the legislators got the message and the bill passed.

In the above case, a simple, inexpensive post card made all the difference. With the pervasive reach of social media, widespread grassroots mobilization is even easier. There is just one problem. In order for a grassroots strategy to work, nonprofit advocates must be consistently engaged in the political process. If we are not out there letting our voices be heard, the causes most important to the people we care about will be drowned out by organizations with deeper pockets and more money to throw around.

There are a number of ways advocates can stay engaged. To make things easier, we have broken them down into two categories; verbal and written strategies. Verbal strategies include things like: 1) in person visits to legislative offices; and 2) telephone calls. Written strategies might include: 1) compiling policy papers and briefs; 2) writing letters; developing factsheets; and presenting sample legislation. This section focuses on written strategies.

Before jumping into the first of the written strategies, let us make a few final points about communication methods in general. As mentioned above, policymakers place a great deal of weight on the volume of correspondence they receive, but it is also important to note that certain methods of communication receive more weight than others. According to legislative staffers, actual in person office visits by constituents are given the most weight, followed by hand written constituent letters, and telephone calls by constituents. Less weight is given to form letters and mass emails with identical wording. Basically, the most effective messages are those that come from constituents who have taken time out of their day to tell the representative in their own words how a particular issue affects them and those they care about. It may not always be practical to have the message come directly from a constituent, and this is not to say that communications from lobbyists have no value, but it is important to work constituent stories into written and verbal materials whenever possible.

Another thing to consider is what kind of relationship you have with the legislator or staffer you are attempting to persuade. If it is the first time you are meeting with or contacting a particular legislator, it may be more productive to lead off with a shorter document, like a factsheet or letter, as opposed to the longer policy brief format. As we have said many times, legislators are pressed for time and they are not likely to read everything they are given. Factsheets or letters can provide a brief introduction to your issues that will hopefully peak the legislator's interest and cause her or him to want to know more. Once this introduction has been made and the legislator requests additional information, then you can follow up with a more detailed policy brief. Similarly, when preparing materials for a meeting, it may be helpful to include an introductory factsheet along with a policy brief, this gives the legislator the option of referring to the longer document for more information as needed. As you build stronger relationships with policymakers over the long term, they will hopefully begin to look to your organization as a resource they can consult before taking actions that are relevant to the people you serve. In this case, the policy brief may be the most effective form of communication.

Writing Policy Briefs & Papers

One of the best mechanisms for nonprofits to get their message in front of legislators is to write a policy brief, which provides an overview of the issue. There are many types of policy briefs. In our experience writing thousands of briefs over the years, the best formats have certain characteristics in common. First and foremost, they are concise and to the point. As we have stated, any politician, whether at the local, state or national level, get thousands of advocacy requests yearly. Chances are that the legislator or staffer you are meeting with has, at best, a superficial knowledge of your issue. The primary purpose of any advocacy tool, therefore, is to both educate and persuade. The best policy briefs present the advocate's key points in an easily digestible manner that allows the reader/legislator to quickly understand the issue and what he or she is being asked to do. The sample briefs included in **Appendix J** are designed to do just that. One of the more widely used formats is a form adapted from legal briefs, known as the CIRAC format.

C -- Conclusion -- write your conclusion up front. What is the issue and what outcomes are you advocating for?
I -- Issue -- lay out the issue clearly and concisely.
R -- Rule/s -- describe current rules and regulations if applicable related to the issue you are advocating for.
A -- Application -- describe how the current rules are interpreted or how the issue is executed or not and why you want to change it. Describe why your issue is important and who would be in favor of what you are advocating for. Also, describe who would be against the issue or rule or regulatory change you are advocating for and why.
C -- Conclusion -- write a persuasive conclusion that acknowledges the opposition, and end with why the advocacy position is the right one for the policy maker to focus on.

Generally, briefs are longer than a letter. However, good letters should follow a CIRAC format.

Examples of Policy Briefs can be found in Appendix K

Policy Fact Sheets and Letters:
Factsheets and letters are a vital piece of the policy toolbox. Generally shorter in length, factsheets and letters are a good way to introduce your organization to a new contact or keep your issues on the forefront of the policy agenda for your existing champions. Because they are so short, usually no more than one or two pages, the most important thing to remember when writing factsheets and letters for policy makers is to be concise and get to the point as quickly as possible. Another thing to keep in mind is that factsheets and letters are used for different purposes. A factsheet is generally used to convey information, point out the benefits of a particular policy, or provide a policymaker with evidence supporting a specific policy position. While letters also convey information and offer evidence for various policy positions, letters contain an ask. They are designed to persuade the policy maker to do something. The information conveyed in the factsheet will certainly support a particular course of action, but there is generally no overt ask. For example, the factsheet in **Appendix L** on the cost effectiveness of retail clinics does not request policymakers to do anything it simply lists a few quick bullet points on how retail clinics can save money. The letter addressed to Speaker Turzai in Pennsylvania, on the other hand, expressly requests the Speaker to bring a bill up for vote in the House as quickly as possible.

Below are a few quick points about each type of document. The factsheets simply provide a few quick bullets supporting whatever point each sheet is attempting to make. It is important to include sources for the facts provided so that whoever is reviewing the sheet knows where to look for more information. In the case of the letters, the ask is included up front usually in the first or second sentence of the letter. Facts offering evidence as to why the request is being made follow the initial ask. These facts are intended to show that the request being made is a sound policy decision and fits within the policy makers priorities. Here again, as with any policy document, it is important to know the priorities of your audience and have a clear idea of what you hope to accomplish. The letter's initial ask is then restated towards the end of the document. Personal stories demonstrating how the policy being advanced will concretely improve the lives of constituents within the policy maker's district or state are very effective. The number one thing staffers want to know up front is how many constituents does the problem or policy being discussed impact? Including a personal story in the letter will help push it to the top of the pile. If no story is available, at the very least the letter should include a sentence or to showing a connection to the policymaker's representatives. For example, the letter to Speaker Turzai states there are 97 retail clinics in Pennsylvania, his home state.

Examples of Policy Fact Sheets can be found in Appendix L

Legislation
The ability of legislation to shape society and change people's lives is unparalleled. Large segments of our nation's history are often associated with an important piece of legislation. In the 1930's, it was the New Deal and in the 1960's there was the Great Society and civil rights legislation, and of course, most recently, the Affordable Care Act (ACA). With this in mind, it is difficult to understate the importance of writing good legislation. President Barak Obama once said, "A good compromise, a good piece of legislation, is like a good sentence. Or a good piece of music. Everybody can recognize it. They say, 'Huh. It works. It makes sense.[vi]"

How does one write good legislation? An article in the *Harvard Journal on Legislation* sheds some light on key essential pointers, some of which, are things we have already talked about (Medows, Deborah Beth, 2016). The first one is something we have mentioned many times, be short and concise. I learned this the hard way. In my role as policy manager with the National Nurse-Led Care Consortium, I was part of a team that wrote legislative language which became part of the ACA. The original bill that we wrote was 12 pages long, however, the final language that made it into the ACA was less than three. That's right, the congressional staffer handling our legislation gave us just one night to cut 12 pages down to three. It pays to be concise.

The article also points out the need to be diligent in research and not to recreate the wheel. Have a good idea of what you want and do some research, chances are somebody at the state or federal level has already written legislation addressing your issue that you can use as a model. Many state legislatures have a search box that allows you to pull up legislation with certain key words. This is a good place to start. I often write legislation dealing with pharmacists. The first thing I do is go to the webpage for the legislature I am working with and type pharmacist into the search box, this usually leads me to previously introduced pharmacist legislation I can use to identify the proper format and citation.

Finally, the article reminds those drafting legislation to keep the big picture in mind. Most legislation is written by partners working in coalitions. Coalitions can be great for generating support for legislation, but they can also make it difficult to draft language. The problem is that each coalition partner often pressures the drafters to include language that benefits the special interests they represent; making too many concessions can water down the legislation and hamper its effectiveness. Keeping the big picture of the legislation in mind helps the drafters strike the right balance between making concessions to partners and maintaining the original goal of the legislation.

Sample Legislation can be found in Appendix M

In conclusion, as you think about policy and systems change remember the primary principles of Lobbying & Advocacy:
1) Be accurate (and don't lie): If you get a question you can't answer, say so.
2) Be brief: For a written communication, try to keep it to a page or less (unless it's an exposé or well-researched position paper).
3) Be clear: Have a specific goal.
4) Know your opposition: Know the main arguments for and against a position or a piece of legislation.
5) Show them how they win: Appeal to enlightened self-interest.
6) See it their way: Try to find a way to make your position and argument fit in with the person's own values, viewpoints, history on the issue, etc.
7) Consider the messenger: This is backed up by the research suggesting that someone is more likely to listen to someone who is like them and who likes them.
8) Follow up: Send a thank you. Make a phone call. Recognize and appreciate any effort made.

We leave you with the importance of thinking about sustainability so that the progress is not lost. Policy and systems change progress can easily be lost if the opposition organizes, and it will, to challenge the changes. The best sustainability plan is to create a membership organization whose responsibility is to monitor and represent the common interests of the group.

We end this chapter and book with case examples of Episcopal Community Services, an anti-poverty regional organization; a Nurse-Led Care National Policy Organization; an International Policy Organization; and a Border Action Network Legislative Policy Influence Case Study.

Case Study: Muddy Boots: Setting the Stage for Policy Change by David Griffith

Episcopal Community Services, a Philadelphia faith-based social service agency founded in 1870, provides services to individuals and families in the Philadelphia Region. The agency currently serves some 2,300 individuals with programs in out of school time, summer camps, youth mentoring, work force development, emergency shelter, emerging housing, wellness, [arenting, and several programs that visit and feed the elderly.

Over the last five years the agency, in response to the changing needs of participants and unpredictable political priorities and funding sources, has undertaken a transformation based on a mandate of innovation and a combination of talents from different non-traditional sectors not typically associated with the social service sector.

In May of 2013, I joined the agency as the first nonsocial worker and nonclergy Executive Director. I have a 40-year background in the for-profit sector as both an executive, director, and as an investor. The mandate from the board was to evaluate the agency and working with the board work through the necessary changes in programs, talent, funding, and focus. To do so in such a way that Episcopal Community Services in both the current and future environment could maintain its leadership and continue to serve the region's most vulnerable individuals as well as to define and sustain its relationship and history with the Episcopal Diocese of Pennsylvania.

My management philosophy is one of the practices of "wear muddy boots." That is you don't manage from behind a desk, you go out into the field, and you talk and listen to the individual doing the work, the users of your services, and you ask two fundamental questions. What is it we do? What should we do better? I believe that the people closest to work, know the most about the work.

Some early lessons and issues occurred as a result and needed addressing. A few examples. On the program side, ECS was a well established medical foster care provider. A month into my assignment the CUA (Community Umbrella Agency) structure was announced in Philadelphia. Medical Foster Care and the design of foster parent, birth parent, and a child's school in the same police district did not match. Rather than wait for the government to end our program we transferred the program and staff to other agencies. Not easy, but it allowed us to focus on programs we had. The message was let's look at the data and make a decision and move on, not the typical process in the sector.

In looking at the finances and specifically the wage and benefit model we found a number of opportunities. First was as an anti-poverty agency we were paying an hourly wage of $10 an hour. We went to the board and found support to raise the hourly wage immediately, and today it stands at $14.00 and is on the way to $18.00. Interestingly workers compensation claims dropped and turnover significantly decreased. We were also able to attract better talent. With soft dollars, we funded hard dollars. Concerning benefits, we were under both a traditional medical plan and a conventional workers compensation plan. We moved both to a self-insured, captive trust model. On an $800,000 medical premium, we were able to preserve coverage and lower costs to $500,000 in the first year. Similar experience with worker compensation and we became eligible for good exposure experience to receive an annual dividend in both programs, which we now enjoy. Some risk garnered some reward which we could reinvest.

We also undertook early on a formal leadership development program that I have used in several other organizations. My observations are we needed to significantly improve the process of both giving and receiving feedback from managers and later employees as well as the ability to have crucial conversations on the severe issues we were working on.

The program is now in its fourth year, is well regarded, and is functioning on several levels. You will see stuffed elephants through the agency locations. We want an environment where elephants can be safely named, and the elephants were props from this leadership training. Learning can be fun.

At the same time, I understood, given my background, I needed significant help with our programs not only current but going forward. It became apparent to me, as it always has that the better the talent, the better the programs we offer our participants. I made a decision early to hire or retain into leadership positions individuals called to this work and second who have the academic and field experience to give them domain experience in the field. Third, those who shared our values of community, dignity, justice, and impact, fourth individuals who have an upside to their careers, and finally, those who could lead others.

Our strategy is to pay individuals reasonably, have a great place to work regarding balance, give them a seat at the table in our decision-making process, and provide them with authority to run their department. All while having a culture of accountability and data to track performance and results.

The combination of our leadership development, values, and hiring process is a team that functions as a team that trusts, is self-accountable, and drives a significant amount of work. Having such a group allows ECS to have a culture of innovation and a critical focus on the task at hand. It also gives us the capacity to deal with stuff as it comes at us. A team can pull a wagon that an individual cannot.

What we have found that seems to work is what we have come to call entrepreneurial social work. In that, a combination of business, social work, field experience adequately focused and leveraging all backgrounds provides solutions to problems and gives an organization the depth to be able to react to changing conditions. The first three years to be clear had mistakes and missteps, but as an organization, we were willing to deal with hard issues, take risks, and look for solutions in creative ways. The board has been supportive, and our results have provided the feedback and results to continue with our approach.

Which sets the stage to talk about our policy and systems work we are currently undertaking. 18 months ago as we had laid the foundation of resetting both our organization and existing programs as well as our building the staff and board relationship we undertook two significant projects. A branding exercise and a strategic plan. We sensed as an organization that our programs were well regarded. The issue for us was the impact we were delivering, or better said not providing. So we launched both projects with the support of our board.

Policy Issue

The poverty rate in America in the mid-1960's as calculated in 1970 dollars hovered around 15 percent. In 2016, still calculated in 1970 dollars, the poverty rate has not changed. Adjusted for inflation the poverty rate is significantly higher. In major cities, specifically Philadelphia, the poverty rate is more than 25 percent. One could conclude that social policy, both public and private has not impacted poverty in America. One can make the argument that public and private social system has primarily been in maintenance mode.

The essential question is how does the "system" move from maintenance to change and break the cycle of intergenerational poverty? In our case how do we as ECS undertake such a change?

Some observations.
1. There are a significant number of organizations working in this space with budgets under five million dollars. The majority of their funding comes from government contracts, as in higher than 85 percent. In Philadelphia, 30 percent of the agencies have less than 90 days cash on hand. The overlap of missions is significant, and the competition for both public and private funding is substantial.
2. Looking at the core funding streams from the public sector one sees there is little room for innovation investment dollars, let alone adequate funding for administrative and compliance functions.
3. In looking at the current environment in Philadelphia, we found:
    i. Long-term high levels of poverty.
    ii. Programs are primarily providing maintenance to individuals and families as opposed to providing pathways out of intergenerational poverty in the form of the long-term sustained change in individuals economic levels.

iii. The challenge of funding overall and lack of access to innovation funding.
iv. The difficulties of creating scale synergies.

One concludes the need for a different approach. Specifically, with the organizational and financial models needed to drive this work efficiently, and the methodology and public policy used by both case managers and organizations with participants to create sustained change in individuals economic status.

Program and organizational scale matters in this work. Overhead as a percent of total agency revenue is more significant in small agencies than in larger ones. The ability to attract talent that is effective in finance, human resources, development, and technology is a function of organizational size. Scale also matters in the ability to create revenue streams other than government contracts, which in turns leads to innovation and investment dollars. A balance of revenue streams can provide more stable funding, and this balance is more accessible with scale. Hence a desire to create such stream is a strategic imperative.

A mix of government contracts, annual fund, foundation and grant funding, endowment, and social impact enterprises provide more stable cash flow, but also the opportunity to support innovation and with a creative approach provide revenues while also being consistent with a mission. Some example that come to mind is the housing and community development space and the emerging urban vertical farming space. Organizations are developing a mix of low-income housing, community incubator space, and traditional commercial space and market housing in a blended portfolio. They are returning to investors a market return while at the same time addressing affordable housing needs and supporting job creation. Shift Capital in Philadelphia is one such example. Another is the emerging urban vertical farm movement where social impact investors are building small urban vertical farms in distressed neighborhoods and providing both jobs and career paths to individuals in these neighborhoods. At the same time, the economic returns are such that these urban farms are profitable and provide a market return. Victory Farms in Philadelphia is one emerging example of such an organization.

An organization at scale allows an organization to create a meaningful development and communication organization that can garner support from individual donors, foundations, and corporate funders. This is also true for the finance, human resource, and technology functions which are vital to the ability to attract and support talent and in turn drive impact. An organization at scale can also drive advocacy, and in turn public policy.

While an agency at scale is critical to support the mission, the vital question of an agency's mission is how impactful are its programs. In the case of intergenerational poverty can one move from the maintenance mode to the change mode with the individuals and families you serve.

In an environment driven by government funding, it is common for an organization to lose focus by chasing the latest contract. To encourage innovation and impact an organization needs to be focused on its mission and more importantly in its approach to its work. We believe that with focus, funding will follow if the work drives impact.

At ECS we stepped back and looked at the poverty data. We concluded while we have active and well-regarded programs they were not lifting the individuals we served out of poverty. We undertook a strategic plan where we reset our mission, vision, and values, and in turn, researched to find the best approach to addressing intergenerational poverty.

Through our branding work we created the following:
- Our mission is to challenge poverty.
- Our vision is a world where prosperity is available to all.
- Our values are Community, Dignity, Justice, and Impact.
- Community, in that we partner with others in this work, especially our participants.
- Dignity, as a bedrock value, is how we interact we all with whom we work.
- Justice, as a guidepost for all. The understanding that Justice is not available to all.
- Impact, in that, if our work does not deliver impact for our participants, then it needs to change.
- These four values reflected in all that we do and that form the filter through which all decisions are driven.

Our research led us to the conclusion we needed to change our case management approach to both our current programs and any future ones we created. We found and embraced the EMPATHY model of our Boston partner which uses the latest brain science and looks to use coaching and incentives to work with participants to help them drive change in their economic status. Our approach includes training everyone at the agency in this model, implementing the model in our current programs and over time creating a new program that focuses on individuals intensively to bring them out of poverty and into a stable economic situation. The model establishes goals in the areas of housing, wellness, education, financial savvy, and workforce development. At its core is the premise that individuals in poverty experience high levels and sustained periods of crisis and that through coaching and incentives an individual's level of crisis can be lowered and in turn their ability to achieve economic stability improved. As we look at the approach, our early analysis suggested funding at the $20,000 level per individual per year and based on other agencies experience a need to work with individuals over a three- to five-year period. This budget requires we create multiple revenue streams and additional revenues.

The data from others in this work suggests the impacts are significant and sustainable and therefore well worth funding. We have decided to move forward while not yet having our own results. Innovation carries risks, but we know the current approach is not working and we trust our research. Based on this focus we are shifting our funding focuses on a mix of contracts, endowment, annual and long-term giving, and social enterprises. This mix of financing will support investment and in turn innovation and we believe over time attract foundation and public support and impact evidence.

In addition to implementing the mobility mentoring model at ECS, we have also undertaken the creation and funding of three additional efforts. The first as I have mentioned is a formal leadership training program within the organization and the intentional structuring of compensation and benefits to attract and train the best available talent. We firmly believe the better the talent, the better the programs and in turn better the ability to draw funding and investment. What we have learned early from this effort is that these works need to be a sustained and defined element of our workflow. Having talent at the table that you listen to, is how high design happens.

The second investment we have made is the creation of an inclusion and advocacy function on the staff and the creation of an advocacy committee of our board. We believe the most significant impact we can have on poverty is focusing voices that drive changes in public policy and funding based on informed and substantiated data and its implications. I also know that as a white male from the world of business I need to be held accountable for inclusion in ways not on my radar and my inclusion officer has this as part of her job description. This has led to some profound experiences and learnings which in turn have made me a better coach.

The third is we have created a learning and evaluation group that collects and provides analytics on all of our program data and outcomes. They host our dashboards and board portal and help us make informed decisions based on data and in turn hold us accountable to our stakeholders and participants. They not only track the data they coach in its use.

We believe that to drive change in intergenerational poverty you need an "all in" and consistent approach to the work and to the messaging of that work and efforts. We asked ourselves the following questions through our efforts and are working on the answers in real time as the environment we live in is fluid.

1. Do you have a clear focus on the mission, the people you serve, and their desired outcomes?
2. Do your actions and spending match up?
3. Do you have a clear focus on talent and talent development?
4. Do you create great alumni networks? Both employees and participants?
5. Do you have the scale to fund the proper level of finance, development, communications, programs, human resources, and technology?
6. Do you invest in innovation and pilots? How do you treat failure?

7. Do you continually look at science-based research to find methodology with the likelihood of success? Do you benchmark?
8. Do you create multiple revenues streams?
9. Can you invest in social impact projects that both drive the mission and generate funding streams?
10. Are you prepared to advocate at a level that inspires change in public policy and informs the broader community as to the real issues surrounding poverty and dispels the urban myths?
11. Are we prepared to share everything we learn?
12. Are you willing to say no?

Our objective and ambition at ECS is to deliver impact to the people we serve and to be around for our second 150 years. This requires a crisp mission: Challenge Poverty, programs that change lives; we believe the Prosperity Model as we call ECS's version of EMPATH does; and talent as a driver of performance, advocacy as a strategic tool, values as a bedrock foundation in all that we do. Finally a willingness to look critically at all we do and be willing to change and figure it out as challenges come at us. What we know is we need to change how we do this work. What I have learned is you learn every day.

We believe that the journey we are on is one that will achieve our ambitions. More importantly, we believe it will best serve the individuals for whom we work.

Case Study: Principles for Changing Policy with Limited Resources: Nurse-Led Care by Brian Valdez

Famous Philadelphia anthropologist Margaret Mead once said, "Never doubt that a small group of thoughtful, committed citizens can change the world; indeed, it's the only thing that ever has." It is particularly important to keep this quote in mind if you are a staff member working in a small not-for-profit or community-based organization. Social innovations are by their nature new and different, which means those supporting innovation will eventually challenge the interest of the status quo. For small organizations with limited resources to dedicate to policy reform, challenging the status quo can often seem like an unwinnable David versus Goliath scenario where the innovators are forced to confront large, often national organizations connected to vast resources, powerful lobbyists, and an entrenched network of supportive elected officials. Although these odds may seem long and at times discouraging, history has shown that Dr. Mead's statement holds true. Time and time again, small groups of committed individuals offering novel solutions to the problems encountered by social policy makers have been able to break through the status quo and force change.

This chapter is intended to suggest some ways small, not-for-profit community-based organizations can utilize strategies that have proven effective in the past to bring about policy reform with limited resources. It will focus on the importance of properly framing the issue, gathering the right data, building effective partnerships, and staying persistent. In an effort to provide some practical knowledge as to how this process plays out in the real world, this chapter will examine how a small group of advocates have been able to increase access to primary care by initiating policy reforms that support innovative models of nurse-led care. Specifically, this chapter will discuss two types of nurse-led clinics: 1) retail clinics and 2) nurse-managed health clinics. Each is defined below.

Retail Clinics -- Retail Clinics are healthcare facilities located inside retail locations, such as pharmacies and grocery stores. There are approximately 2,300 of these clinics in operation across the country. The majority of retail clinics are run by nurse practitioners with a small percentage being run by physician assistants and other providers. The clinics offer high-quality, low-cost, accessible healthcare that encompasses basic primary care, preventive and wellness services, and some chronic disease monitoring and treatment. Generally open seven days a week, with extended weekday hours, appointments are not necessary, and visits generally take 15-20 minutes. Services include: things like treatment for cold/flu, rashes/skin irritation, and muscle strains or sprains, as well as physicals, vaccinations and other preventive health screenings.

Nurse-Managed Health Clinics -- A nurse-managed health clinic (NMHC) is a nurse-practice arrangement, managed by advanced practice nurses, that provides primary care or wellness services to underserved or vulnerable populations, and that is associated with a school, college, university or department of nursing, federally qualified health center (FQHC), or independent nonprofit health or social services agency. There are approximately 250 nurse-managed clinics nationwide. NMHC care is directed by nurse practitioners and other advanced practice nurses offering a wide range of primary care, health promotion, and disease prevention services to low-income, vulnerable patients living in medically underserved areas. Nationally, NMHCs record about 250,000 patient encounters each year. The majority of NMHC patients are either Medicaid recipients, uninsured, or self-pay.

Step 1: Background: Framing the Issue -- You may have heard the saying, "perception is reality." The quote was actually coined by the highly sought after presidential campaign strategist, Lee Atwater. His point, I think, is that the way advocates and innovators frame a particular issue effects the way policymakers think about that issue and will ultimately impact how likely they support the policy changes being requested. One way that small organizations can increase their influence on policy is to understand the priorities of their elected officials and craft their messaging to fit those priorities, as much as possible. Take for example, the issue of nurse-led care. Innovative models of nurse-led care, like nurse managed health clinics (NMHC) and retail clinics, offer several possible advantages, but the organizations supporting these models are relatively small with limited resources to dedicate to policy. In order to spend these resources effectively, advocates have had to decide which benefits of the various nurse-led innovations to highlight when approaching particular legislators, or policymakers. They have also had to be flexible enough to refresh their messaging when a previously successful line of reason no longer has the desired impact.

It is generally accepted that nurse practitioners and other advanced practice nurses offer high quality care.[1] In addition to the quality care, advocates of nurse-led care tend to highlight three primary benefits of the model. First, NMHCs and retail clinics increase healthcare access by offering care at times and locations that are easily accessible. They also utilize nurse practitioners, which expands the number of available providers, particularly in rural and intercity medically underserved areas.

---

[1] Maria, Schiff et al. "The Role of Nurse Practitioners in Meeting Increasing Demand for Primary Care." National Governors Association. [Accessed 2012].

In fact, a 2018 study found that the supply of nurse practitioners is about 50 percent higher in less affluent counties where the population has more health problems.[2] Second, nurse-led models reduce overall costs by diverting patients from emergency rooms and hospitals, while making less expensive primary and preventative services more widely available. These cost savings are especially evident for Medicare patients where evaluation and management costs are about 29 percent lower when nurse practitioners are involved.[3] Third, nurse-led models increase completion and consumer choice by giving consumers access to non-traditional healthcare providers, like nurse practitioners. The Federal Trade Commission (FTC) has made numerous statements supporting this view, including this one from a 2016 report, "When advanced practice nurse access to the primary care market is restricted, health care consumers -- patients -- and other payors are denied some of the competitive benefits that advanced practice nurses, as additional primary care service providers, can offer.[4]"

It might be tempting to assume it's always best to emphasize every possible advantage of your innovation, but there are situations when this is not the case. Nurse-managed health clinics scored a big victory when the Affordable Care Act (ACA) defined the model in federal law and created a new grant program appropriating funding for the clinics, but this victory was short lived. The Republicans soon seized control of the Congress due in large part to a backlash against the ACA. Prior to the passage of the act, both Republican and Democratic policymakers had been receptive to the message that NMHCs can increase access to care and cut costs, indeed this had been the message used by advocates arguing for the ACA's recognition of NMHCs. As congress moved to the right, however, Republican leaders became very reluctant to release any NMHC grant funding, especially since the NMHC grant program was associated with the ACA.

---

[2] Matthew A. Davis, Rebecca Anthopolos, Joshua Tootoo, Marita Titler, Julie P. W. Bynum and Scott A. Shipman. "Supply of Healthcare Providers in Relation to County Socioeconomic and Health Status." Journal of General Internal Medicine. [Accessed 2018].

[3] Jennifer Perloff, Catherine M. DesRoches and Peter Buerhaus. "Comparing the Cost of Care Provided to Medicare Beneficiaries Assigned to Primary Care Nurse Practitioners and Physicians." Health Services Research. [Accessed 2016].

[4] Federal Trade Commission. Policy Perspectives Competition and the Regulation of Advanced Practice Nurses. Available at:
https://www.ftc.gov/system/files/documents/reports/policy-perspectives-competition-regulation-advanced-practice-nurses/140307aprnpolicypaper.pdf. [Accessed 2014].

This change in the balance of power has forced NMHC advocates to rethink and reframe their messaging around the importance of nurse-led care. Instead of concentrating on the argument that money for NMHCs can increase access to care in medically underserved areas at a lower cost, advocates began highlighting the FTC's assertion that nurse practitioner-led models of care increase competition within the healthcare market, while lowering costs, and enhancing consumer choice.

This shift in emphasis brings the message more in line with conservative ideals like free market economics, fiscal conservatism, and limited government. Although the reframing of the issue has not led to new funding for NMHCs, it has brought additional support to another key piece of the nurse-led care policy agenda, namely the campaign to gain independent practice or full practice authority for nurse practitioners.

Several states have laws and regulations on the books that prevent nurse practitioners from practicing without some form of physician supervision. Supporters of nurse-led care have long tried to remove these restrictions, because requiring a nurse practitioner to enter into a supervisory or collaborative relationship with a physician limits patient access to nurse practitioners and creates additional costs for patients and providers without improving the overall quality of care. The FTC has said, "when an APRN is required to secure and maintain a collaborative practice agreement with a physician in order to practice independently, at least some costs are imposed on both contracting parties. Either sort of cost may harm patients, to the extent that higher costs diminish access to care, and may harm health care consumers, as well as public and private third-party payors to the extent that some increased costs may be passed along as higher prices.[5]"

By reframing the issue around the FTC's desire to promote competition in health care, nurse-led care advocates have gained the support of conservative organizations, like the Heritage Foundation, which is calling for the removal of state regulations that prevent the independent practice of nurse practitioners, because these regulations are viewed as an unlawful restraint of trade. The addition of conservative voices that would not be in favor of the ACA is one factor that has led to a growth in number of states granting nurse practitioners independent practice. Today, 22 states and the District of Columbia allow nurse practitioners to practice independently, which is up from 14 states and DC in 2010.

---

[5] Federal Trade Commission. Policy Perspectives Competition and the Regulation of Advanced Practice Nurses. Available at:
https://www.ftc.gov/system/files/documents/reports/policy-perspectives-competition-regulation-advanced-practice-nurses/140307aprnpolicypaper.pdf. [Accessed 2014].

Step 2. Gathering the Right Data: The retail clinic industry is another innovative model of nurse-led care with relatively small policy resources that has achieved great success. At the time the industry first obtained visibility in the early 2000's there were around 150 clinics nationwide. Today, that number has ballooned to nearly 3,000. Most of these clinics are run by nurse practitioners. In the early years, retail clinics, like other clinics built around nurse practitioners, faced considerable opposition from organized medicine. Organized medicine represented by groups, such as the American Medical Association (AMA), has a large well-established lobby with a long list of supporters. Retail clinic leaders have employed a number of strategies to overcome, deflect, and defuse the AMA's antagonism. One strategy, which should be part of every small organization's policy toolbox is to prioritize the collection and utilization of data.

When one thinks of data in a private sector business context, perhaps the image that most often comes to mind is one of sales executives poring over reports full of information used to analyze spending habits, match consumers with popular products, and build effective marketing strategies; all done with the goal of increasing profits. For retail clinics and other social innovations, the goal is different. Of course, maintaining a solid bottom line is important to all businesses, but for most social innovations the use of data is inextricably tied to the accomplishment of a social mission. For retail clinics, their mission is to increase access to convenient, high-quality, affordable healthcare. But, in contrast to not-for-profit NMHCs, retail clinics are, for the most part, an innovation born of the private sector and linked companies with a for-profit business model. Their connection to business allows retail clinics to bring together the best of both worlds, using private sector data analysis and tools to provide the ideal patient healthcare experience, an experience that offers patients the services they want and need, while ultimately leading to improved health outcomes. The capacity of retail clinics to highlight these outcomes has been key to the success of the industry's policy agenda.

Retail clinic operators realized early on that data was going to be vital to not only the accomplishment of their mission, but also the survival and acceptance of the model, in general. Early opposition to the retail clinics coalesced around the fear that retail clinics would lead to a disruption of the primary care provider relationship and a lower quality of care. To overcome this obstacle, one of the first things clinic operators did was found a trade association, known as the Convenient Care Association (CCA), to give voice to the industry. CCA and its members quickly moved to build connections with top researchers that could produce peer-reviewed, evidence-based studies showing the high quality of retail clinic services. One advantage of the retail clinic business model is that all retail clinics use electronic health records (EHR), which makes data more accessible and easy to transmit. The wealth of data available to retail clinics made, and continues to make, the clinics an attractive option for researchers and government agencies searching for answers to America's most pressing healthcare problems.

One of the first researchers to recognize the disruptive potential of retail clinics was RAND Health. Researchers analyzing de-identified data from retail clinic EHRs concluded that the quality scores and rates of preventive care offered at retail clinics are similar to the scores and rates in other delivery settings.[6]
Other researchers found that retail clinics had a 92.72 percent compliance with the quality measure for appropriate testing of children with pharyngitis as compared to HEDIS average of 74.7 percent; they also found that the clinics had an 88.35 percent compliance score for appropriate testing of children with URI compared to the HEDIS average of 83.5 percent.[7] Findings like these coupled with several later studies attesting to the high quality of care at retail clinics have effectively silenced opposition based on the industry's quality of care.

---

[6] Ateev Mehrotra, Liu Hangsheng, John L. Adams, et al. Comparing Costs and Quality of Care at Retail Clinics with that of Other Medical Settings for 3 Common Illnesses. Annals of Internal Medicine 151, no. 5. Pages: 321-328. [Accessed 2009].

[7] Richard Jacoby, Albert G. Crawford, et al. Quality of Care for 2 Common Pediatric Conditions Treated by Convenient Care Providers. American Journal of Medical Quality 26, no. 1. Pages: 53-58, doi: 10.1177/1062860610375106. [Accessed 2010].

[8] CTS Household Survey and HSC Health Tracking Household Surveys. Center for Studying Health System Change. http://www.hschange.com/index.cgi?data=02. [Accessed 12 November 2016].

[9] Blue Cross and Blue Shield of Minnesota Offers No Co-Pay for Use of Retail Clinics. Business Wire. http://www.businesswire.com/news/home/20080729006230/en/Blue-Cross-Blue-Shield-Minnesota-Offers-Co-Pay. [Accessed 14 November 2016].

[10] The Future of Nursing: Leading Change, Advancing Health. Institute of Medicine. Page: H-18 (2010).
https://www.nationalacademies.org/hmd/~/media/Files/Report%20Files/2010/The-Future-of-Nursing/Future%20of%20Nursing%202010%20Recommendations.pdf. [Accessed 12 November 2016].

[11] The Future of Nursing: Leading Change, Advancing Health. Institute of Medicine (2010). Page: H-18 (2010).
https://www.nationalacademies.org/hmd/~/media/Files/Report%20Files/2010/The-Future-of-Nursing/Future%20of%20Nursing%202010%20Recommendations.pdf. [Accessed 12 November 2016].

Another key finding to emerge during early research showed that more than half of retail clinic patients reported not having access to a regular source of care.[8] This demonstrated that, rather than disrupting the primary care relationship, retail clinics are serving to strengthen access to primary care by connecting patients without a regular source of care to primary care and other critical services. Another watershed moment came when the Blue Cross Blue Shield Association released a study showing that retail clinics had produced a cost savings of $1.2 million for patients enrolled in Blue Cross and Blue Shield of Minnesota.[9] The cost savings was so great, in fact, that Blue Cross and Blue Shield of Minnesota decided to lower copays for retail clinic users. Data from the Blues helped to open the door for retail clinics to contract with the nation's major managed care insurers, many of whom had previously been reluctant to contract with the relatively new industry.

Research conducted by government and quazi-government agencies, like the Institute of Medicine (IOM), now called the National Academy of Medicine, has served to further emphasize the benefits of the retail clinic model for policymakers seeking to reform healthcare systems. For example, retail clinics are mentioned more than 30 times in IOM's report entitled, "The Future of Nursing: Leading Change, Advancing Health," published in 2010. The report especially highlights patient satisfaction with retail clinic services and calls the clinics, "a desirable service-delivery mechanism providing accessible, less costly, evidence-based services.[10]" The report goes on to say, "the Centers for Medicare and Medicaid Services should encourage state Medicaid programs to cover health care services provided by retail or convenient care clinics.[11]" Endorsements from such widely respected agencies paved the way for greater acceptance and expansion of the model, but such endorsements would not have been possible without the retail clinic industry's emphasis on the collection and use of data.

While data is not the only factor driving retail clinic expansion, it is clear that easy access to data showing the capacity of retail clinics to accomplish the triple aim of increased access, lower costs, and improved health outcomes was essential in establishing the legitimacy of the industry at a time when opposition could have stopped retail clinics in their tracks. In other words, the retail clinic experience has shown that a policy agenda built around timely and well researched data can survive and thrive even in the face of entrenched opposition.

Step 3: Building Effective Partnerships: The 2018 movie, "12 Strong" tells the true story of twelve U.S. green berets sent to Afghanistan to lay the ground work for the fight against the Taliban. Although the green berets are highly trained and have access to advanced technology, twelve soldiers are no match for the overwhelming numbers of Taliban fighters. The green berets employ a principle called force multiplication, namely they link up with partners who can increase their numbers and help accomplish their mission.

In the business world, force multipliers are defined as tools that amplify your effort to produce more output, which basically means they enable you to get more done with the same amount of effort or resources. This whole chapter is in a way an exploration of various force multipliers smaller organizations can employ to amplify their policy impact. The ability to identify and establish partnerships with influential organizations or individuals is in my experience, the most important force multiplier available to policy staff representing small organizations.

Partnerships in the policy context basically fall into three categories: 1) partnerships formed with individual champions; 2) partnerships with individual organizations; and 3) partnerships with coalitions. An individual champion is an elected representative or policymaker who uses their position of influence to highlight your innovation or shepherd your policy agenda through the political process. Along with identifying individual champions, smaller organizations can extend their reach by partnering with larger organizations that can dedicate more policy staff time and take advantage of well-established connections with elected officials. A coalition further broadens this impact by bringing together multiple organizations that agree to utilize their collective resources in an effort to advance a common policy agenda. A brief look at the history of the NMHC movement beginning in the late-1990s offers a glimpse into just how essential these types of partnerships can be in moving policies friendly to social innovation forward.

The nurse-managed health clinic policy agenda has been championed by the National Nurse-Led Care Consortium (NNCC), a membership association founded by a group of NMHC leaders, since the mid-1990s. NNCC is a relatively small organization with a limited policy staff. To make up for its lack of size, NNCC focused on identifying individual champions and joining coalitions made up of other nursing organizations that wanted to see greater independence for advanced practice nurses, like the nurse practitioners practicing in NMHCs. This strategy served two purposes. First, in the early days very few policy makers knew what NMHCs or nurse practitioners were and what they did. Identifying and educating key individual champions in state and federal legislatures helped NNCC staff bring visibility to the innovative nature of the NMHC model and its benefits for patients. Second, joining existing coalitions of nursing groups advocating for advanced practice nurses, allowed NNCC staff to make the NMHC policy agenda part of the coalition's overall strategy and thereby bring additional policy resources to bear in advancing the agenda.

One of the first congressional leaders to champion the NMHC cause was former U.S. Senator Arlen Specter (R-PA), a man who NNCC's executive director first met on a train. Senator Specter was at the time the chairman of the Senate Labor and Health and Human Services Appropriations Committee. In this position, Senator Specter could insert language favorable to the NMHCs into the committee report that accompanies each appropriations bill. NNCC's policy agenda at the federal level has always been to place NMHCs on equal footing with other safety-net providers, like federally qualified health centers (FQHC) and secure additional funding for the model. Below is an example of the type of language that was inserted into the committee reports:

"The Committee recognizes that Nurse-Managed Health Centers [NMHCs] serve a dual function in strengthening the health care safety net by providing health care to populations in underserved areas and by providing the clinical experiences to nursing students that are mandatory for professional development. Recognizing that NMHCs are frequently the only source of health care to their patients and that a lack of clinical education sites for nurses is a contributing factor to the nationwide nursing shortage, the Committee encourages HRSA to provide alternative means to secure cost-based reimbursement for NMHCs, by providing that reimbursement or by granting university-based CHCs. In addition, the Committee encourages HRSA to research the effectiveness of nurse-managed health centers as a national model to reduce health disparities. S. Rpt. 109-103 (p.34) 2006."

Although, this language carried no legal significance it did add visibility to NMHCs and keep them on the congressional radar screen. Another thing Senator Specter did was appropriate funding for the Centers for Medicare and Medicaid Services to conduct a nationwide study evaluating the capability of NMHCs to increase access, lower costs, and provide high quality care. This study gave NMHC advocates access to valuable data, like the kind discussed in the previous section of this chapter. To further increase visibility NNCC also hosted yearly legislative briefings to educate House and Senate staffers on the benefits of the NMHCs model and to discuss the policy agenda. Other individual champions NNCC staff have relied on include: 1) former Senator Daniel Inouye (D-HI), who became a strong supporter of nursing after Navy nurses helped him recover from injuries sustained during World War II; 2) Senator Lamar Alexander (R-TN), who is the current chairman of the U.S. Senate Committee on Health, Education, Labor and Pensions and is a strong supporter of NMHCs, especially those connected to Vanderbilt University; 3) retired U.S. Representative Lois Capps (D-CA), who is a former nurse. Each one of these individuals played a crucial role in increasing NMHC visibility, sponsoring legislative briefings, and moving NMHC legislation forward.

After almost 10 years of education and advocacy at the federal level, NNCC felt confident enough to introduce its first piece of federal legislation in 2006. The push to pass this language, which took the form of an amendment to the Community Health Center Reauthorization Act, clearly demonstrates the importance of partnering with the right organizations. The purpose of the amendment was to give a NMHC applying for community health center, or FQHC funding a temporary waiver of certain FQHC requirements, so that the clinic staff could put the necessary systems in place to comply with the regulations. Unfortunately, introducing the amendment brought NNCC into direct conflict with the National Association of Community Health Centers (NACHC), which saw the amendment as a threat to community health center program's funding and structure. NACHC has a large, well-entrenched, well-funded lobby, their opposition effectively caused the amendment strategy to stall.

NNCC, not wanting to clash with NACHC again, set to work developing a strategy that would move NACHC from an opponent to an ally. After much discussion, NNCC's leadership and congressional champions convinced NACHC to work with NNCC on a new piece of legislation that would give NMHCs access to grants coming from a separate pool of funding not connected to the community health center program. The shift ensured that NACHC's interest in protecting the integrity of community health center program would not be threatened. NNCC further reassured NACHC by allowing NACHC staff to be directly involved in the drafting of the NMHC grant program legislation, which would be called the Nurse-Managed Health Clinic Investment Act. The decision to include NACHC in the decision-making process ultimately convinced the organization to lift its opposition to the NMHC legislation and allowed it to proceed. This episode, I think, illustrates an important lesson for policy staff supporting novel and innovative ideas. Whenever possible, it is better to connect with and address the concerns of any potential opponents to your innovation prior to initiating a strategy of policy reform. This is not always possible, of course, but when it is the process runs much smoother.

The final push to make the NMHC Investment Act law would require the intersection of all three types of partnerships. NNCC began this part of the campaign by forming a coalition made up of NACHC, several national nursing groups, and other stakeholders. Coalition members quickly set about drafting legislation that would legally recognize NMHCs as safety net providers and bring badly needed grant funding to the clinics. While working in partnership with a coalition did increase the appeal of the legislation, it also came with some drawbacks. NNCC staff had to balance the needs of the NMHCs we severed, while also catering to the competing interests within the group. Each organization wanted special recognition given to their constituents and, or a pool of money set aside for their own use. Not all of these suggestions could be accommodated without lessening the legislation's overall impact and some requests from well-meaning, supportive organizations had to be denied.

The coalition eventually agreed upon legislation, which our congressional champions finalized and introduced. After multiple legislative visits by NNCC staff and coalition members, it took outstanding work from staffers working with Senator Daniel Inouye (D-HI) and Representative Lois Capps (D-CA) to get the legislation in front of the House and Senate leaders drafting the final version of the ACA. Thankfully, NNCC's language was included in the ACA and the NMHC grant program became law in 2010 when President Obama signed the legislation. Here again the decision to include NACHC in the planning was key, because former Senator Edward Kennedy (D-MA), a staunch supporter of NACHC and community health centers, was ultimately responsible for inserting the NMHC language into the Senate version of the ACA. It would not have happened without his support. The legislation resulted in $15 million in grants going to 10 NMHCs around the country. One NMHC director in rural Mississippi called her grant, "a dream come true" for her patients. More importantly, the visibility NMHCs gained as a result of the campaign and through legal recognition as safety net providers opened the door for many more NMHCs to qualify for FQHC funding.

Step 4: Staying Persistent: As a Philadelphian, I can't help but close this chapter with one more quote by a famous city resident, Rocky Balboa, who said, "Every champion was once a contender who refused to give up." It might be a little overly dramatic, but I think it is important for small organizations to remember that almost every, if not all, successful social innovations have had to start small. The retail clinics, for example, have grown from 150 to nearly 3,000 clinics in a little over 10 years. Every organization no matter their size can benefit from a policy agenda that clearly frames the issues, utilizes data, and takes full advantage of partnerships. The thing that makes social innovators special and sets them apart from more traditional entrepreneurs is their steadfast belief in the worthiness of their mission and a willingness to push the innovation forward in spite of opposition.

Change did come quickly for NMHC innovators. The ACA victory in 2010 was preceded by nearly 15 years of policy advocacy in the states and DC. Progress was slow and there were many setbacks. Throughout this time, NMHC leaders never lost sight of their vision, to improve people's health, lower costs, and increase access. The fact that the innovation is connected to such a critical social mission has given nurses a unique persistence in pursuing their policy agenda. The vision driving social innovators from other disciplines is just as compelling and should be harnessed. As Dr. Meade said, a small group of thoughtful, committed citizens can change the world, but I might add only if they persist.

Maria, Schiff et al. "The Role of Nurse Practitioners in Meeting Increasing Demand for Primary Care." National Governors Association. [Accessed 2012].

Matthew A. Davis, Rebecca Anthopolos, Joshua Tootoo, Marita Titler, Julie P. W. Bynum and Scott A. Shipman. "Supply of Healthcare Providers in Relation to County Socioeconomic and Health Status." Journal of General Internal Medicine. [Accessed 2018].

Jennifer Perloff, Catherine M. DesRoches and Peter Buerhaus. "Comparing the Cost of Care Provided to Medicare Beneficiaries Assigned to Primary Care Nurse Practitioners and Physicians." Health Services Research. [Accessed 2016].

Federal Trade Commission. Policy Perspectives Competition and the Regulation of Advanced Practice Nurses. Available at: https://www.ftc.gov/system/files/documents/reports/policy-perspectives-competition-regulation-advanced-practice-nurses/140307aprnpolicypaper.pdf. [Accessed 2014].

Case Study: Providing Nursing Leadership in a Community Residential Mental Health Setting in New Zealand by Frances Hughes

Strong leadership is emerging as a core component of good mental health nursing. The ways in which nurses meet the challenges faced by mental health services, are often at the heart of effective leadership skills and strategies. Nurse leadership in mental health services is not new; our colleagues are delivering a range of services in the UK, Canada, Australia, and the USA. However, it is still relatively uncommon to see residential services for "high needs" individuals being led by nurses. This chapter discusses ways in which nurses can provide strong and consistent leadership, together with an illustration of leadership in a community residential mental health service.

Mental Health

Despite clear evidence that there can be no health without mental health, nowhere in the world does mental health enjoy parity with physical health in national policies and budgets or in medical education and practice. Globally, it is estimated that less than seven percent of health budgets is allocated to address mental health. In lower-income countries, less than $2 per person is spent annually on it. Most investments are focused on long-term institutional care and psychiatric hospitals, resulting in a near total policy failure to promote mental health holistically for all. The arbitrary division of physical and mental health and the subsequent isolation and abandonment of mental health has contributed to an untenable situation of unmet needs and human rights violations (UN 2017), including of the right to the highest attainable standard of mental and physical health. The move to community support and primary care is the way of the future for prevention and recovery of those with mental illness

Overview of the New Zealand Health Care System

The Minister of Health has the overall responsibility for the health care system in New Zealand. The Minister works through the Ministry of Health, which employs civil servants to enter into management agreements with District Health Boards (DHBs); determines the health strategy for the country; and decides with government colleagues how much public funding will be spent on the public delivery of health service (N.Z. MOH, 2003b). The Ministry of Health provides policy advice on improving health outcomes and reducing health disparities, acts as the Minister's agent, monitors the performance of DHBs and other health entities, implements, administers, and enforces legislation and regulations, provides health information, facilitates collaboration across sectors, and plans and funds public health, disability support services, and other services.(N.Z. MOH, 2003b).

While the New Zealand belief is that health care is a right for all its citizens, over the last decade the health care sector in New Zealand has undergone four major structural changes that have had an impact on access to care for many New Zealand residents. The changes have ranged from a purchaser/provider market-oriented model in 1994, to a more community-oriented model that is currently in place to promote access (World Health Organization [WHO], 2005a). In December 2000 New Zealand launched a new health care strategy to ensure that all citizens have access to health care services, including primary, secondary, and tertiary care. The goal of the plan is for New Zealand to have healthy and thriving communities by 2010. Up until 2000, the health care system had focused on a more traditional medical model, emphasizing treatment of illnesses, and not prevention. Care was provided under a fee-for-service arrangement under the direction of a physician with little acknowledgement of the role of nursing, and services were provided in a western manner, without recognition of cultural competence or local ethnicities, like the Maori and Pacific Island populations (King, 2001). To change the direction of the medical model, the first major policy step was to create a strategy to build a strong primary health care system. (King, 2001) Accordingly, the New Zealand Ministry of Health under the leadership of the then Minister of Health, Annette King, decentralized the delivery of health care in the country through the establishment of 21 local DHBs, giving them full responsibility of providing health care in a designated service area. (WHO, 2005a).

DHBs report and are responsible to the Minister of Health. Each DHB Board of Directors has up to eleven members, seven of which are elected by the community. The Minister of Health appoints four members. In recognition of the unique status of Maori in New Zealand, each DHB must have at least two Maori members. DHBs function as a cross between a state health department and a large county or city health department in the U.S. and are primarily responsible for planning, funding, and guaranteeing the provision of health and disability services to a geographically defined population in 21 regions. The Ministry of Health provides broad guidelines on what services the DHBs must provide, and national priorities have been set in the New Zealand Primary Health Care strategy. Health care services, such as assessment, treatment, rehabilitation, and some public health services, come directly under the arm of DHBs, whereas primary care provided by general practitioners(GPs), Primary Healthcare Organizations (PHOs), nursing homes, and independent midwifery services are independent and are contracted by DHBs to supply services. Currently, there are 80 public hospitals in New Zealand. (N.Z. MOH, 2003b) DHBs control all the funding and are responsible for managing their budgets, which are created on a fairly complicated population health formula. The NGOs, which the DHBs fund, often serve the indigent populations, and those who for cultural or other reasons are not comfortable using mainstream health services.

Health Disparities in New Zealand

Maori and South-Pacific Island populations suffer the most health disparities in New Zealand. Maori have a higher rate of smoking, especially among younger women, than non-Maori. The cancer mortality and diabetes rates are higher, oral health is poor, vaccine-preventable diseases among children are higher, and obesity is higher particularly among men (WHO, 2005b). The Maori mortality rate in the 35-64-year age group was 3.4 times as high as that of non-Maori and non-Pacific Islanders. For the 65-74-year old Maori males the mortality rate was twice the rate of non-Maori. For female Maori in the 35-64-year age group, the mortality rate was 5.6 times as high as that of non-Maori, and in the age group of 65-74 the mortality rate was 3.3 times the non-Maori rate (Ajwani et. al, 2005). To address health disparities in Maori health, the principles of the New Zealand Primary Health Care Health Strategy include acknowledging the special relationship between Maori and the English Crown under the Treaty of Waitangi. In the Treaty the New Zealand Government committed to work with Maori communities to develop strategies for Maori health gains and appropriate services. The Government involved Maori at all levels of health care decision-making, planning, development, and delivery of health services. The treaty ensured the safeguarding of Maori cultural concepts, values, and practices (King & Turia, 2002). Maori and Pacific communities have also demonstrated considerable leadership in developing and pursuing their own health initiatives. Maori are over-represented under the Mental Health Act. Reducing the disparity in mental health outcomes for Maori is a priority action for the Ministry of Health and district health boards (DHBs).

Mental Health services are funded through the Ministry of Health through the DHB's. All DHB's have a responsibility to meet the needs of their population areas. There are range of mental health services within each DHB and it is the DHB would contracts with NGO to deliver residential, day programs for mental health clients. IN 2016 a commissioning framework was developed for providing services for those with mental health and addictions.

Commissioning Framework for Mental Health and Addiction

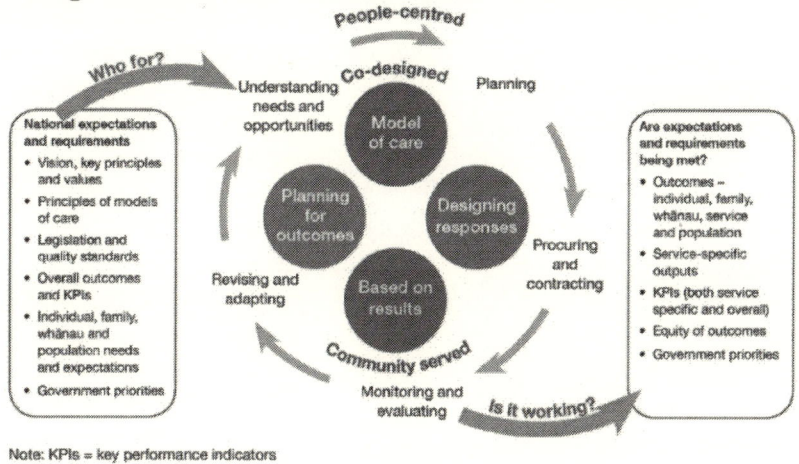

Note: KPIs = key performance indicators

What is nursing leadership?
We can all agree that "leadership" is an essential practice, but it remains a concept that has different meanings irrespective of the particular nursing discipline in which we work. Nursing leadership is a critical part of the ways in which we address issues facing people with mental illness and in the ways in which mental health services are developed and delivered. It is central to the ways in change is managed and in our relationships with other health professionals, with our consumers and their families and with the public and the political system (Hughes, 2006).

Leadership is not always associated with a formal title (e.g. manager) and can happen within or between services; between colleagues, and external to formal management or accountability structures. At its most narrow definition, leadership is reliant on formal hierarchical structures and provides little scope for the development of excellence. However, at its best, leadership has the potential to provide positive change.

A useful definition of "leadership" involves understanding that it is "a process ordinary people use when they are bringing forth the best from themselves and others" (*Nursing Now,* 2005). In this context, leadership is not reliant on formal structures, but is based on a series of themes, including

- Courage
- Change
- Vision and goal setting
- Enabling and inspiring
- Enlisting others to get things done
- Relationships
- Honesty and integrity; and
- Fostering leadership in others (*Nursing* Now 2005).

With growing evidence about the burden of disease, and disparities in health status of those with mental illness, it is important that nursing take a more active role in addressing this key health issue. Nurses are an important component of the health and disability workforce and in many countries they are the most common providers of health care (WHO, 2010). As such, they are well-placed to tackle the issues facing mental health consumers and their families, and to provide a "point of reference" for other health professionals and health care workers. Mental health nursing is a specialist area and combines professional therapeutic people skills with technical skills. This combination involves specialist, evidenced-based knowledge, skills, and attitudes in patient observation, assessment, individual, and group interventions and care. Nurses also provide support to families and communities and work within a wider health team with other disciplines

Mental Health nursing is a profession of courage and conviction, not only do mental health nurses work with the most vulnerable individuals who are subjected to stigma and discrimination, yet, the nurses are often subjected to the same within the nursing profession. Mental health nurses often need the courage to step up and argue for the inclusion of their clients within main stream services, i.e. access to primary health care. Mental health internationally is often the "Cinderella service" to main acute orientated services. An important component now of mental health is a focus on recovery -- one of the most important themes of leadership in mental health services. Recovery is defined as "the ability to live well in the presence or absence of one's mental illness (or whatever people choose to name their experience)" (Mental Health Commission 2001).

Leadership in Community Mental Health Services
I believe that the "Cinderella status" of mental health services contributes to a lack of recognition of mental health nurses as leaders (Hughes 2008). This is by no means an excuse for poor leadership and it is in spite of this that mental health nurses are emerging as leaders in the service provision, policymaking, and education (Hughes, Duke, Bamford and Moss 2006).

I believe there is a range of factors that have led to this high standard of leadership in mental health nursing. Some of these factors are within nursing itself, while others reflect changes in the ways in which mental health services are provided.

Mental health nurses have traditionally had to work extra hard to get recognition and inclusion, resulting in one of two attitudes -- a defensive and entrenched position whereby we feel that "the world is against us" or the view that mental health nurses need to be "out there" supporting our colleagues and seeking continuous improvement of services for consumers of mental health services. For the most part, mental health nurses take the latter view. This view fosters leadership and I believe has resulted in the mental health nursing workforce developing a style of leadership that is often beyond that of our colleagues in other nursing disciplines.

However, mental health nurses are not always well-recognized by our other nursing colleagues; an ongoing reflection of the deep-grained stigma towards people with mental illness that includes those involved in their care. There are all too many examples of this, from the policy level where mental health nurses were excluded from a working group on primary health (Bennis et al) to inpatient surgical facilities where nursing staff feel incapable of "managing" a patient whose needs in that facility are surgical, but who also has a mental illness (Hughes, 2008). These attitudes demand our response as mental health nurses. Although it might be argued that it is the responsibility of nursing leaders in those disciplines to show leadership, the very lack of such leadership requires us to take action.

So, in view of the factors influencing mental health nurse leadership, how best might we promote and improve our skills in this regard? Returning to the introduction to this article, I think it is critical to remember that true leadership occurs across, within, and between organizations, and is not necessarily dependent on hierarchy (although we should of course expect managers to exhibit leadership). The competencies for mental health nurses articulated by the NZ College of Mental Health Nurses (Te Ao Maramatanga) reflect the themes of leadership listed above, thus strongly indicating that we expect leadership of all mental health nurses (New Zealand College of Mental Health Nurses, Inc, 2004).

Having a clear understanding of leadership and developing expectations of mental health nurses are important in developing our services. However, there is a corresponding need to ensure that formal training is available, to enable nurses to develop and take advantage of their leadership skills, in the provision of independent mental health services.

The move towards enabling nurses to become independent nurse practitioners has been a significant contribution towards the development of nurse-led services. The competencies for nurse practitioners set out by the Nursing Council of New Zealand include a specific focus leadership, require nurse practitioners to "demonstrate(s) nursing leadership that positively influences the health outcomes of client/population group and the profession of nursing" (Nursing Council of New Zealand, 2008). This quite clearly indicates that we have an expectation that nurses can, and should, provide leadership including in an independent practitioner role.

New Zealand has also responded to this need through the development of formally recognized training. For example, Te Pou o Te Whakaaro Nui (The National Centre of Maternal Health Research, Information, and Workforce Development) has recently (2004-2007) delivered the first national mental health leadership and management development program for District Health Board and NGO managers, and clinical and service use leaders. Te Pou believes there are only two programs of this type in the world -- programs that see leaders, who are service users and health professionals, learning alongside each other.

Mental health nursing has come a long way in the last 30 years, and the changes have been even more rapid in recent times. Mental health nurses now take an active role in service provision and continue to lead service development. The expansion of services in the community has both enabled, and been enabled by, the ability of nurses to provide leadership in the care and recovery of people with mental illness. Mental health services are now predominantly provided in the community rather than in inpatient settings and nurses are often at the forefront of the delivery of these services. Such services range from clinic-based services (e.g. diabetes and primary care clinics) to the provision and management of residential services in the community. This is of course not unique to New Zealand, with nurse-led mental health services being provided in the UK, Canada, Australia, and increasingly in developing countries where there are few doctors.

I note here, that the focus of this chapter on nurse-led services, is not intended to argue against a range of other services that are delivered by other providers, including service users/consumers. The focus on appropriate service delivery should ideally be sufficiently broad to ensure a range of services that meet the needs and wishes of all consumers.

The increased ability of non-government organizations (NGOs) to provide services in the community has also been a driver in the development of nurse-led mental health services. An example of this kind of service is Hillcrest Lodge 2000 Ltd, a nurse-led, residential service in Raumati South, north of Wellington, New Zealand.

Case Study -- Nurse-led Service (Hillcrest Lodge)
Hillcrest Lodge demonstrates effective nurse leadership in the delivery of a residential mental health service that is part of its community. Hillcrest provides a range of services, including acute recovery services and has been successful in transitioning residents back into their communities, without subsequent intervention from acute mental health services.

The residents of Hillcrest come from many sources, including other NGO providers where residents were no longer suitable, forensic medium secure units, and acute inpatient units. This means that the service is experienced in supporting and managing residents with complex needs, including people who are;
- on compulsory treatment orders (CTOs) under the Mental Health (Compulsory Assessment and Treatment) Act 1992
- have complex physical and aged-related conditions
- are dying and chose to stay in familiar surroundings (with the support of district nurses)

Although Hillcrest was originally an all-male facility, it now includes five women. Residents are a mixture of cultures -- Eastern Block European, British, Irish, and New Zealand European and Maori.

Hillcrest Lodge has established extensive relationships with the surrounding community, the Kapiti PHO, other mental health NGOs, the Kapiti mental health team and the Regional Forensic Mental Health Service. For those of us involved at Hillcrest, the concept of "leadership" includes a strong focus on recovery, and as part of that, we need to constantly advocate for our residents to be respected and treated fairly.

The services offered by Hillcrest include a strong focus on recovery. Recovery principles are apparent from the fact that Hillcrest residents have few readmissions to inpatient mental health. For example, in August 2006 Hillcrest provided services for five residents who were living in accommodations that had its license revoked. All these residents were successfully transitioned into Hillcrest and have not needed intervention from the acute mental health services since that time.

Sadly, there are also instances that provide stark contrast between the leadership demonstrated by many mental health nurses and those working on other services. In a June 2008 article in the *Nursing Review*, I provided an example of how other health services can fail to meet the needs of people with mental illness. This demonstrates the extent to which those of us working in mental health services have an obligation to continually extend our leadership into other services.

Broker: Arrange complex supports with various agencies to meet residents' identified needs. Encourage institutions - ACC, DHBs, WINZ- to think outside the box.
Coordinator: Visits, activities, social events, leave entitlements.
Personal carer: Assist with daily activities, so that I understand the requirements needed, observe physical health and follow post-op discharge instructions.
Domestic help: Assist with preparing food, shopping with residents and providing guidance on household chores
Therapist Support through cognitive and diversional approaches.
Dietician: Support healthy options and advocate for resources to maintain healthy diets.
Advocate: Stand up to community discrimination, eg, challenging unfair trespass orders in local shops. Being assertive with mainstream health providers to ensure those with mental illness receive the appropriate service in a timely manner, eg, challenging attitudes of staff in medical wards over care, or lack of it.
Pharmacist: Work with pharmacists and multiple prescribers to ensure safe practices. Question from an informed base, supporting residents to provide narratives of their experiences with medications. Ensure safe administrative practices with all staff.
Educator: Provide materials and opportunities for discussion to both staff and residents. Provide competency training to, and assessment of, community mental health support workers (CMHSWs).
Delegator, supervisor, supporter: All of these things in relation to key care plan areas with CMHSWs, and also when residents are developing and reclaiming skills, such as self-medication of insulin etc.

The following two vignettes are examples of the impact of this service are outlined below. Both these residents had been cared for by community teams, living in the community, but both physically and mentally at risk of [further] serious illness.

Mrs. T has had a long history of bipolar disorder and type 2 diabetes, which she is insulin dependent. Over the years her management of her bipolar symptoms combined with diabetes has been challenging, her dietary regime combined with her unstable behavior meant she was on large doses of insulin twice daily, and it required external administration. She historically has had many different primary care providers, this made continuum of management difficult not only for her but her mental health care team who worked with her on managing her mental wellbeing. She lived at home with her family, but this proved too difficult and she was placed in varying types of residential care facilities. She continues to be under a Community Treatment Order under the 1992 Mental Health compulsory treatment act. Mrs. T came into our community houses eight months ago with no permanent primary health care provider and 25 kg over weight, 56 units of insulin a.m. and 22 units in p.m. Her blood sugars average was 18.6. Her mental state was labile and volatile, she spent large amounts of time in a distressed state. Her diet existed of large amounts of processed foods and soft drinks, her main snacks were biscuits and potato chips. She had long history of PRN medication utilization to manage her acute symptoms.

A life style and care plan were established by the RN in conjunction with Mrs. T, regular assessment and monitoring occurred with mental health team and her family in regards to Mrs. T's goals. She became enrolled in our local Primary Health Care provider and had access to diabetes nurse specialist and full physical reviews by GP. She was now experiencing the benefits of integrated MH and PH care. The challenge was the everyday lifestyle choices particularly around diet, weight management, and exercise. Her day to day in home support to assist her with these within her mental health recovery was contact with a RN and CMHSW's.

Mrs. T lived in a house with three other women. From the day of arrival, she experienced a change in her dietary regime, she was introduced to fresh foods, cooked from scratch. She was given choices within healthy food options and substitutions, she was also encouraged to take responsibility, she became involved in determining what would grow in the vegetable garden and shopped with staff at the local market gardens. Slips occurred, and she was given support and positive reinforcement. As her blood sugars started to lower and with that her mental state improved, she particularly became less agitated, demanding, and aggressive in her engagement with others.

Access to healthy food, both grown on site and bought with a variety of options but emphasis on low fat and low sugar combined with increased exercise was the platform to establishing her diabetes. RN liaised frequently with GP and diabetic nurse, also provided regular monitoring and education not only to Mrs. T but also CMHSW. Psychiatrist was advised of progress when Mrs. T had three out of 12 consultations and this resulted in medication being decreased. Within six weeks Mrs. T's insulin was reduced down to 24 units of insulin in the a.m. and 10 units in p.m. Her blood sugar average was 8.5. Weight loss occurred and was down 10 kg within 10 weeks.

The key to addressing the physical health issues of Mrs. T is the commitment of the people that live and interact with her on a day to day basis, the oversight of RN's who are able to support, apply integrated knowledge, translate into practical day to day care activities, liaise, and advocate for residents to access services.

Mr. X, in his late 50's, had a long-standing forensic mental health history and treatment under different aspects of the N.Z. Mental Health Act. He had been living in the community with six hours a day of support worker input, but now required more oversight and support. His team was multidisciplinary (MDT) but no nurses were involved. He had trouble walking due to medical conditions and his mental health appeared to be deteriorating.

Arriving at our residence, his documents outlined his mental health support requirements, and risk and relapse plan, but there was little about ADLs and physical concerns. The RN involved discussed this with his prior care team and noted that things were unclear about the "human and physical aspects of living day to day." The first two days were a steep learning curve. Despite Mr. X apparently having had very close oversight, he arrived in a physically neglected state. The RN worked with him to establish a supportive and supervised ADL program. He had multiple fungal infections, calloused and infected feet, untreated infected burns, severe constipation, and high blood sugar. To summarize, the RN worked with him and other health providers to resolve his issues. His walking stick is no longer needed; he no longer buys and applies his own enemas; he has regular podiatry input; he enjoys trips into the community, which he had not been able to do, and he is enjoying his meals. He recently commented that he had not had this kind of thorough support before.

The focus on leadership at Hillcrest includes continuous quality improvement, designed to enhance the lives of staff and residents. This involves strong clinical support and oversight for residents and a proactive approach to all health-related areas of residents' lives -- screening, monitoring, and early intervention. Furthermore, it involves a belief that the residents of Hillcrest can, and should, live well and walk tall in the wider community.

Continuing to Develop Leadership Among Mental Health Nurses
Having determined the value and active presence of strong leadership among mental health nurses, it is equally as important to ensure that our leadership continues to grow and develop (*Nursing Now,* 2005*)*.

One of the strengths of effective leadership is its ability to identify and respond to challenges. It is tempting to perceive "challenges" as being negative and requiring some sort of struggle to overcome. Rather, challenges are inevitable and may be positive in nature -- for example, the availability of a new medication, preparing a service user for transition into a new environment, taking on a new role, or establishing a new service. The emergence of a robust mental health consumer movement in New Zealand is a challenge and a delight -- and I firmly believe it has resulted in better services. Our strength as leaders is reflected by our ability to adapt to change and to foster leadership in others.

As noted in the preceding discussion, there is a need for formal training and recognition of leadership, as well as a common understanding of its principles and purpose. There is also the need for leadership to be an active process. Part of our role as nursing leaders, and as service providers, is to continue the debate on leadership and to articulate what it is that we expect from those involved in establishing training policy, competencies, and standards (Hughes et al, 2006).

In terms of developing nurse-led services, we also need nurses who are prepared to understand the business aspect of health services, and who can have a sense of "entrepreneurship." Perhaps this is yet a further theme that can be added to those outlined previously!

Conclusion
The continuing development of strong and effective leadership by mental health nurses is, I believe, a critical factor in the emerging provision of nurse-led services, including an increasing number and range of residential services for people with long-term mental health problems.
I believe that mental health nursing provides our colleagues with the skills to provide leadership within mental health services, and that these skills are not only valuable, but are *critical* in ensuring that services (including health, disability and social services) meet the needs of the people we serve. Effective leadership also ensures that staff are well-supported and are able to participate as leaders in their own right, irrespective of their job-title or position in an organization.

The article demonstrates some of the ways in which a nurse-led service can provide effective residential services for people with long-term mental health and disability issues. Leadership within this context is not solely about management or ownership -- rather, it is about demonstrating and enabling other people to perform at their best, towards common goals.

As leaders, we must have the courage to respond to challenges and build the resilience needed to ensure that our responses are timely and appropriate. Such challenges arise at all levels -- policy, legislation, service delivery, and through our relationships with our clients and various communities. Not only should we be prepared to address these many challenges, but we should have sufficient strength to welcome them, honesty and integrity to face them, and courage to address them.

Case Study References
1. Mass H. Nursing Leadership. Nursing BC; 2005. Available at: www.findarticles.com (accessed June 2008).
2. Bennis W, Nanus B. Leaders: The strategies for taking charge. New York: Harper and Row Publishers Inc; 1985.
3. O'Neil E. Nursing Leadership: Challenges and Opportunities. Policy, Politics and Nursing Practice:2003;4(3):173-9. Available at: http://www.ppn.sagepub.com (accessed June 2008).
4. Geedey, NM. Following a new roadmap to leadership success. Nursing Management:2004;35(8): 49-51.
5. Hughes, F. Policy, "A Practical Tool for Nurses and Nursing." *Journal of Advanced Nursing*, 49(4):331.
6. Hughes, F., Bamford, A., Porter-O'Grady (2006). "Interface Between Global Health Care and Nursing Leadership." *Nurse Leader*.
7. Hughes, F.A., Duke, J., Bamford, A., Moss, C (2006). "The Centrality of Policy Entrepreneurship and Strategic Alliances to Professional Leadership Within Key Nursing Roles," *Nurse Leader*. Vol 4, Issue 2, pp 24-27.
8. *Nursing Leadership in a Changing World* (2005). Canadian Nurses Association *Nursing Now* No. 18 January 2005 (Author unspecified)
9. Hughes, F.A. RN, DNurs (2008). "In Search of a Place at the Table," *Nursing Review*, pp.11-12.
10. Te Pou o Te Whakaaro Nui (The National Centre of Mental Health Research, Information and Workforce Development) www.tepou.co.nz.
11. Nursing Council of New Zealand (2008) Te Kaunihera Tapuhi O Aotearoa *Competencies for Nurse Practitioners.*
12. UN Special Rapporteur on the Right to Health (2017).
13. World Health Organisation (2010). "Mental Health Gap Action Programme: Scaling up Care for Mental, Neurological and Substance Abuse Disorders," *World Health Organisation Press, Geneva.*

Case Study: Border Action Network Case Study: Advocating Policy Change to Elected Officials by Justin Harlem

Any comprehensive strategy to effect policy change entails working with elected officials. That is, building relationships with legislators and their staff, developing leaders and credibility within your organization or network, and establishing a foundation for ongoing advocacy. Meeting with your elected official does not have to be an intimidating process. After all, you hold a great deal of influence as a constituent! The fact is, legislators, want your help and advice. There are simply too many issues and areas of work for any elected official and their staff to master themselves. Legislators want to know who is in their districts, what you do, and how they can help. After all, that is how they get reelected! Successful advocacy campaigns, however, do not materialize effortlessly. They require careful planning and purposeful execution. To achieve any successful policy change, your efforts must be based on facts; draw on practical experience; offer proof to support your arguments; be carefully and strategically planned, and actively involve the group on whose behalf it is undertaken.

Before scheduling a meeting, it is important to do your homework about both the issue at stake and the elected official(s) you would like to meet with. Successful advocacy in policy change involves an integrated strategy devised to create a positive response to your proposal, thereby increasing the chances of achieving your overarching objectives. This requires a more comprehensive approach than simply submitting a request. In order to lay the foundation for an effective advocacy program, you must begin by looking at what is possible and achievable. Every organization must be cognizant of its own political strength, infrastructure, priorities, and key issues. For some, the goal may be a hearing where diverse views can be equally articulated, and legislators better educated. Others may seek the creation of new legislation, support for or opposition to existing legislation, an amendment to a larger bill, or change in existing regulations. Each of these goals can have a distinct strategy and campaign behind them. It is therefore critical to begin with your goal clearly in mind. Focus on answering these questions: what specifically are we going to ask for; what is the minimum result we are willing to accept; what is our desired outcome; and what would need to occur to declare total success?

With your groundwork complete, it is time to plot a legislative strategy to advance your proposal. It is important to identify the key officials and politicians who can influence the outcome of your campaign. Who are the key decision-makers (e.g. committee chairs or members, caucus leaders, party leadership)? This includes knowing your legislator's party affiliation, whether your lawmaker is a champion on certain issues, the demographics of their district, and when they are up for re-election. Timelines should be dictated by events. Political events, such as an upcoming election, where you can maximize any political opportunity to achieve your objectives, should be decisive markers in establishing your timeline.

Another key step in launching a new issue is to identify potential key supporters, most importantly lead sponsors for the measure, focusing first on majority party members of the relevant committees, but always looking to secure bipartisan support. Voting records, speeches, relevant past positions, and discussions with staff all provide a foundation for selecting leaders for the issue. Find out which government officials are active in the area you are advocating change. More importantly, find out which of these officials, if any, have the ability to make actual decisions. What is the committee of jurisdiction? Who is lobbying in support of the issue and who is lobbying against the issue? What are their arguments and messages? Find out if your elected official generally supports or opposes your issue. What is your lawmaker's voting record on the issue at stake and on similar issues?

Knowing how the political landscape relates to your issue is also important. What is the legislative history of the issue? Where were any impediments to enactment in the past? Who have been the past leaders, supporters, and opponents? Is the issue or legislation anticipated to come up for a hearing or vote? A good resource for voting records and issue ratings is Project Vote Smart: www.votesmart.org. If you are meeting about a specific piece of legislation, is your elected official is a co-sponsor? This information can be located by visiting the Library of Congress website: http://thomas.loc.gov and entering the bill name or number and clicking on the co-sponsor list. Ideally, you would have a member of both political parties sponsor any legislation, in both the House and Senate. Understanding the political and legislative background can provide a significant basis from which to develop a path forward.

Regardless of what you are advocating for, you can expect to be asked the question: "How much will it cost and where will the money come from?" Often, advocates simply request "new," "full," or "increased" funding for programs. Such broad statements can be inconsequential in the context of advocacy, as they do not help lawmakers understand the underlying significance of the request, especially when contrasted to every other request they are called upon to consider. You must not only justify why your request is vital but why a lesser amount will not suffice in the current fiscal climate. Focus instead on the question: "How much will these changes save?" Be sure to highlight any potential future cost savings as part of any advocacy programs. Rough calculations of these cost-benefit assessments can be extremely valuable for justifying underlying costs.

Contacting your Legislators
Most legislators are eager to meet with their constituents. Remember, as a voter and advocate your opinions are valuable! Keep in mind that you do not need to be an expert to get your point across. Begin simply by introducing yourself as well as the name and mission of your organization.

Typically, you will only be contacting your own elected officials, so be sure to mention where you live so they know you're a constituent. Feel free to indicate any additional personal connections, such as family, social or business ties, that you may have with the legislator. Being able to provide a brief background about the issue, a personal story and a clear "ask" is much more effective than presenting a ten-point plan or a litany of facts. There is also power in numbers -- setting up a meeting along with three or four like-minded individuals can help showcase even stronger support for your issue.

Do not be discouraged if you are unable to schedule a meeting with your elected official personally. Rarely will anyone initially get a meeting with the legislators on their own. Through personal connections, campaign relationships, and persuasion over constituents have been known to can help expedite the process. Lawmakers rely heavily on their staff to meet with constituents on their behalf, draft legislation, acquire in-depth knowledge about issues, and make policy recommendations. Staff will have more time to get to know you and your issues and will serve as your gateway to the elected official. Request a meeting with the legislative director or legislative staff member responsible for your issue area. Take the time to get to know and develop a relationship with the staff member, so they begin to view you as a resource and a reliable base of information.

Though it may seem obvious, always be polite and professional. Not everyone is. You can state your views firmly and forcefully without being hostile or belligerent. Always be friendly and courteous, even if the legislator disagrees with your position. Dress nicely and be on time. First impressions matter -- do not let your appearance detract from your message or credibility. If you are not able to favorably convince the staff member, your issue may never advance any further. So be sure to treat the staffer with the same respect you would the elected official themselves.

If your organization is locally or regionally based, it is often good to reach out to the local district office first. Get to know their district director, invite them to see your organization in action. Your goal here should not be to push your legislative or advocacy goals, per se, rather introduce yourself, your organization and what services you provide. Think of this as community outreach. After meeting with the district office staff, ask if it would be possible to host the member for a visit next time they are in the district. This can be an excellent channel for getting your name and organization in front of the legislator. If you are able to bring your elected official to your office, remember again, legislation is not the primary purpose of the visit. This is your opportunity to educate them first-hand about who you are and how you serve the community. Then you can begin to discuss any areas of difficulties. Discuss your desire to work with their office to find a solution to issues of concern. Ask which member of their staff would be best to follow-up with. Then email that staffer member informing them their boss has just visited your office and asked you to contact them to discuss your issues. This will help ensure the legislative staff member speaks to their boss about taking further actions.

Be Prepared, Be Clear, Be Concise:
Expect to have a maximum of 30 minutes for any meeting you schedule and expect those thirty minutes go by faster than you anticipate! So, you need to plan accordingly. If you are meeting as part of a small coalition, it is important to determine prior to the meeting who your spokesperson or lead speaker will be, who will answer specific questions, who will take notes, and who will write a follow-up thank you letter.

Prepare your arguments based on your experience, consultations, research, and an assessment of what is possible and achievable. Begin with a supportive statement. For instance, mention if the legislator recently voted in favor of a related issue you care about, or if they recently made a speech, attended an event, put out a press release, cosponsored legislation, etc. At a minimum, be sure to thank your elected official for taking the time to meet with you. Clearly and concisely state what issue you are there to discuss, your position, and what action you would like your elected official to take. Use straightforward, understandable terms bolstered by supporting facts and examples. Your goal is to present your argument with enough factual data to rationalize your objectives, but not so much detail that it overwhelms or becomes overly time-consuming for the elected official or their staff.

Emphasize why this issue is important to you personally. While lawmakers are interested in data and statistics, they are more concerned with how the issue directly affects their constituents. A personal story is always more compelling than charts and graphs. Share a story or concrete examples that highlight personal experience with the issue. How many of their constituents would be affected by your proposal? Few bills can successfully move through the complex process without major efforts by a broad group of supporters, no matter the importance of the policy or the benefits that might be achieved by enactment. It is always useful to engage allies in this process, both to ensure that planning is informed by diverse perspectives and to prevent competing efforts could prove counterproductive. Support can come in many forms: shared economic interests, professional interests, common policy, or ideology. Is there already a coalition or organization in existence that is supporting the issue in a focused, current manner? Consider how to link your arguments to other organizations, influential people, government officials and lawmakers that support your position.

If a coalition already exists, you will need to ask: What are the coalition's strengths and weaknesses, and how would your advocacy efforts integrate with those of the other groups comprising the coalition? If there is no coalition, would it be beneficial to create a coordinating organization? The political strengths and weaknesses of potential allies on an issue should be assessed, as well as how the coalition would function should compromises be needed to advance the issue. Coalitions, like any organization, can fail because they lose sight of their original mission and goals. At what point might your organization's interests diverge from the coalition's? It is not unusual for a coalition to alter their objectives over time. Should the interests of coalition begin to diverge from your own, how will you know when it is time to part ways, preserving your own expert voice and efforts?

Elected officials and their staff will often tell you it is easier to be the minority party in a legislature than the majority party. That is because it is generally easier to defeat a legislative proposal than to enact one. Be cognizant of any arguments and data that can be used to counter your position and be prepared to respond to them. In today's political climate, there will undoubtedly be people opposed to your position. Legislators will want to know who they are, and what their influence is when weighing their decisions. Which industries, interests, organizations, agencies, government entities are likely to oppose the proposal? Is their opposition based upon direct economic interest or another impact, or on policy or ideological grounds? Is there already a coalition or organization that opposes the issue? What are their strengths and weaknesses? What is likely to be the most effective arguments or activities of opponents to the policy, and might there be any way to anticipate, counter or undermine their arguments?

Your meeting is intended to influence what other people believe, think, and do in order to achieve an objective. To accomplish this, you must engage your legislators in conversation, not present a sermon. So, anticipate being interrupted with questions and comments. Their remarks will give you cues on how to adjust your arguments and what additional information might be useful. Always be prepared to bring the conversation back to your message if (or when) the lawmaker goes off tangent. It is crucially important not to lie or mislead an elected official. Points of view are subjective, facts are not. If you make up facts and figures or stretch the truth, it will come back to haunt you. I do not say this as a lesson in morality, rather because it happens all too often. Being caught making dishonest statements is the quickest way to be rendered inept and extraneous. Answer questions to the best of your ability. If you do not know the answer, say so and offer to get back to them promptly with the information. You are not expected to be an expert in every facet of an issue.

Always have and present a specific "ask." Pose a direct, yes-or-no question to which the legislator can respond." Can we count on you to co-sponsor the bill?" Be prepared for how you will respond to your member's position. Have a plan to turn a "yes" into a public victory, a "maybe" into a yes, and to learn from the objections of a "no."

Before committing to any action, staff may suggest you also consult with additional public, private or nonprofit organizations. Be sure to ask them to share any contact information they have. They may also request you get back to them on issues concerning your proposal.

Whether it is about gaining support or countering potential opposition, staff will often see the issue through a much more political lens. Some may even request additional information in order to gauge your own dedication. Too often organizations give an aggressive one-time lobbying pitches, only to never respond to any additional requested information. Simply scheduling another meeting six months, a year later, with an identical request and no additional progress, does nothing to progress your goals.

Always thank your legislator for their time at the end of the meeting, even if they did not agree with your position. If a legislator does agree to your request, such as co-sponsor or vote for a bill, be sure to thank them for taking that action. Positive reinforcement is the most effective way to develop a good relationship for future issues. Be prepared to give the lawmaker a leave behind or fact sheet outlining your position, talking points and why they should support your position. The more help you are able to provide staff, the more readily accessible the information is for them, the more likely they are to use it. Staff, just like the elected officials themselves, are extremely busy. At one point I handled all trade, foreign policy, national defense, government reform, education, veterans' affairs, immigration, homeland security, judiciary, appropriations, housing, telecommunications, labor, and agriculture issues for my boss simultaneously. Ideally, your goal should not just be to present the justifications, but also to demonstrate how your request may provide notoriety, support, distinction and recognition, and to do so in the easiest possible way.

After the Meeting
After the meeting, be sure to document what happened and any information you learned about the member's position, so you can share it with others and modify your advocacy strategy appropriately. Always follow up with a timely thank you letter. In the letter, reiterate your key points and any commitments you received and include any follow-up information you promised to provide.

Proposals typically move through Congress VERY slowly. Do not get discouraged if you do not immediately obtain your objectives. Any initial meeting where you receive guidance from the staff is a positive meeting. You have engaged them, which means they are at least open to the idea. If they ask questions or need more information, you have a concrete reason to follow up with them at a later date. Legislators may not do what you want one hundred percent of the time, however, they can still help advance your cause. If you discuss three bills and they agree to support two, you've made progress. A legislator might agree to vote for a bill when it comes to the floor but doesn't want to be a co-sponsor for political reasons. In essence, you must be willing to do what our legislators seem increasingly incapable of -- be prepared to compromise.

Application of Effective Lobbying by the Border Action Network
The Border Action Network, in Tucson, Arizona, was formed in 1999 as an all-volunteer, membership-based organization human rights organization in border and immigrant communities. Their mission is to promote safety, equality, dignity, understanding, and justice within the human environment and across cultures regardless of race, sexual orientation, religious beliefs, or country of origin. They combine grassroots organizing, leadership development, litigation, and legislative advocacy. However, advocacy was not always a part of their mission.

In 2005, immigration reform precipitously became a central focus of the government and national debate. The President pushed immigration reform as a principle priority, initiating Congressional consideration of multiple pieces of legislation. As border security and immigration control bills began to work their way through Congress, the Border Action Network recognized the extent to which their community could be affected. As one Border Action staff member put it: "...this was an issue we pretty much couldn't ignore; we were in it by virtue of where we live." If Congress and the White House wanted to change immigration policy, the Border Action Network wanted a way to influence the outcome.

At the time, the Border Action Network had four full-time employees, some dedicated volunteers, and almost no advocacy experience in at the federal level. Initially, the idea that such a small, local organization should actually lobby at the federal level was met with a lot of unease. Most had never even considered the idea that a charity would lobby. Lobbying activity and charitable activity seemed completely separate. Was it even legal for a charity to lobby? They learned that it is indeed legal for charities to lobby, that Congress even encouraged it in a law passed in 1976 and that Internal Revenue Service regulations give charities wide latitude to lobby and do other types of advocacy. Lobbying cannot be the primary activity of a charity, but it can be an important part of its work.

The Border Action Network's goal was ambitious. Their objective was to ensure language protecting immigrants' human rights was included in any immigration reform legislation moving through the U.S. Congress. An intimidating undertaking for an organization new to federal lobbying and crafting legislative lobbying.

As Congress worked through legislative proposals, the Border Action Network recognized many of the same policies and guidelines Congress was considering did not require the creation of additional legislation. Some of the Executive Branch agencies had the ability to craft regulations capable of dramatically affecting the human rights of immigrants without any change in the laws. However, this would require working with Department of Homeland Security officials, White House Staff, in addition to members of Congress and their staffs. Thus, an intimidating undertaking for a four-person staff became an impossible task.

In order to manage the scope of work, the Border Action Network embarked on a campaign to engage allies in the process, both to ensure that action was planned and informed by diverse perspectives and to prevent competing efforts that could prove counterproductive. Together with community supporters, they helped create a US-Mexico Border & Immigrant Task Force that included: local elected officials, local law enforcement, attorneys, faith community members, businesspeople, and academics from Arizona, New Mexico, California, and Texas. Task Force members traveled to Washington, D.C., several times in order to speak directly with federal officials about the need for comprehensive immigration reform.

In order to get the critical players on the same page, the Border Action Network began with a training session regarding the advocacy and lobbying rules for nonprofits. Central to their action was a belief in the strength of the diversity of the nonprofit sector and its ability to tell compelling local stories about the importance of advocating on behalf of the people and issues they serve. The campaign worked with similar organizations, providing information and analyses to them to distribute to their membership and affiliates. Each organization brought credibility to the campaign and provided various strengths, including bringing players to be part of the coalition that traditionally had not worked together before.

Throughout 2006 and 2007 the Border Action Network and its Task Force allies played an active role in the debate. Some campaign activities helped build grassroots support: one rally in Tucson drew over 1,200 attendees. One campaign utilizing "portapostales" kits at participating businesses, generated over 13,000 postcards. Other actions involved lobbying visits in Washington, DC and press conferences at the U.S. Capitol and Congressional members' local offices.

The task force brought together stakeholders in a multi-faceted coalition, to articulate a sensible and effective approach to immigration policy. Their efforts helped influence the national debate and the proposed legislation in Congress. Five of the Task Force language recommendations made it into both the House and Senate versions of the Immigration bill that Congress debated in 2007 when progress on the bills came to a halt.

Today, the Border Action Network still works for a sensible and humane resolution to the immigration debate, that takes into account our border communities. They are not only able to build on-the-ground organizing and leadership capacity within heavily militarized, criminalized, and marginalized immigrant and border communities, but continue to carry the local lessons from the border directly to policymakers at a state and national level. Their experience in organizing, research, communications, and advocacy, enables them to continue to argue the ineffectiveness, high cost, and cruelty of border and immigration enforcement, and their dedication to policy change empowers them to put concrete solutions before policymakers.

ABOUT THE AUTHORS/EDITORS

Nicholas Torres, M.Ed. has more than 20 years of experience in executive management. He built and led one of the largest and nationally recognized human services organizations; founded/governed/led two charter schools and a nonprofit dedicated to scaling high-impact social enterprises (e.g. school based health centers; college access and completion pipelines; and early literacy technology platform); founded and currently leads a social sector "think-tank" organization; and teaches at UPENN Fels Institute of Policy and the Wharton School. From 2000 – 2010 Nicholas served as President of Congreso de Latinos Unidos, where he transformed the organization from a traditional social services agency into a comprehensive children and family-oriented human services nonprofit by integrating behavioral health, education, and primary health care into the service model. Under his leadership, Congreso was one of just six national leadership investments ($5 million) from Edna McConnell Clark Foundation to demonstrate multi-service organization impact on young people aged 16-24. As a result of this investment, he created a first-of-its-kind performance management system to measure organizational effectiveness for more than 50 service lines and 17,000 clients/customers that would later be used as a model for Social Solutions' Efforts To Outcome (ETO) to scale in nonprofits nationally. He then served as a member of the National Alliance for Effective Social Investments that led the nation on integrating Social Impact Indicators into nonprofit best practices.

Currently, Mr. Torres serves as Interim Executive Director of The Network: TUFH. The Network: TUFH convenes the world's leading Academic Institutions, Health Systems, Community Health Associations and Industry Field Builders to collectively tackle the world's global health challenges by collectively sharing (abstracts and research) and designing (live challenges, expert panels, position papers) innovative approaches, and developing policy recommendations toward universal access and equitable health delivery. He also serves as CEO/Co-Founder of Social Innovations Partners that manages the Social Innovation Journal, Institute, and Lab; manages Parent Reading Coach, an Education Technology Early Literacy Company; and teaches Policy; Leading Not-for-profits; and Social Enterprise at the University of Pennsylvania Fels Institute of Policy and the Wharton School. He has co-authored several books and serves on many regional and national foundations, government; and private boards. He has received several advocacy and leadership awards including the prestigious Eisenhower Fellowship, the Business Journal 40 under 40; and Leadership Philadelphia's 101 Connectors. Mr. Torres received his BA from Carleton College and his Master's in Educational Psychology from the University of Texas at Austin.

Tine Hansen-Turton, MGA, JD, FCPP, FAAN, was appointed President and Chief Executive Officer of Woods Services in October 2016. Ms. Hansen-Turton is an Executive with more than 20 years of experience in health and human services senior management, executive leadership, and consulting. She has founded and led several nationally recognized organizations and trade associations. A proven results-oriented strategic leader, Ms. Hansen-Turton is known for being an effective organizational change agent and policy and health and human services systems reform advocate. Woods Services is a $230 million leading nonprofit multi-service healthcare and human services organization that provides innovative, comprehensive, and integrated health-and-behavior, education, workforce, and care management services to children and adults in the intellectual/developmental disability, child welfare, behavioral and acquired brain injury public health sectors. Woods has more than 3,500 staff that serve more than 4,000 individuals primarily from Pennsylvania, New Jersey, and New York, but also has national reach given its expertise in serving people who are medically and behavioral frail and vulnerable. Ms. Hansen-Turton also oversees Woods' four subsidiary corporations in Pennsylvania and New Jersey (Brian's House and Tabor Services in Pennsylvania and Allies and Archway Programs in New Jersey).

Previously, Ms. Hansen-Turton served as the Chief Operating Officer and Chief Strategy Officer at Public Health Management Corporation, where she oversaw and led corporate strategy, operations, business development, and M&A. Additionally, Ms. Hansen-Turton served as CEO of the National Nurse-led Care Consortium, a not-for-profit organization supporting the growth and development of more than 500 nurse-managed and school health clinics, serving more than five million vulnerable people across the country in urban and rural locations. For the past two decades she has also been instrumental in positioning Nurse Practitioners as primary health care providers globally. Ms. Hansen-Turton still serves as the founding Executive Administrator for the Convenient Care Association (CCA), the national trade association of more than 2,300 private-sector retail clinic industry, serving 30 million people with basic health care services across the country. Ms. Hansen-Turton also teaches public and social innovations, leading nonprofits, health policy and the social innovations lab at University of Pennsylvania Fels Institute of Government and School of Nursing. Ms. Hansen-Turton is founder and publisher of a social impact/innovation journal and has co-published eight books and is known as a serial social entrepreneur who has started several national social and public innovations in the health and human services sector. She has received several advocacy and leadership awards, the prestigious Eisenhower Fellowship, the Business Journal 40 under 40 Leadership and Women of Distinction Awards. She was named one of the 101 emerging Philadelphia connectors by Leadership, Inc. and American Express NextGen Independent Sector Fellow. Ms. Hansen-Turton received her BA from Slippery Rock University, her Master of Government/Public Administration from University of Pennsylvania Fels Institute, and her Juris Doctor from Temple University Beasley School of Law.

ABOUT THE CASE STUDY AUTHORS

Lauren Buckheit is the Assistant Director, Young Alumni Development for The Penn Fund at the University of Pennsylvania. She holds a BA in Political Science with a concentration in Gender & Sexuality Studies from Bryn Mawr College. Passionate about development and curious about the future of philanthropy, she is hoping to pursue a Masters in Nonprofit Leadership from Penn's School of Social Policy & Practice. In her free time, she enjoys exploring cities through their restaurants and art museums.

Katie Chisholm has dedicated her career to working in the nonprofit sector. Katie has worked for human services nonprofits both in New York City and Philadelphia. She has also worked as an educator abroad teaching English as a second language. Currently, Katie is working for a nonprofit focused on international medical education. Katie obtained her degree in Psychology Based Human Relations from Connecticut College and is currently pursuing her Masters in Nonprofit Leadership Development from UPenn. She also completed the Non Profit Executive Leadership Institute at Bryn Mawr.

Jennifer Chu has served as Director of Young Quakers Community Athletics (YQCA), a partnership between Netter Center for Community Partnerships and Penn Athletics, since 2014. Prior to her work at Netter Center, Jennifer was the Girls Wrestling Program Director at Beat the Streets Philadelphia, a sports based youth development program that engages and empowers students through the sport of wrestling. A current student in Penn's School of Social Policy and Practice (SP2), Jennifer is a candidate for a Master's in Nonprofit Leadership.

Dave Griffith is the Executive Director and Head Coach of Episcopal Community Services of Philadelphia. ECS is a 148-year-old faith-based social service agency focused on the issues of intergenerational poverty. He is the first nonclergy, non-MSW to lead the organization. In addition to his work at ECS, he is the Chairman of The Modern Group LTD., Chairman of Delaware Valley Floral Group, Chairman of Verus LLC., Chairman of Hoober Inc., Director of the JJ Haines Company, Manager of Mountain Laurel Spirits, LLC. He also serves on the board of the Economy League of Greater Philadelphia, the World Affairs Council of Philadelphia, the Academy of Natural Sciences of Drexel University where he chairs the Governance Committee and Friends of Foundation Academy as secretary. He is the Chairman of the McEwen Family Scholarship Foundation and a director of the Griffith Family Foundation. He also serves as an advisor to the Journal of Social Innovation, The Caliper Corporation, and the IBM Customer Advisory Council. Dave is the author of The Muddy Boots Blog, www.wearmuddyboots.com.

He is also a lecturer at the Center for High Impact Philanthropy at the University of Pennsylvania as well as the Non-Profit Leadership Program at the School of Social Policy and Practice and the Fox School of Business and the Rutgers School of Engineering. He is a nationally recognized speaker and author on governance, compensation, and leadership. He is past President of the Material Handling Equipment Dealers Association and a previous Director of the National Association of Wholesales Institute for Distribution Excellence. He served as an officer and trustee of The Westminster School, trustee of the Pennsylvania Biotechnology Center, senior warden of Trinity Episcopal Church and clerked the Development Committee at Buckingham Friends School. He has served on search committees for the Presidents of the Academy and World Affairs Council as well as the Episcopal Bishop of the Diocese of Pennsylvania. He is an alumnus or member of MHEDA, ARA, NAW, YPO and the Alliance for Strong Families and Communities. He was President and CEO of the Modern Group Ltd, VP of Marketing for MCI National Accounts, Regional Manager for The ROLM Corporation, and served in several executive positions at IBM including Regional Manager, Branch Manager, Administrative Assistant to the President, and Director of Marketing. In 1979 he was recognized as IBM's top marketing representative in the US. He is a graduate of Kenyon College and The Westminster Schools. At Kenyon, he received his BA with honors in Economics and History. While at Kenyon he played DIII Soccer and Lacrosse. Volunteered with the local Fire Department and served as both an EMT and line officer and worked as a resident advisor. He is also a member of the Lambda chapter of Delta Kappa Epsilon. He is married, and he and his wife have two adult children and one old dog. He is an adequate golfer and avid fly fisherman.

Justin Harlem is a rare public servant and advocate who has risen above politics time and again to take on the status quo and protect all of society. Mr. Harlem has an extensive track record in government relations fundamentals and emerging trends, grassroot advocacy, stakeholder engagement and federal, state and local policy development. As a Congressional staffer for nearly a decade, he worked on behalf of members on the Senate Armed Services Committee, the Senate Committee on Homeland Security and Governmental Affairs, the House Ways and Means Committee, the House Committee on the Budget, the NATO Parliamentary Assembly, and the House Democracy Partnership. In Pennsylvania, Mr. Harlem helped lay the groundwork for a newly formed Montgomery County Department of Commerce, creating a "one stop shopping" tool for businesses seeking capital, asset, workforce development services. Through extensive internal reorganization, grassroot advocacy, mentoring in government relations and increased technology capabilities, he identified opportunities for new strategic partnerships, while expanding existing relationships This clarity of organization allowed the County to more effectively and transparently fulfill the needs of the community.

Compassionate and forward-thinking, Mr. Harlem's career has focused the development, leadership, and management of organizations and their intersection with the public sector. Hailed as a resourceful problem-solver with collaborative orientation and entrepreneurial approach, Mr. Harlem has always worked on behalf of the public interest. Mr. Harlem earned a Bachelor of Arts degree in political science from Franklin and Marshall College, a Master's of Public Administration and professional certifications in Nonprofit Administration and Politics from the University of Pennsylvania.

Dr. Frances Hughes is the Executive Director of Cutting Edge Oceania across both Australia and New Zealand. Through this she provides strategic, business and operational advice and services for various USA and European organisations wanting to develop increased market share in Oceania. This has included involvement with tech companies on application of blockchain and credentialing evaluation systems. Prior to this she held the position of CEO of the International Council of Nursing (ICN) in Geneva Switzerland for the past two years. Prior to ICN, Dr Hughes spent four years as the Chief Nursing and Midwifery Officer, Department of Health, Queensland Australia. During this time, she developed policy briefs and programmes to the value of 500m for nursing in Queensland. Frances was the first nurse to be awarded the Harkness Fellowship in Health Care Policy (US equivalent of Rhode Scholar) from the Commonwealth Fund in New York. She spent a year in 2001 studying at the Centre for Hospital and Patient Outcomes, University of Pennsylvania with Professor Linda Aitken. During this time, she was involved in research relating to nurse practitioners, costing nursing turnover and the effects of nursing on patient outcomes. Frances served as the Commandant Colonel for the Royal New Zealand Nursing Corp for seven years, providing strategic nursing leadership to the New Zealand Army. From 1998 -2004 Frances held the position, Chief Nurse for New Zealand, for 8 years and during this time played a major leadership role in health care policy and nursing. Frances was instrumental in the development of government policy around nurse prescribing, primary health care, health line and rural schemes, mental health and nurse practitioners. In 2004 Frances was appointed as the first Professor of Nursing at Auckland University, Chair of Mental Health Nursing and established the centre for mental health policy, research and service development. From 2005 through to 2011 Frances worked for World Health Organisation (WHO) as the Facilitator for the Pacific Island Mental Health Network (PIMHNet). During this time she worked with 16 governments, supporting them to develop policy and plans to improve mental health. Frances has a BA, MA and Doctorate in Nursing and was awarded the Queen's birthday -New Zealand Order of Merit in 2005 for her Services to Mental Health. In 2011, Frances received a Fulbright Senior Scholarship followed by a Distinguished Alumni Service Award from Massey University in New Zealand in 2013. In 2016 she received the Chancellors Award for Excellence and the Faculty Alumni award from the University of Technology Sydney

Alyssa Kaminski is a graduate student of Nonprofit Leadership at the University of Pennsylvania's School of Social Policy and Practice. She received her BFA from the University of Delaware in 2012, with a concentration in photography and video practice. Since moving to Philadelphia in 2012, Alyssa has worked for several arts and humanities organizations within the city. She chose to continue her education in the study of nonprofits after having first-hand-experience with the problems that face the nonprofit community. Her educational focus has been on identifying structural issues common in organizational operations, ethical nonprofit practices and planning for future challenges. Alyssa is currently employed as a digital media developer at the Penn Museum, working to enhance the Museum's online presence and develop new video content.

Sam Margolius is a graduate student in the School of Social Policy and Practice at the University of Pennsylvania and will graduate in 2019 with a clinical Masters of Social Work and a Masters in Nonprofit Leadership. Over the past two years, he has worked with victim/survivors of violent crime and adults battling substance use disorders in the Philadelphia area. Sam has consulted for the Massachusetts' Commission on Unaccompanied Homeless Youth and co-authored a proposal to prevent future cases of opioid use disorder that won first place in the Wharton Public Policy Case Competition. Prior to his graduate education, Sam worked with young adults aging out of state custody and as Program Director of YouthHarbors, an early intervention and prevention program at the intersection of education and unaccompanied youth homelessness. Sam grew up in the Philadelphia area, goes on road trips whenever possible, and received his Bachelor's degree in Psychology from Skidmore College.

Megan R. Osvath is a young nonprofit professional based in Philadelphia. While completing her BS in Psychology at the Pennsylvania State University, she first began her nonprofit career as a student leader for the Penn State Dance Marathon (THON). As the 2014-2015 Executive Director, Megan led more than 15,000 student volunteers as they supported families impacted by childhood cancer. Throughout the year, Megan worked with THON volunteers to build meaningful relationships with families, spread awareness of childhood cancer, and raise more than $13 million for Four Diamonds, an organization based at Penn State Hershey Children's Hospital. Today, Megan is building on her passion for healthcare philanthropy by serving as Associate Director of Development for Biomedical Research at the University of Pennsylvania. In this role, she works to accelerate scientific discovery by working with philanthropic partners who are interested in supporting basic and translational research across Penn Medicine. She is also a part-time student in the Nonprofit Leadership Master's Program at the University of Pennsylvania. Inside and outside of professional responsibilities, Megan is passionate about advancing biomedical science and learning more about the social determinants of health, aiming to gain a deeper understanding of how they impact society broadly, and how we can address them to improve human health.

Callie Perrone is a current graduate student at the University of Pennsylvania's School of Social Policy and Practice, where she is pursuing master's degrees in Social Work and Social Policy. Committed to community-driven anti-poverty work, Callie has interned at the Center for Hunger-Free Communities, Project HOME, AFSC, and the Philadelphia Mayor's Office of Community Empowerment & Opportunity. Callie received her bachelor's degree in Political Science and Peace, Justice, & Human Rights from Haverford College, and is a former Haverford House Fellow.

Brian Valdez serves as the Law and Policy Director of the Convenient Care Association (CCA), the National Trade Association for Retail Health Clinics. Before this role, Brian served as the Law and Policy Manager for the National Nurse-led Care Consortium for 15 years, when he joined the organization as an AmeriCorps VISTA volunteer. In these roles, he is responsible for monitoring and responding to federal and state laws and regulations affecting nurse-led and convenient care clinics throughout the country. He also educates policymakers at all levels about the importance of nurse-led care by meeting with elected officials, drafting and presenting comments at legislative hearings, as well as creating fact sheets and other informational materials. He engages CCA members in policy initiatives around scope of practice, telehealth, provider credentialing and other issues, while also keeping members informed through monthly policy updates. In addition to his policy work, Brian is an accomplished grant writer with over 10 years of experience. His work has helped to bring in millions of dollars in support of public health programs serving low-income children and families. In 2015 Brian was named an Americorps VISTA, "Champion of Change", an honor given to individuals from across the nation who have done "extraordinary things to empoer and inspire members of their communities in all areas of community service". Brian is currently earning his Masters in Public Administration from the Harvard Kennedy School, he has a law degree from Temple University and is licensed to practice law in Pennsylvania and New Jersey.

Allison Wortley is an experienced development professional passionate about working in the social sector.

APPENDIX A
IRS CODE

IRS CODE
List of the types of not-for-profits that the IRS recognizes. This information comes from IRS Publication 557, if you are considering filing for not-for-profit status. In addition, IRS Publication 526 provides information about which of these organization can accept tax-deductible contributions.

- **501(c)(1)** These are corporations organized under Act of Congress. Federal Credit Unions are a good example of this type of not-for-profit. These not-for-profits do not have to file an annual return. Tax-exempt contributions are allowed if they are made for exclusively public purposes.
- **501(c)(2)**. These are holding corporations for exempt organizations. That is, they can hold title to property of an exempt group. They apply for not-for-profit status using IRS form 1024. They annually file forms 990 or 990EZ.
- **501(c)(3)**. This is the most common type of not-for-profit. It includes organizations that are religious, educational, charitable, scientific, and literary; groups that test for public safety, that foster national or international amateur sports competition; or organizations engaged in the prevention of cruelty to children or animals.

This type of not-for-profit applies for its status using IRS form 1023, and files annually form 990, 990EZ, or 990-PF. Contributions are usually tax-exempt.
All 501(c)(3) organizations are considered either:
1. A private foundation. These are not-for-profits that don't qualify as public charities. Foundations may be sub-classified as private operating foundations or private non-operating foundations and receive some of the advantages of public charities.
2. Or a public charity.

501(c)(3) are formed exclusively for benefit of the public good and include:
1. Charitable
2. Educational
3. Religious
4. Literary
5. Scientific
6. Testing for public safety
7. Prevention of cruelty to children or animals
8. Fostering national or international amateur sports competition

- **501(c)(4)** These organizations are civic leagues, social welfare organizations, and local associations of employees. They promote community welfare, charitable, education, or recreational goals. They apply using IRS Form 1024. They file annually 990 or 990EZ.

- **501(c)(5)**. Labor, agricultural, and horticultural organizations fit under this classification. They are educational or instructive, with the goal of improving conditions of work, and to improve products and efficiency. They apply by using IRS Form 1024, and file annually form 990 or 990EZ.
- **501(c)(6)**. These organizations are business leagues, chambers of commerce, real estate boards, etc. They seek to improve business conditions. They apply using IRS form 1024 and file annually the 990 or 990EZ.
- **501(c)(7)**. Social and recreation clubs fall into this category. They promote pleasure, recreation, and social activities. They apply using IRS form 1024 and file annually the 990 or 990EZ.
- **501(c)(8)**. This category includes fraternal beneficiary societies and associations. They provide for the payment of life, sickness, accident, or other benefits to members. They apply using IRS form 1024 and file annually the 990 or 990EZ.
- **501(c)(9)**. These are voluntary employees' beneficiary associations. They provide for the payment of life, sickness, accident, or other benefits to members. They apply using IRS form 1024 and file annually the 990 or 990EZ.
- **501(c)(10)**. Domestic Fraternal Societies and Associations. A lodge devoting its net earnings to charitable, fraternal, and other specified purposes. No life, sickness, or accident benefits to members. Apply using IRS form 1024 and file annually the 990 or 990EZ.
- **502(c)(11)**. Teacher's Retirement Fund Associations. Associations for payment of retirement benefits. Apply using IRS form 1024 and file annually the 990 or 990EZ.
- **501(c)(13)**. Cemetery Companies. Loans to members. Uses Form 1024 for application. Files annually the 990 or 990EZ.
- **501(c)(14)**. State Chartered Credit Unions, Mutual Reserve Funds. Loans to members. No application form. Files annually the 990 or 990EZ.
- **501(c)(15)**. Mutual Insurance Companies of Association. Provide insurance to members, mostly at cost. Applies using Form 1024. Files annually the 990 or 990EZ.
- **501(c)(16)** Cooperative Organizations to Finance Crop Operations. Finance crop operations in conjunction with activities of a marketing or purchasing association. No form to apply. Files annually the 990 or 990EZ.
- **501(c)(17)**. Supplemental Unemployment Benefit Trusts. Provides for payment of supplemental unemployment compensation benefits. Applies using Form 1024. Files annually the 990 or 990EZ.
- **501(c)(18)**. Employee Funded Pension Trust (created before June 25, 1959). Payment of benefits under a pension plan funded by employees. No form. Applies using Form 1024. Files annually the 990 or 990EZ.
- **501(c)(19)**. Post or Organization of Past or Present Members of the Armed Forces. Activities according to the nature of organization. Applies using Form 1024. Files annually the 990 or 990EZ.

- **501(c)(20)**. Group Legal Services Plan Organizations.
- **501(c)(21)**. Black Lung Benefit Trusts. Funded by coal mine operators to satisfy their liability for disability or death due to black lung diseases. No form for filing. Reports on tax form 990-BL.
- **501(c)(22)**. Withdrawal Liability Payment Fund. Provides funds to meet the liability of employers withdrawing from a multi-employer pension fund. No form to file. Tax forms 990 or 990EZ.
- **501(c)(23)**. Veterans Organization (created before 1880). Provides insurance and other benefits to veterans. No form to apply. Uses tax forms 990 or 990EZ.
- **501(c)(25)**. Title Holding Corporations or Trusts with Multiple Parents. Holding title and paying over income from property to 35 or fewer parents or beneficiaries. Applies with form 1024. Files tax forms 990 or 990EZ.
- **501(c)(26)**. State-Sponsored Organization Providing Health Coverage for High-Risk Individuals. Provides health care coverage to high-risk individuals. No form for applying. Files tax forms 990 or 990EZ.
- **501(c)(27)**. State-Sponsored Workers' Compensation Reinsurance Organization Reimburses members for losses under workers' compensation acts. No form for applying. Files tax forms 990 or 990EZ.
- **501(d)**. Religious and Apostolic Associations. Regular business activities. Communal religious community. No application form. Files tax form 1065.
- **501(e)**. Cooperative Hospital Service Organizations. Performs cooperative services for hospitals. Use 1023 to apply. Files tax forms 990 or 990EZ.
- **501(f)**. Cooperative Service Organizations of Operating Educational Organizations. Performs collective investment services for educational organizations. Applies with form 1023. Files tax forms 990 or 990EZ.
- **501(k)**. Child Care Organizations. Provides care for children. Apply with 1023. Files tax forms 990 or 990EZ.
- **501(n)**. Charitable Risk Pools. Pools certain insurance risks of 501(c)(3). Apply with form 1023. Use tax forms 990 or 990EZ.
- **521(a)**. Farmers' Cooperative Associations. Cooperative marketing and purchasing for agricultural producers. Applies using Form 1028. Tax form 990-C.

APPENDIX B
NOT-FOR-PROFIT GOVERNANCE TEMPLATES

BYLAWS TEMPLATE

BYLAWS OF NOT-FOR-PROFIT LEGAL NAME, Inc.

ARTICLE I

Name

The name of the Corporation is NOT-FOR-PROFIT LEGAL NAME.

ARTICLE II

Purpose and Operation

Section 1. Purposes. The Corporation is incorporated under the Nonprofit Corporation Law of the **STATE NAME**, and the Corporation does not contemplate pecuniary gain or profit, incidental or otherwise. The nature of the activities to be conducted, and the purposes to be promoted or carried out by the corporation, shall be exclusively those within the purview of Section 501(c)(3) of the Internal Revenue Code of 1986, as amended ("Code") or the corresponding provisions limiting the generality of the foregoing, the purposes of the Corporation shall be:

   a. To promote, advocate and deliver an array of human services to the ……….. community of the Delaware Valley.
   b. To stimulate and encourage the social, economic and cultural advancement of the community for common achievement and accomplishment.
   c. To serve as advisors to local, state and federal institutions to assure the needs of the …………. community are met, subject in all cases, to the restrictions set forth in Article II, Section 5 hereto.
   d. To represent the ………….. community before the civic and governmental authorities of the City of Philadelphia, State of Pennsylvania, and Federal Government subject in all cases, to the restrictions set forth in Article II, Section 5 hereof.

e. No part of the net earnings of the Corporation shall inure to the benefit of, or be distributable to its directors, officers or other private persons, except that the Corporation shall be authorized and empowered to pay reasonable compensation for services rendered and to make payments and distributions in furtherance of the purposes set forth in the preceding paragraphs and in the articles of incorporation of the Corporation (the "Articles"). Except as may be permitted under the provisions of Section 501(h) of the Code, or corresponding provisions of any subsequent tax laws of the United States, no substantial part of the activities of the Corporation shall be the carrying on of propaganda or otherwise attempting to influence legislation, and the Corporation shall not participate in, or intervene in (including the publishing or distribution of statements) any political campaign on behalf of any candidate for public office.

f. Notwithstanding any other provision of these bylaws or the Articles, the Corporation shall not carry on any other activities not permitted to be carried on (a) by a corporation exempt from Federal income tax under Section 501(a) and Section 501(c)(3) of the Code (or the corresponding provision of any future United States Internal Revenue Law) or (b) by a corporation, contributions to which are deductible under Section 170(a) and Section 170(c)(2) of the Code (or the corresponding provision of any future United State Internal Revenue Law).

g. Upon any dissolution or termination of the existence of the Corporation, all of its property and assets shall, after payment or making provision for payment of the lawful debts of the Corporation and the expenses of its dissolution or termination, be delivered, conveyed and paid over to such one or more qualified organizations as the Board of Directors of the Corporation (the "Board of Directors" or the "Board") shall determine. In the event the Board of Directors fails to make a determination, such property and assets shall be delivered, conveyed and paid over to such one or more qualified organizations as may be ordered by the court having jurisdiction over the dissolution and liquidation of the Corporation, pursuant to the appropriate subchapter of chapter 59 of Title 15 of the Pennsylvania Consolidated Statutes annotated. Any provision of law to the contrary notwithstanding, the Corporation shall not be merged or consolidated with any Corporation other than a qualified organization. As used in this subsection (g), the term "qualified organization" shall mean an organization exempt from Federal Income Tax under Section 501(a) and Section 501(c)(3), and describe in Section 170(b)(1)(A) (other than in clauses (vii) and (viii) of the Code, or corresponding provisions of any subsequent tax laws of the United States, and which has been in existence and so described for a continuous period of at least sixty (60) calendar months.

Section 2. Operation. The Corporation shall operate on a non-stock and non-membership basis and it shall not distribute any part of its income or profits to its Directors or Officers.

Section 3. Limitation of Corporation Activities. The activities of the Corporation shall at all times be so conducted and limited as to enable the Corporation to meet the requirements for:

a. a corporation exempt from Federal Income Tax under Section 501(c)(3) of the Code or corresponding provisions of any subsequent tax laws of the United States;

b. a corporation, the contributions to which are deductible under Section 170(c)(2) of the Code, or corresponding provisions of any subsequent tax laws of the United States.

Section 4. Offices. The registered office of the Corporation shall be **LEGAL ADDRESS**. The Corporation may also have offices at such other places as the Board of Directors may from time to time determine.

Section 5. Lobbying. No substantial part of the activities of the Corporation shall consist of carrying on propaganda or otherwise attempting to influence legislation.

ARTICLE III
Members
The Corporation **shall or shall** not have members.

ARTICLE IV
Directors

Section 1. Number and Powers. The business and affairs of the Corporation shall be managed by a Board of no less than and no more than fifteen (15) directors. The Board may exercise all powers of the Corporation and do all lawful acts and things as are not proscribed by statue, by the Articles, or by these bylaws.

Section 2. Qualifications. Directors shall be natural persons at least 18 years of age, with demonstrated interest in the Latino community.

Section 3. Election of Directors. A meeting of the Board shall be in November of each year (the "Annual Meeting") at such time and place as the Board shall determine for the election of directors and for the transaction of such other business as may properly come before the meeting. Directors may, but need not, be elected from the nominees presented to the Board by the Selection/Nominating Committee at the Board's meeting immediately prior to the Annual Meeting. Election of Directors shall be by the vote of majority of Directors present at an Annual Meeting at which a quorum is present.

Section 4. Term of Office of Directors. The term of office for each Director shall be two (2) years. The Board shall seek to ensure that a nucleus of experienced Directors is always in office. Each Director elected at the Annual Meeting of the Board shall serve until the expiration of the term for which she or he was selected and her or his successor is elected and qualified or until her or his earlier death, resignation or removal. No Director shall serve for more than two (2) consecutive terms without the approval of the Board.

Section 5. Leave of Absence. In the event that a Director, for personal, health, professional or other reason(s), desires to take a leave of absence from the Board of Directors, such Director may request that the Board of Directors approve such a leave of absence. Leave of absence ("Leave") shall be approved by the affirmative vote of the Board of Directors' provided that, the Directors requesting Leave shall not be entitled to vote. Leave shall only be granted in extraordinary circumstances, and the granting of Leave shall be the exception and not the rule. Only two (2) Directors at any one time may be on Leave. A Director on Leave shall be considered to have resigned from the Board of Directors pursuant to Article IV, Section 7 of these bylaws; provided, that (i) seats on the Board of Directors held by persons on leave shall not be considered vacant for purposes of Article IV, Section 5 of these bylaws, and (ii) upon the end of the period for which the person has been granted leave, the Board of Directors shall re-elect such person to the Board of Directors. Leave may be granted for a period of up to a one (1) year; provided, that the Board of Directors may approve an extension of leave beyond one (1) year under appropriate circumstances. In the event a Director shall serve for a period of one (1) year or less during any one (1) term in office due to the time spent on Leave, such service shall not constitute one of the two (2) consecutive terms permitted to be served by Directors, under Article IV, Section 4 of these bylaws.

Section 6. Vacancies. Vacancies in the Board of Directors, including vacancies resulting from an increase in the number of Directors constituting the whole Board, shall be filled by a majority of the remaining Directors, even though less than a quorum. Each person so elected shall be a Director until his successor is elected and qualified at the next (applicable) Annual Meeting of the Board, or at any special meeting of the Board duly called for that purpose and held prior thereto. In the event a Director is so elected, and such Director shall serve for a period of one (1) year or less, such service shall not constitute one of the two (2) consecutive terms permitted to be served by Directors, under Article IV, Section 4 of these bylaws.

Section 7. Removal.
    a.   Any Director or Directors may be removed from office pursuant to the provisions of Section 5726 of the Pennsylvania Nonprofit Corporation Law of 1988, as amended (15 Pa.C.S.A. §5726), or the corresponding provision of any future law.
    b.   In addition to the foregoing, a Director may be removed from office as follows:

(1) Upon the occurrence of three (3) consecutive unexcused absences from the regular announced meetings of the Board, a Director shall automatically and without further action on the part of the Board, be removed from office. Absences may be excused either prior to a meeting by the Chair of the Board or following a meeting by the approval of the Board.

(2) Any Director may be removed from the Board for "cause" at a duly organized meeting of the Board of Directors called expressly for that purpose. For purposes hereof, "cause" shall include, but not be limited to, acts of misfeasance or non-feasance, including conviction by a criminal court or any Federal or State jurisdiction, any conduct on the part of a Director which shall constitute a conflict of interest with respect to the official policy or programs of the Corporation, or a Director engaging in any of the conduct prohibited by Article XI of these bylaws.

Section 8. Resignation. Director may resign at any time by giving written notice to the Chair of the Board or the Secretary of the Corporation. Any such resignation shall take effect on the date of receipt of such notice or any other time specified therein.

Section 9. Liability of Directors. No person who is or was a Director of this Corporation shall be personally liable for monetary damages for any action taken, or any failure to take any action, as a Director unless:

a. the Director has breached or failed to perform the duties of his office as set forth in Subchapter B of Chapter 57 of Title 15 of the Pennsylvania Consolidated Statutes Annotated, as amended, or the corresponding provisions of any future law; and

b. the breach or failure to perform constitutes self-dealing, willful misconduct or recklessness.

This provision of the bylaws shall not apply to:
(1) the responsibility or liability of a Director pursuant to any criminal statute; or
(2) the liability of a Director for the payment of taxes pursuant to local, state or federal law.

If **Name of State** law hereafter is amended to authorize the further elimination or limitation of the liability of Directors, then the liability of a Director of the Corporation, in addition to the limitation on personal liability provided herein, shall be limited to the fullest extent permitted by the amended Pennsylvania law.

Section 10. Services from Directors. Any Director may perform services for or on behalf of the Corporation, but without the prior approval of the Board of Directors (upon which matter the Director to perform such services may note vote); such services may be performed only on a voluntary basis and without compensation.

Section 11. Staff. Directors may become employees/staff members of the Corporation provided; however, upon her or his appointment or hiring as much, the Director must resign from the Board. Resignations will be effective immediately upon appointment as an employee/staff member.

Section 12. Compensation. No monetary compensation for attendance at regular meetings shall be authorized. Reimbursement for out-of-pocket expenses may be authorized for official activities related to the Corporation; provided such activity was duly authorized by the Executive Committee or the Board.

ARTICLE V
Director's Meetings

Section 1. Reorganizational Meeting. The first meeting of each newly constituted Board (the reorganizational meeting) may be held at the same place and immediately after the meeting at which Directors were elected and no notice need be given to the newly elected Directors in order to legally constitute the meeting; or it may convene at such time and place as may be fixed by the consent or consents in writing of all the directors.

Section 2. Regular Meetings. Regular meetings of the Board shall be held at such time and place as shall be determined from time to time, by resolution of the Board. The Board shall use reasonable efforts to have regular meetings at least once a month, but in no event shall the Board have regular meetings less than quarterly. Notice of each regular meeting of the Board shall specify the date, place and hour of the meeting and shall be given each Director at least one (1) week before the meeting personally or by mail, courier or telegram.

Section 3. Special Meetings. Special meetings of the Board may be called by the Chairperson of the Board on 48-hours notice to each Director; either personally or by mail, courier or telegram; special meetings shall be called by the Chairperson of the Board or Secretary in like manner and on like notice on the written request of at least one-third of the Directors in office. Notice of such special meeting of the Board shall specify the date, place and hour of the meeting. The notice need not state the general nature of the business to be conducted at such special meeting.

Section 4. Quorum. At least a majority of the persons entitled to vote at any meeting of the Board shall constitute a quorum for the transactions of business at that meeting, and the acts of a majority of the Directors present at a meeting at which a quorum is present shall be the acts of the Board. Quorum, once constituted, shall hold and cannot be defeated by one or more Director(s) leaving the meeting.

Section 5. Informal Action by Directors. Any action which may be taken at a meeting of the Directors of the Corporation may be taken without a meeting if consent or consents in writing setting forth the action so taken shall be signed by all of the Directors and shall be filed with the secretary of the Corporation.

ARTICLE VI
Committees

Section 1. Committees. Other than the standing committees of the Board which shall be established as provided in this Article VI below, the Board may, but shall not be required to, provide for appropriate committees of the Board of such number of Directors as determined by the Board. In addition, individuals that are not Directors may be asked to serve on committees (subject to the provisions of this Article VI of these bylaws) as non-voting members of each such committee. Only Directors may serve as voting members of committees. Subject to the provisions of these bylaws, the Chairperson and members of every committee shall be chosen by the Board. Subject to the provisions of these bylaws, the powers and duties of all such committees shall be as prescribed by the Board. Each committee, other than standing committees, shall automatically dissolve upon completion of the task assigned to that committee.

Section 2. Standing Committees. There shall be the following Standing Committees of the Board: Executive Committee, Finance Committee, Fundraising Committee, and a Selection/Nominating Committee.

Section 3. Executive Committee.
- a. There shall be an Executive Committee of the Board to advise and assist the Board in managing the Corporation's affairs. The voting members of the Executive Committee shall consist of the Chairperson of the Board, the Vice-Chair of the Board, the Treasurer and the Secretary. The Executive Director shall serve as the sole non-voting member of the Executive Committee. The Chairperson of the Board shall be the Chairperson of the Executive Committee.
- b. The Executive Committee shall meet whenever required between meetings of the Board, with full power and authority to act for the Board between such meetings, except for those powers specifically reserved by the Board from time to time, and except as may be provided in these bylaws. The Executive Committee shall also generally perform such duties and exercise such powers as may also be directed or delegated by the Board from time to time.
- c. Special meetings of the Executive Committee shall be called at the direction of its Chairperson or any three (3) members of the Executive Committee and shall be held at such time and place as shall be designated in the notice calling said meeting. Written notice of the time, place and object of every special meeting of the Executive Committee shall be given to each member thereof at last with 24-hour notice prior to the day named for the meeting and no business shall be considered except such as is stated in the notice of the meeting.

      d.   Three (3) voting members of the Executive Committee shall be necessary to constitute a quorum for the transaction of business. The acts of a majority of the members of the Executive Committee present at a meeting which a quorum is present shall be the acts of the Executive Committee. If a quorum is not present, a majority of the members of the Executive Committee present may adjourn the meeting. No notice of such adjourned meeting shall be required.

Section 4. Finance Committee. There shall be a Finance Committee consisting of such Directors (and non-Directors) as determined by the Board from time to time. The Finance Committee shall advise and aid the Board in all matters concerning the Corporation's finances. The Finance Committee shall also generally perform such duties and exercise such powers as may be directed or delegated by the Board from time to time.

Section 5. Fund Raising Committee. There shall be a Fundraising Committee consisting of such Directors (and Non-Directors) as determined by the Board from time to time. The Fundraising Committee shall advise and aid the Board in all matters concerning the Corporation's fundraising activities. The Fundraising Committee shall also generally perform such duties and exercise such powers as may be directed or delegated by the Board from time to time.

Section 6. Selection/Nominating Committee.
      a.   There shall be a Selection/Nomination Committee of the Board consisting of such Directors (and non-Directors) as determined by the Board from time to time. The Selection/Nominating Committee shall review resumes and/or applications of candidates who desire to be nominated for Board membership. The Selection/Nominating Committee shall consider candidates for Director from various fields, including but not limited to the following: representatives from governmental units, elected officials, consumers, business professionals in the field of human services delivery, representatives from other Latino organizations, organized labor, youth, senior citizens, and clergy. The Selection/Nominating Committee shall also generally perform such duties and exercise such powers as may also be directed or delegated by the Board from time to time.
      b.   The Selection/Nominating Committee shall meet whenever appropriate in order to perform its tasks and fulfill its function. The Selection/Nominating Committee shall present their nominees to the Board at the Board's regularly scheduled meeting immediately prior to the month of November, so that the Board may, at its regularly scheduled November meeting (i.e., its Annual Meeting), elect its new members.

Section 7. Program Evaluation Committee. The Board may establish a Program Evaluation Committee of the Board consisting of such Directors as determined by the Board from time to time. The Program Evaluation Committee shall evaluate the programs in which the Corporation has an opportunity to participate from time to time and shall also generally perform such duties and exercise such powers as may also be directed or delegated by the Board from time to time.

ARTICLE VII

Officers

Section 1. Qualification and Election. The officers of the Corporation shall be elected by the Board at the Reorganization Meeting, immediately after the Annual Meeting, and shall be a Chairperson of the Board, Vice-Chair of the Board, Secretary, Treasurer and Executive Director. The Chairperson of the Board, the Vice-Chair of the Board, Secretary, Treasurer and Executive Director shall be natural persons of full age. The Treasurer may be a corporation but, if the Treasurer is a natural person, the Treasurer shall be a person of full age. Any number of other offices may be held by the same persons, except the Chairperson of the Board, the Vice-Chair of the Board, the Treasurer, the Secretary and the Executive Director must be different persons. All of the Chairperson of the Board, the Vice-Chair of the Board, the Treasurer and the Secretary shall be Directors of the Corporation as well.

Section 2. Term. The Officers of the Corporation shall hold office until their successors are chosen and qualified. Any officers or agent elected or appointed by the Board of Directors may be removed by the Board of Directors whenever, in its judgment, the best interest of the Corporation will be served thereby, but such removal shall be without prejudice to the contract rights, if any of the person so removed. In the office of any officer becomes vacant for any reason, the vacancy shall be filled by the Board.

Section 3. Chairperson of the Board. The Chairperson of the Board shall preside at all meetings of Directors. The Chairperson of the Board may execute bonds, mortgages and other contracts requiring a seal, under the seal of the Corporation except where required by law to be otherwise signed and executed and except where the signing and execution thereof shall be expressly delegated by the Board to some other officer or agent of the Corporation. He shall also perform such other duties as the Board of Directors may from time to time assign to him.

Section 4. Vice-Chair. In the absence of the Chairperson of the Board or in the event of his inability or refusal to act, the Vice-Chair shall perform the duties of the Chairperson of the Board and when so acting, shall have all the powers of and be subject to all the restrictions upon the Chairperson of the Board. The Vice-Chair shall perform such other duties and have such other powers as the Board of Directors may from time to time prescribe or the Chairperson of the Board may from time to time delegate to him.

Section 5. Executive Director. The Executive Director shall be the Chief Executive and Chief Operating Officer of the Corporation; shall have general management of the business of the Corporation; shall maintain active supervision over the day-to-day business and activities of the Corporation; and shall see that all orders and resolutions of the Board are carried into effect. She or he shall execute bonds, mortgages and other contracts requiring a seal, under the seal of the Corporation, except where required or permitted by law to be otherwise signed and executed and except where the signing and execution thereof shall be expressly delegated by the Board to some other officer or agent of the Corporation. The Executive Director shall be considered the statutory President of the Corporation for purposes of §5732(a) of the Nonprofit Corporation Law of 1988 and shall have sufficiently broad authority to enable him or her to carry out his or her responsibilities and she or he shall act as the duly authorized representative of the corporation whenever appropriate.

Section 6. Secretary. The Secretary shall attend all sessions of the Board and record all the votes of the Corporation and the minutes of all the transactions and shall perform like duties for other committees of the Board, when required. She or he shall give, or cause to be given, notice of all meetings of the Board and its committees, and shall perform such other duties as may be prescribed by the Board or by the Chairperson of the Board, under whose supervision she or he shall be. She or he shall keep in safe custody the corporate seal of the Corporation and, when authorized by the Board, affix the same to any instrument requiring it and, when so affixed, it shall be attested by his signature or by the signature of the Treasurer or an Assistant Secretary or an Assistant Treasurer.

Section 7. Treasurer. The Treasurer shall be the chief accounting officer of the Corporation and shall arrange for the keeping of adequate records of all assets, liabilities and transactions of the Corporation. He or she provide for the establishment of internal controls and see that adequate audits are currently and regularly made. He or she shall submit to the Chairperson of the Board and the Board timely statements of the accounts of the Corporation and the financial results of the operations thereof. The Treasurer shall also be responsible to the Board for properly carrying out fiscal, accounting and internal-external auditing policies and programs, all as prescribed by the Board from time to time. The Treasurer shall be bonded as provided in Article XII, Section 5 of these bylaws.

ARTICLE VIII
Advisory Council
There may be, at the election and in the sole discretion of the Board, established an Advisory Council of the Corporation which shall report to the Board. The Advisory Corporation shall identify, evaluate and prioritize projects in which the Corporation may engage, and shall assist the Board and the Corporation in the manner and for the purposes for which the Advisory Council may be formed.

ARTICLE IX
Administration

Section 1. Executive Director. The Board of Directors shall appointment an Executive Director who shall serve the Corporation, subject to the provisions of any contractual arrangement, until terminated by the Board of Directors. The Executive Director shall have the custody of the custody of the corporate funds and shall keep full and accurate accounts of receipt and disbursements in books belonging to the Corporation and shall deposit all moneys and other valuable effects in the name and to the credit of the Corporation in such depositories as shall be designed by the Board. The Executive Director shall also perform such other duties as shall be specified by the Board of Directors from time to time.

Section 2. Finance Director. The Executive Director shall designate a Finance Director who shall serve the Corporation, subject to the provisions of any contractual arrangement, until terminated by the Executive Director. The Finance Director shall have the custody of the corporate funds and shall keep full and accurate accounts of receipts and disbursements in books belonging to the Corporation and shall deposit all moneys and other valuable effects in the name and to the credit of the Corporation in such depositories as shall be designed by the Board. The Finance Director shall also perform such other duties as shall be specified by the Executive Director from time to time.

Section 3. Other Officers. The Board may provide for and designate such other officers and assistant officers, including assistant vice president, assistant secretaries, and assistant treasurers as the needs of the Corporation may require. There officers shall hold their offices for such terms and shall have such authority and perform such duties as, from time to time, shall be specified by the Board.

Section 4. Employees. The Corporation may retain or employ and compensate such employees, professional or otherwise, as may be deemed necessary to carry out the purpose of the Corporation. All such employees, professionals or otherwise shall be employed and/or retained by the Executive Director, and their respective employment and/or retention may be terminated by the Executive Director in the exercise of his or her sole discretion.

ARTICLE X
Indemnification

Section 1. Terms. The Corporation shall indemnify, to the extent permitted by and under Pennsylvania law and under these bylaws, any person who was or is a party (other than a party plaintiff suing on her or his own behalf or in the right of the Corporation), or who is threatened to be made such a party, to any threatened, pending or completed action, suit or proceeding, whether civil, criminal, administrative or investigative (including, but not limited to, an action by or in the right of the Corporation) by reason of the fact that she or he is or was a director, officer or employee of the Corporation, or is or was serving at the request of the Corporation as a director, officer or employee of another corporation, partnership, joint venture, trust or other enterprise (such person being herein called an "Indemnified Person"), against expenses (including attorneys' fees), judgments, fines and amounts paid in settlement actually and reasonably incurred by her or him in connection with such action, suit or proceeding (herein called collectively the "Indemnified Liabilities"), unless the act or failure to act giving rise to the claim for indemnification is determined by a court to have constituted self-dealing, willful misconduct or recklessness.

In addition, the Corporation shall indemnify any Indemnified Person against the Indemnified Liabilities to the full extent otherwise authorized by Pennsylvania law, including, without limitation, the indemnification permitted by Section 5741, et seq., of the Nonprofit Corporation Law of 1988.

Section 2. Powers. The Corporation shall have the power to indemnify any person who is or was an agent of the Corporation, or is or was serving at the request of the Corporation as an agent of another corporation, partnership, joint venture, trust or other enterprise, against expenses (including attorney's fees), judgments, fines and amounts paid in settlement actually and reasonably incurred by her or him by reason of her or his services on behalf of the Corporation, except as prohibited by law.

Section 3. Ability to Advance Expenses. Expenses incurred by an officer, director, employee or agent in defending a civil or criminal action, suit or proceeding may be paid by the Corporation in advance of the final disposition of such action, suit or proceeding, as authorized in the manner provided in Section 4 of this Article, upon receipt of an undertaking by or on behalf of such person to repay such amount if it shall ultimately be determined that she or he is not entitled to be indemnified by the Corporation as authorized in this Article.

Section 4. Determination of Indemnification and Advancement of Expenses.
   a. Any indemnification under Section 1 of this Article (unless ordered by a court) shall be made by the corporation unless a determination is reasonably and promptly made that indemnification of the director, officer or employee is not proper in the circumstances because she or he has not satisfied the terms set forth in Section 1.

b. Expenses shall be advanced by the Corporation to a director, officer or employee upon a determination that such person is an Indemnified Person as defined in Section 1 of this Article and has satisfied the terms set forth in Section 3 of this Article.
c. Any indemnification under Section 2 of this Article or advancement of expenses to an agent under Section 3 of this Article (unless ordered by a court) may be made upon a determination that the agent has satisfied the terms of Section 2 or 3, as applicable, and in view of all the circumstances of the case, such person is fairly and reasonably entitled to indemnity or advancement of expenses.
d. All determinations under this Section 4 shall be made:

   (1) By the Board of Directors by a majority vote of a quorum consisting of Directors who were not parties to such action, suit or proceeding or
   (2) If such a quorum is not obtainable, or even if obtainable, if a majority vote of a quorum of disinterested directors so directs, by independent legal counsel is written opinion.

Section 5. Other Rights of Indemnified Person. The indemnification provided by this Article shall not be deemed exclusive of any other rights to which those seeking indemnification may be entitled under any agreement, vote of disinterested directors or otherwise, both as to action in her or his official capacity and as to action in another capacity while holding such office, and shall continue as to a person who has ceased to be a director, officer, employee or agent and shall inure to the benefit of the heirs, executors and administrators of such person.

Section 6. Insurance. The Corporation shall have power to purchase and maintain insurance on behalf of any person who is or was a director, officer, employee or agent of the Corporation, or is or was serving at the request of the Corporation as a director, officer, employee or agent of another corporation, partnership, joint venture, trust or other enterprise against any liability asserted against her or him and incurred by her or him in any such capacity, or arising out of her status as such, whether or not the Corporation would have the power to indemnify her or him against such liability under the provisions of this Article.

ARTICLE XI
Conflicts of Interest
Section 1. Use of Corporate Name. It is a violation of a Director's fiduciary relationship to the Corporation for such Director to use the Corporation's name for personal gain or profit.
Section 2. Personal Interest. It is a violation of a Director's fiduciary relationship to the Corporation for such Director to vote on any question in which he/she has a direct financial interest.

Section 3. Filial Relationship. Members of a Director's immediate family may not serve as a Director until the current director no longer serves in such capacity. For purposes hereof, members of a Director's immediate family shall include such Director's spouse (or "domestic partner"), brother, sister, mother, father, son or daughter.

Members of a Director's immediate family may not serve as an employee unless a majority of Board approves Executive Director's recommendation to hire. The Director will not be able to vote on matters related to that employee's compensation benefits or terms of employment.

ARTICLE XI
Commercial Transactions

Section 1. Contracts. Contracts of the Corporation can be signed by any Officer as authorized by a resolution of the Executive Committee or the Board of Directors.
Section 2. Loans. Only the Executive Director, with the concurring signature of the Treasurer, Chairperson of the Board of Vice-Chair of the Board, shall be authorized to borrow money on behalf of the Corporation, and only after Board approval thereof has been obtained.
Section 3. Checks, Drafts, Etc. All checks and drafts, or other orders for the payment of money, notes or other evidences of indebtedness issued in the name of the Corporation will be signed by two (2) officers of the Corporation.
Section 4. Corporate Funds. All funds received by the Corporation, whether acquired by gifts, contract or any other means, not otherwise employed, shall be deposited to the credit of the Corporation in such bank, trust companies, or other depositories as the Board of Directors may select. The Board may accept on behalf of the Corporation any contribution, gift, bequest or devise for the general purposes or for any special purpose of the Corporation.
Section 5. Bonds. All Officers and employees of the Corporation who are charged with handling money on behalf of the Corporation shall be bonded in an amount which will indemnify the Corporation in case or misappropriation or misconduct.
Section 6. Auditors. Auditors shall be designed by the Board, prior to the close of business in each fiscal year, who shall audit and examine the books of account of the Corporation and shall certify to the Board the annual balances of said books which shall be prepared at the close of the fiscal year under the direction of the Treasurer, or his designee. No director or officer of the Corporation and no firm or corporation of which such officer or director is a member, shall be eligible to discharge the duties of auditor.

Section 7. Financial Report to Board. The Board shall insure that the books and finances of the Corporation are in proper order at all times. The Directors of the Corporation shall direct the Executive Director, or his (or her) designee, and the Treasurer to present annually to the Board a report, the contents of which are prescribed in Section 5553 of the Pennsylvania Nonprofit Corporation Law of 1988 (or any successor Act or provisions), a copy of which report shall be filed with the minutes of the Annual Meeting of Directors. Financial Reports shall also be furnished at each regular Board of Directors meeting by the Treasurer, or his designee.

Section 8. Fiscal Year. The fiscal year of the Corporation shall be July 1 to June 30.

ARTICLE XIII
Miscellaneous

Section 1. Seal. The seal of the Corporation shall be circular in form, setting forth the name of the Corporation, the year of its organization and the words "Corporate Seal".

Section 2. Waiver of Notice. Whenever any notice of any meeting is required as aforesaid, a waiver thereof in writing signed by the person or persons entitled to such notice, whether before or after the time stated therein, shall be deemed equivalent to the giving of such notice.

Section 3. Meetings Involving Telephone. One or more Directors or members of Board committees may participate in a meeting of the board or a committee of the Board (as the case may be) by means of conference telephone or similar communications equipment, whereby all persons participating in the call can hear each other. Providing all notice requirements for holding the meeting involved have been met, action may be taken at such a telephone meeting to the same extent and in the same manner as if all persons participating were physically present at the same location.

Section 4. Adjournment. If any meeting of the Board, or member of any committee of the Board cannot be organized because less than a quorum of the persons involved is in attendance, those persons in attendance may adjourn the meeting to such time and place as they may determine and it shall not be necessary to give any notice of the adjourned meeting or of the business to be transacted, other than the announcement to the meeting at which such adjournment is taken.

Section 5. Procedure. Subject to the provisions of the Articles of Incorporation and these bylaws, procedures of the Board or committees thereof, shall be in accordance with Robert's Rules of Order, unless a more simplified and useful manual of procedures is adopted by such body.

Section 6. Amendment of Bylaws. These bylaws may be altered, amended or repealed by the vote of two-thirds (2/3rds) or Special Meeting, duly convened after due notice to the Directors of that purpose.

BOARD POLICY TEMPLATES

ORGANIZATIONAL CODE OF CONDUCT TEMPLATE
NOT-FOR-PROFIT LEGAL NAME, Inc. (Not-for-profit) and its Directors, officers, and employees must, at all times, comply with all applicable laws and regulations. Not-for-profit will not condone the activities of Directors, officers, and employees who achieve results through violation of the law or unethical business dealings. This includes any payments for illegal acts, indirect contributions, rebates and bribery. Not-for-profit does not permit any activity that fails to satisfy the highest standards of ethical and professional conduct.

All business conduct should be well above the minimum standards required by law. Accordingly, Directors, officers, and employees must ensure that their actions cannot be interpreted as being, in any way, breaking the laws and regulations governing Not-for-profit's operations. Employees uncertain about the application or interpretation of any legal requirements should refer the matter to their superior, who, if necessary, should seek the advice of the Internal Audit Director, the VP of Administration. Directors and officers seeking assistance in the interpretation or application of legal requirements should seek the advice of the Chairperson of the Board of Directors.

General Employee Conduct
See section 8.10 of Not-for-profit's Personnel Policies Manual, "Behavior of Employees."

Outside Activities, Employment and Directorships. All Directors, officers, and employees share a serious responsibility for Not-for-profit's good public relations, especially at the community level. Readiness to help with religious, charitable, educational and civic activities brings credit to Not-for-profit and is encouraged. Directors, officers, and employees must, however, avoid acquiring any business interest or participating in any other activity outside Not-for-profit that would, or would appear to:
- Create an excessive demand upon his or her time and attention, thus depriving Not-for-profit of his or her best efforts on the job.
- Create a conflict of interest-an obligation, interest or distraction-that may interfere with the independent exercise of judgment in Not-for-profit's best interest.

Conflicts of Interest
Affiliated Persons. The term "affiliated persons" applies to certain parties related to Directors, officers, and employees, and includes the following:
    a. Spouse, domestic partner, child, mother, father, brother or sister, or spouse of a brother or sister;
    b. Any corporation or organization of which one is a board member, an officer, a partner, participates in management or is employed by, or is, directly or indirectly, a debt holder or the beneficial owner of any class of equity securities; and

    c.   Any trust or other estate in which one has a substantial beneficial interest or as to which one serves as a trustee or in a similar capacity.

Relationships with Clients and Suppliers

Directors, officers, employees, and affiliated persons should avoid investing in or acquiring a financial interest for his or her own accounts in any business organization that has a contractual relationship with Not-for-profit, or that provides goods or services (or both) to Not-for-profit, if such investment or interest could influence or create the impression of influencing their decisions in the performance of his or her duties on behalf of Not-for-profit.

Kickbacks and Secret Commissions

Regarding Not-for-profit's business activities, Directors, officers, employees, and affiliated persons may not receive payment or compensation of any kind, except as authorized under Not-for-profit's compensation policies. In particular, Not-for-profit strictly prohibits the acceptance of kickbacks and secret commissions from suppliers or others. Any breach of this rule will result in immediate termination and prosecution to the fullest extent of the law. Small items, including trade show giveaways such as key chains, notepads, etc., may be retained for personal use. It is recognized that some vendors such as caterers or printers might provide "samples" of their goods to give staff a better idea of their product. This practice is considered acceptable.

Gifts, Entertainment, and Favors

Directors, officers, employees, and affiliated persons should not accept entertainment, gifts, loans, or personal favors that could, in any way, influence, or appear to influence, business decisions in favor of any third parties dealing or competing with Not-for-profit. Receipt of any gift is disapproved except gifts of a value less than $50, which could not be refused without discourtesy. No personal gift of money should ever be accepted.

Similarly, Directors, officers, employees, and affiliated persons should not accept any other preferential treatment under these circumstances because their position with Not-for-profit might be inclined to, or be perceived to, place them under obligation.

In cases of uncertainty about whether or not a transaction is considered influential, employees should contact the Internal Audit Director for advice. The CEO/President, Directors, and officers should contact the Chairperson of the Board of Directors, who may bring the matter before the Board of Directors.

Organization Funds and Other Assets

Directors, officers, and employees who have access to Not-for-profit's funds in any form must follow the prescribed procedures for recording, handling and protecting money as detailed in Not-for-profit's Agency Operations Manual. Not-for-profit imposes strict standards to prevent fraud and dishonesty. If employees become aware of any evidence of fraud and dishonesty, they should immediately advise their superior or the Internal Audit Director, the VP of Administration, so that Not-for-profit can promptly investigate further. If the complainant suspected of fraud is the Internal Audit Director or CEO/ President, the complainant may contact a member of the Board of Directors. If Directors or officers become aware of any evidence of fraud and dishonesty, they should immediately advise the Chairperson of the Board of Directors.

When a Director's, officer's, or employee's position requires spending organization funds or incurring any reimbursable personal expenses, that individual must use good judgment on Not-for-profit's behalf to ensure that good value is received for every expenditure. Organization funds and all other assets of Not-for-profit are for organization purposes only and not for personal benefit. This includes the personal use of organizational assets such as computers.

Organization Records and Communications
Accurate and reliable records of many kinds are necessary to meet Not-for-profit's legal and financial obligations and to manage the affairs of Not-for-profit. Not-for-profit's books and records must reflect in an accurate and timely manner all business transactions. The Directors, officers, and employees responsible for accounting and record-keeping must fully disclose and record all assets, liabilities, or both, and must exercise diligence in enforcing these requirements.
Directors, officers, and employees must not make or engage in any false record or communication of any kind, whether internal or external, including but not limited to:
- False expense, attendance, production, financial or similar reports and statements
- False advertising, deceptive marketing practices, or other misleading representations

Prompt Communications
In all matters relevant to clients, suppliers, government authorities, the public and others in Not-for-profit, all Directors, officers, and employees must make every effort to achieve complete, accurate and timely communications-responding promptly and courteously to all proper requests for information and to all complaints.
Privacy and Confidentiality
When handling financial and personal information about clients, employees, or others with whom Not-for-profit has dealings, employees, Directors, and officers should observe the following principles:

1. Individuals should collect, use, and retain only the personal information necessary for Not-for-profit's business. Whenever possible, relevant information should be obtained directly from the person concerned. Only reputable and reliable sources should supplement this information.
2. Information should be retained only for as long as necessary or as required by law and in full compliance with Not-for-profit's Document Retention Policy. The physical security of this information must be protected. Employees should refer to individual departmental operations manuals for document storage information.
3. Access to personal information of clients should be limited to those with a legitimate business reason for seeking that information. Personal information is to be used only for the purposes for which it was originally obtained. Consent must be obtained of the person concerned before externally disclosing any personal information, unless legal process or contractual obligation provides otherwise.
4. Not-for-profit employee records and information, including medical, compensation, and legal information, must be maintained with the highest confidentiality. Consent must be obtained by the person concerned before externally disclosing any personal information, unless legal process provides otherwise. Refer to Not-for-profit's Human Resources policy for maintaining employee records.

CONFLICT OF INTEREST POLICY TEMPLATE

Section 1. Purpose

NOT-FOR-PROFIT LEGAL NAME, Inc. (Not-for-profit) is a not-for-profit, tax-exempt organization. Maintenance of its tax-exempt status is important both for its continued financial stability and for public support. Therefore, the IRS as well as state regulatory and tax officials view the operations of Not-for-profit as a public trust, which is subject to scrutiny by accountable to such governmental authorities as well as to members of the public.

Consequently, there exists between Not-for-profit and its Board of Directors, officers, and management employees and the public a fiduciary duty, which carries with it a broad and unbending duty of loyalty and fidelity. Directors, officers, and management employees have the responsibility of administering the affairs of Not-for-profit honestly and prudently, and of exercising their best care, skill, and judgment for the sole benefit of Not-for-profit. Those persons shall exercise the utmost good faith in all transactions involved in their duties, and they shall not use their positions with Not-for-profit or knowledge gained from the agency for their personal benefit.

Section 2. Persons Concerned

This statement is directed to Directors, officers, and all employees who can influence the actions of Not-for-profit (including all who make purchasing decisions, and all management personnel), anyone who has proprietary information concerning Not-for-profit, and affiliated persons of all persons named above. For the purposes of this policy, the term "affiliated persons" applies to certain parties related to Directors, officers, and employees, and includes the following:
   a. Spouse, domestic partner, child, mother, father, brother or sister, or spouse of a brother or sister;
   b. Any corporation or organization of which one is a board member, an officer, a partner, participates in management or is employed by, or is, directly or indirectly, a debt holder or the beneficial owner of any class of equity securities; and
   c. Any trust or other estate in which one has a substantial beneficial interest or as to which one serves as a trustee or in a similar capacity.

Section 3. Areas in which Conflict May Arise
Conflicts of interest may arise in any number of scenarios. For example, in the relations of Directors, officers, management employees, and affiliated persons with any of the following third parties:
   1. Persons and firms supplying goods and services to Not-for-profit.
   2. Persons and firms from whom Not-for-profit leases or is planning to lease property and equipment.
   3. Persons and firms with whom Not-for-profit is dealing or planning to deal in connection with the gift, purchase, or sale of real estate, securities, or other property.
   4. Competing or affinity organizations.
   5. Donors and others supporting Not-for-profit.
   6. Agencies, organizations, and associations which affect the operations of Not-for-profit.
   7. Family members, friends, and other employees.

Section 4. Nature of Conflicting Interest
A conflicting interest may be defined as an interest, direct or indirect, with any persons or firms mentioned in Section 3. Such an interest might arise through:
   1. Owning stock or holding debt or other proprietary interests in any third party dealing with Not-for-profit.
   2. Holding office, serving on the Board, participating in management, or being otherwise employed (or formerly employed) with any third party dealing with Not-for-profit.
   3. Receiving remuneration for services with respect to individual transactions involving Not-for-profit.
   4. Using Not-for-profit's time, personnel, equipment, supplies, or good will for other than Not-for-profit approved activities, programs, and purposes.

5. Receiving personal gifts or loans from third parties dealing or competing with Not-for-profit. Except for gifts of a value less than $50 which could not be refused without discourtesy, no employee, Director, officer, or affiliated person should accept gifts, entertainment or other favors from any person or entity which:
   - Does or seeks to do business with Not-for-profit, or
   - Does or seeks to compete with Not-for-profit, or
   - Has received, is receiving, or is seeking to receive a contract or transaction with Not-for-profit. "Contract or Transaction" is any agreement or relationship involving the sale or purchase of goods, services or rights of any kind, receipt of a loan or grant, or the establishment of any other financial relationship. The making of a gift to Not-for-profit is not a "contract" or "transaction."

Section 5. Interpretation of the Conflict of Interest Policy

The areas of conflicting interest listed in Section 3, and the relations in those areas which may give rise to conflict, as listed in Section 4, are not exhaustive. Conflicts might arise in other areas or through other relations. It is assumed that the Directors, officers, and employees will recognize such areas and, by analogy where need be, use their best efforts to comply with this policy.

In cases of uncertainty about whether or not a transaction may give rise to conflict, employees should contact their immediate supervisor, or the Internal Audit Director for advice. The CEO/ President, Directors, and officers should contact the Chairperson of the Board of Directors, who may bring the matter before the Board of Directors.

The fact that one of the interests described in Section 4 exists does not necessarily mean that a conflict exists, or that the conflict, if it exists, is material enough to be of practical importance, or if material, that upon full disclosure of all relevant facts and circumstances it is necessarily averse to the interests of Not-for-profit.

However, it is the policy of the Board that the existence of any of the interests described in Section 4 shall be disclosed before any transaction is consummated. It shall be the continuing responsibility of Directors, officers, and management employees to scrutinize their transactions and outside business interests and relationships, and those of their affiliated persons, for potential conflicts and to immediately make such disclosures.

Section 6. Disclosure Policy and Procedure
Transactions with parties with whom conflicting interest exists may be undertaken only if all of the following are observed:
1. The conflicting interest is fully disclosed;
2. The person with the conflict of interest is excluded from the discussion and approval of such transaction;

3. If applicable, contractual requirements regarding competitive bids are met; and
4. The Board of Directors has determined that the transaction is in the best interest of the organization.

Disclosure in the organization should be made to the CEO/ President (or if he or she is the one with the conflict, then to the Board Chair), who shall bring the matter to the attention of the Board of Directors. Disclosures involving Directors should be made to the Chairperson of the Board of Directors, (or if he or she is the one with the conflict, then to the Board Vice-Chair) who shall bring these matters to the Board of Directors.

The Board of Directors shall determine whether a conflict exists and in the case of an existing conflict, whether the contemplated transaction may be authorized as just, fair, and reasonable to Not-for-profit. The decision of the Board of Directors on these matters will rest in their sole discretion, and their concern must be the welfare of Not-for-profit and the advancement of its purpose.

CONFLICT OF INTEREST DISCLOSURE STATEMENT TEMPLATE

To be completed annually by all members of the Board of Directors, and NOT-FOR-PROFIT LEGAL NAME, Inc. (Not-for-profit) management personnel.

PLEASE NOTE: In order to be more comprehensive, this statement of disclosure/questionnaire also requires you to provide information with respect to certain parties that are related to you. These persons are termed "affiliated persons" and include the following:
1. Your spouse, domestic partner, child, mother, father, brother or sister, or spouse of a brother or sister;
2. Any corporation or organization of which you are a Board member, an officer, a partner, participate in management or are employed by, or are, directly or indirectly, a debt holder or the beneficial owner of any class of equity securities; and
3. Any trust or other estate in which you have a substantial beneficial interest or as to which you serve as a trustee or in a similar capacity.

1. Name of Employee or Board Member: (Please print)

    _____

2. Capacity: Board of Directors
   Executive Committee
   Officer
   Committee Member (please list committee(s)
   Staff (please list position)

3. Have you or any of your affiliated persons provided services or property to Not-for-profit in the past year?

_____YES   _____NO

If yes, please describe the nature of the services or property and if an affiliated person is involved, the identity of the affiliated person and your relationship with that person:

_____

4. Have you or any of your affiliated persons purchased services or property from Not-for-profit in the past year?

_____YES   ____NO

If yes, please describe the purchased services or property and if an affiliated person is involved, the identity of the affiliated person and your relationship with that person:

_____

5. Please indicate whether you or any of your affiliated persons had any direct or indirect interest in any business transaction(s) in the past year to which Not-for-profit was or is a party?

_____YES   _____NO

If yes, describe the transaction(s) and if an affiliated person is involved, the identity of the affiliated person and your relationship with that person:

_____

6. Were you or any of your affiliated persons indebted to pay money to Not-for-profit at any time in the past year (other than travel advances or the like)?

_____YES   _____NO

If yes, please describe the indebtedness and if an affiliated person is involved, the identity of the affiliated person and your relationship with that person:

_____

7. In the past year, did you or any of your affiliated persons receive, or become entitled to receive, directly or indirectly, any personal benefits from Not-for-profit or as a result of your relationship with Not-for-profit, that in the aggregate could be valued in excess of $1,000, that were not or will not be compensation directly related to your duties to Not-for-profit?

_____YES _____NO

If yes, please describe the benefit(s) and if an affiliated person is involved, the identity of the affiliated person and your relationship with that person:

_____

8. Are you or any of your affiliated persons a party to or have an interest in any pending legal proceedings involving Not-for-profit?

_____YES _____NO

If yes, please describe the proceeding(s) and if an affiliated person is involved, the identity of the affiliated person and your relationship with that person:

_____

9. Are you aware of any other events, transactions, arrangements or other situations that have occurred or may occur in the future that you believe should be examined by Not-for-profit's Board of Directors in accordance with the terms and intent of Not-for-profit's Conflict of Interest policy?

_____YES _____NO

If yes, please describe the situation(s) and if an affiliated person is involved, the identity of the affiliated person and your relationship with that person:

_____

10. At this time, I am a Board member, Committee member, or employee of the following organizations (please list organizations and the position held):

_____

I HEREBY CONFIRM that I have read and understand Not-for-profit's conflict of interest policy, and that my responses to the above questions are complete and correct to the best of my knowledge and beliefs. I agree that if I become aware of any information that might indicate that this disclosure is inaccurate or that I have not complied with this policy, I will notify the President/ CEO (employees) or Chairperson of the Board of Directors (Directors and officers).

FRAUD RESPONSE POLICY TEMPLATE

NOT-FOR-PROFIT LEGAL NAME, Inc. (Not-for-profit) is committed to the highest possible standards of openness, integrity, and accountability in all its affairs. It is determined to maintain a culture of honesty and opposition to fraud and corruption.

In line with that commitment, Not-for-profit's Fraud Response Policy outlines the principles to which Not-for-profit is committed in relation to preventing, reporting and managing fraud and corruption.

This Fraud Response Policy reinforces Not-for-profit's approach by setting out the ways in which individual Directors, officers, employees, or members of the public can voice their concerns about suspected fraud or corruption. It also outlines how Not-for-profit will deal with such complaints.

Implementation
This plan is to be implemented where suspicions of fraud or corruption have been raised.

Fraud is defined as:
"The intentional distortion of financial statements or other records by persons internal or external to Not-for-profit which is carried out to conceal the misappropriation of assets or otherwise for gain."
Corruption is defined as:
"The offering, giving, soliciting or acceptance of an inducement or reward, which may influence the action of any person."

Fraudulent or corrupt acts may include:
• Systems Issues - Where a process/system exists which is prone to abuse by either employees or public.
• Financial Issues - Where individuals or companies have fraudulently obtained money from Not-for-profit.
• Equipment Issues - Where Not-for-profit's equipment is used for inappropriate personal use.
• Resource Issues - Where a misuse of resources exists (e.g. theft of materials).

• Other Issues- Activities undertaken by employees, Directors, or officers of Not-for-profit which may be: unlawful, against Not-for-profit's policies, fall below established standards or practices, or amount to improper conduct.

This is not an exhaustive list. The Internal Audit Director (VP of Administration) will provide advice and guidance if any doubt exists about the seriousness of a concern.

Safeguards
Harassment or Victimization - Not-for-profit recognizes that the decision to report a concern can be a difficult one, not least because of the fear of retaliation from those responsible for the malpractice. Not-for-profit will not tolerate harassment or victimization and will take action to protect those who raise a concern in good faith.
Confidentiality -- Not-for-profit will do its best to protect an individual's identity when he or she raises a concern and does not want his or her name to be disclosed. It must be appreciated, however, that the investigation process may reveal the source of the information and a statement by the individual may be required as part of the evidence.
Anonymous Allegations -- This policy encourages individuals to put their name to allegations. Concerns expressed anonymously are much less powerful, but they will be considered at the discretion of Not-for-profit. In exercising this discretion, the factors to be taken into account would include: the seriousness of the issues raised, the credibility of the concern, and the likelihood of confirming the allegation from reliable sources.
Untrue Allegations - If an allegation is made in good faith, but it is not confirmed by the investigation, no action will be taken against the complainant. If, however, an individual makes a malicious or vexatious allegation, action may be considered against the individual making the allegation.

Employee Actions
Employees are often the first to realize that there is something seriously wrong within an organization. However, they may not express their concerns because they feel that speaking up would be disloyal to their colleagues or to Not-for-profit. They may also fear harassment or victimization. Not-for-profit's Whistleblower Protection Policy is intended to encourage and enable staff to raise serious concerns within Not-for-profit rather than overlooking a problem or blowing the whistle to the media or other external bodies.

Employees should first address their concern with their immediate supervisor. However, if an individual is not comfortable speaking with his or her supervisor or is not satisfied with the supervisor's response, the individual should report the concern to the Internal Audit Director, the VP of Administration. Supervisors and managers are required to report suspected violations of the Code of Conduct to Not-for-profit's Internal Audit Director, who has specific and exclusive responsibility to investigate all reported violations. For suspected fraud, or when an individual is not satisfied or uncomfortable with following the above-mentioned steps, individuals should contact Not-for-profit's Internal Audit Director directly. Individuals may make confidential or anonymous reports to the Whistleblower Hotline at 000-000-0000, ext. XXXX, or by writing directly to the Internal Audit Director at the following address:

If an individual wants to make a report concerning the Internal Audit Director or CEO/ President, he or she may make a report to the Board of Directors at the following address:

Board of Directors
Not-for-profit Address

Individuals making such reports should ensure enough information is supplied to conduct an investigation.

Board of Directors' Actions

Members of the Board of Directors are required to report suspected violations of the Code of Conduct to the Chairperson of the Board of Directors, who will bring the matter to the attention of the audit committee of the Board of Directors.

Public Actions

Not-for-profit encourages members of the public who suspect fraud and corruption to contact the Internal Audit Director.

The Internal Audit Director can be contacted by phone at 000-000-0000, ext. XXXX or by writing to the Internal Audit Director at the address below:

VP of Administration
Not-for-profit Address

If an individual wants to make a report concerning the Internal Audit Director and/ or CEO/ President, he or she may make a report to the Board of Directors at the following address:

Board of Directors
Not-for-profit Address

GIFT POLICY AND GIFT STATEMENT TEMPLATE

As part of its Conflict of Interest Policy, NOT-FOR-PROFIT LEGAL NAME, Inc. (Not-for-profit) requires that officers, employees and Directors decline to accept certain gifts, consideration or remuneration from individuals or companies that seek to do business with Not-for-profit or are a competitor of it. This policy and disclosure form is intended to implement that prohibition on gifts.

Prohibited Gifts, Gratuities and Entertainment.

Except for gifts of a value less than $50 which could not be refused without discourtesy, no employee, Director, officer, or family member (spouse, domestic partner, parent, child or spouse of a child, or a brother, sister, or spouse of a brother or sister) should accept gifts, entertainment or other favors from any person or entity which:

1. Does or seeks to do business with Not-for-profit, or
2. Does or seeks to compete with Not-for-profit, or
3. Has received, is receiving, or is seeking to receive a contract or transaction with Not-for-profit. "Contract or Transaction" is any agreement or relationship involving the sale or purchase of goods, services or rights of any kind, receipt of a loan or grant, or the establishment of any other financial relationship. The making of a gift to Not-for-profit is not a "contract" or "transaction."
No gift of money should ever be accepted.

Gift Statement
The following Gift Statement is to be signed by all Directors, officers, and employees upon hire or appointment to the Board of Directors, and annually. Copies of signed statements of employees will be held in individual employees' personnel files, and copies of signed statements of Directors and officers shall be held with the Board Minutes.

I certify that I have read the above policy concerning gifts, and I agree that I will not accept gifts, entertainment or other favors from any individual or entity, which would be prohibited by the above policy. Following my initial statement, I agree to provide a signed statement at the end of each calendar year certifying that I have not received any such gifts, entertainment or other favors during the preceding year.

WHISTLEBLOWER PROTECTION POLICY TEMPLATE
NOT-FOR-PROFIT LEGAL NAME, Inc. (Not-for-profit)'s Organizational Code of Conduct ("Code") requires Directors, officers, and employees to observe high standards of business and personal ethics in the conduct of their duties and responsibilities. As representatives of Not-for-profit, all must practice honesty and integrity in fulfilling responsibilities and comply with all applicable laws and regulations.

Purpose
The objectives of Not-for-profit's Whistleblower Protection Policy are to establish policies and procedures for:
- The anonymous and/ or confidential submission of concerns regarding questionable accounting or auditing matters, and violations and suspected violations of Not-for-profit's Code by employees, Directors, officers, and other stakeholders of Not-for-profit.

- The method for reporting, tracking, and responding to complaints received by Not-for-profit regarding accounting, internal controls, auditing matters, or violations of the Code.
- The protection of employees, Directors, officers, and members of the public reporting concerns from retaliatory actions

Reporting Responsibility
It is the responsibility of all Directors, officers, and employees to comply with the Code and to report violations or suspected violations in accordance with this Whistleblower Policy.

No Retaliation
No employee, officer, or Director who in good faith reports a violation of the Code shall suffer harassment, retaliation or adverse employment consequence. An employee who retaliates against someone who has reported a violation in good faith is subject to discipline up to and including termination of employment. A Director or officer who retaliates against someone who has reported a violation in good faith is subject to discipline, including removal from the Board of Directors. This Whistleblower Policy is intended to encourage and enable Directors, officers, and employees and others to raise serious concerns within Nonprofit prior to seeking resolution outside Not-for-profit.

Reporting Violations
An employee should first address his or her concern with his or her immediate supervisor. However, if an individual is not comfortable speaking with his or her supervisor or is not satisfied with the supervisor's response, the individual should report the concern to Not-for-profit's Internal Audit Director, the VP of Administration. Supervisors and managers are required to report suspected violations of the Code to Not-for-profit's Internal Audit Director, who has specific and exclusive responsibility to investigate all reported violations. For suspected fraud, or when an individual is not satisfied or uncomfortable with following the above-mentioned steps, individuals should contact Not-for-profit's Internal Audit Director directly. Individuals may make confidential or anonymous reports to the Whistleblower Hotline at 215-763-8870, ext. XXXX, or by writing directly to the Internal Audit Director at the following address:

VP of Administration
Not-for-profit ADDRESS

If an individual wants to make a report concerning the Internal Audit Director and/ or CEO/ President, he or she may make a report to the Board of Directors at the following address:
Board of Directors
Not-for-profit ADDRESS
Individuals making such reports should ensure enough information is supplied to conduct an investigation.

Members of the Board of Directors are required to report suspected violations of the Code of Conduct to the Chairperson of the Board of Directors, who will bring the matter to the attention of the audit committee of the Board of Directors.

Internal Audit Director
Not-for-profit's Internal Audit Director, the VP of Administration, is responsible for investigating and resolving all reported complaints and allegations concerning violations of the Code. At the Internal Audit Director's discretion, he or she shall advise the President/ CEO and/or the audit committee of reported violations. The Internal Audit Director reports directly to the audit committee of the Board of Directors and is required to report to the audit committee annually with a summary of any significant violations.

Mandated Reporting to the Audit Committee
The audit committee of the Board of Directors shall address all reported concerns or complaints regarding corporate accounting practices, internal controls, fraud, auditing, or theft of money or equipment valued at $5,000 or more. The Internal Audit Director shall immediately notify the CEO/ President and the audit committee of any such complaint, and work with the committee until the matter is resolved.

Untrue Allegations
If an allegation is made in good faith, but is not confirmed by the investigation, no action will be taken against the complainant. Any allegations which prove to have been made maliciously or knowingly to be false will be viewed as a serious disciplinary offense.

Confidentiality
Violations or suspected violations may be submitted on a confidential basis by the complainant or may be submitted anonymously. Reports of violations or suspected violations will be kept confidential to the extent possible, consistent with the need to conduct an adequate investigation.

Handling of Reported Violations
The Internal Audit Director will notify the sender and acknowledge receipt of the reported violation or suspected violation within five business days. All reports will be promptly investigated, and appropriate corrective action will be taken if warranted by the investigation. In addition, action taken must include a conclusion and/or follow-up with the complainant for complete closure of the concern.
The audit committee has the authority to retain outside legal counsel, accountants, private investigators, or any other resource deemed necessary to conduct a full and complete investigation of the allegations.

DOCUMENT RETENTION AND DESTRUCTION POLICY TEMPLATE

Purpose

In accordance with the Sarbanes-Oxley Act, which makes it a crime to alter, cover up, falsify, or destroy any document with the intent of impeding or obstructing any official proceeding, this policy provides for the systematic review, retention and destruction of documents received or created by NOT-FOR-PROFIT LEGAL NAME, Inc. (Not-for-profit) in connection with the transaction of organization business. This policy covers all records and documents, regardless of physical form. The policy is designed to ensure compliance with federal and state laws and regulations, to eliminate accidental or innocent destruction of records, and to facilitate Not-for-profit's operations by promoting efficiency and freeing up valuable storage space. Not-for-profit shall not knowingly destroy a document with the intent to obstruct or influence an investigation. If an official investigation is underway or even suspected, document purging must stop immediately. It is the VP of Administration's responsibility to inform employees to cease document destruction, to ensure employees comply, and to inform employees when document destruction may commence again after the investigation is complete.

Document Retention

Not-for-profit follows the document retention procedures outlined below. Documents that are not listed but are substantially similar to those listed in the schedule will be retained for the appropriate length of time. Federal contract requirements take precedence over the following minimum requirements. The following table provides the minimum requirements:

Type of Document	Minimum Requirement
Accident Reports and Worker's Compensation Records	5 years
Annual Reports to Secretary of State/ Attorney General	Permanently
Appraisals	Permanently
Articles of Incorporation	Permanently
Accounts Payable Ledgers and Schedules	7 years
Audit Reports	Permanently
Bank Reconciliations	7 years
Bank Statements	7 years
Board Policies/ Resolutions	Permanently
Business Expense Records	7 years
Cash Receipts	3 years
Checks (for important payments and purchases)	Permanently
Client Files	7 years minimum, or longer as dictated by funding source
Conflict of Interest Disclosure Statements	4 years
Construction Documents	Permanently

Contracts, Mortgages, Notes and Leases (expired)	7 years
Contracts (still in effect)	Permanently
Correspondence (general)	2 years
Correspondence (legal and important matters)	Permanently
Correspondence (with customers and vendors)	2 years
Credit Card Receipts	3 years
Deeds, Mortgages, and Bills of Sale	Permanently
Depreciation Schedules	Permanently
Donor Records and Acknowledgement Letters	7 years
Duplicate Deposit Slips	2 years
Electronic Fund Transfer Documents	7 years
Employment Applications	3 years
Employment and Termination Agreements	Permanently
Expense Analyses/Expense Distribution Schedules	7 years
Facility Logs (Fire Marshall, Security, etc.)	5 years
Year End Financial Statements	Permanently
Garnishment Records	7 years
Grant Applications and Funding Contracts	5 years after completion
I-9 Forms	3 years after termination
Incident Reports	5 years
Insurance Policies	Permanently
Insurance records, current accident reports, claims, policies, etc.	Permanently
Internal Audit Reports	3 years
Inventories of Products, Materials, and Supplies	7 years
Invoices (to customers, from vendors)	7 years
IRS 990 Tax Returns	Permanently
IRS 1099s	7 years
IRS Application for Tax-Exempt Status (Form 1023)	Permanently
IRS Determination Letter	Permanently
Journal Entries (Accounting)	7 years
Leases	6 years after expiration
Minute Books, Bylaws and Charter	Permanently
Patents and Related Papers	Permanently
Payroll Records and Summaries	Permanently
Personnel Files	7 years after termination
Petty Cash Vouchers	3 years
Retirement and Pension Records	Permanently
Salary Schedules	5 years
State Unemployment Tax Records	Permanently
Tax Returns and Worksheets	Permanently
Timesheets / Timecards	7 years
Trademark Registrations and Copyrights	Permanently
W-2 Statements	7 years
Withholding Tax Statements	7 years

Electronic Documents and Records
Any electronic files, including records of donations made online, that fall into one of the document types on the above schedule will be maintained for the appropriate amount of time. Backup and recovery methods will be tested on a regular basis.

Document Destruction: Not-for-profit's VP of Administration is responsible for document retention, and annual review and destruction of records. Financial and personnel-related documents will be destroyed by shredding.

Compliance: Failure on the part of employees to follow this policy can result in disciplinary action against responsible individuals. The VP of Administration and Chair of the audit committee will periodically review these procedures with legal counsel to ensure they are in compliance with new or revised regulations.

EXECUTIVE COMMITTEE DELIVERABLES TEMPLATE

The executive committee advises and assists the Board in managing Not-for-profit's affairs. The executive committee consists of the Chairperson of the Board, the Vice-Chair of the Board, the Treasurer and the Secretary. The President serves as the sole non-voting member of the executive committee. The Chairperson of the Board chairs the executive committee.

The work of Not-for-profit's executive committee revolves around the following six major areas:

1. Policy work: Carries out specific directions of the board, and takes action on policies when they affect the work of the executive committee or when the full board directs the committee to do so. Acts on behalf of the board on all issues related to Not-for-profit business between board meetings, with responsibility to report actions to the board for ratification or further board action at the next meeting
2. President/ board relations: Nurtures the President by providing counsel, feedback, and support when needed. Plans and conducts annual assessment of the President and reports the results of the assessment to the board and President. Reviews compensation and benefits for the President
3. Strategic/ Business planning: Initiates the board's involvement in establishing a strategic framework or direction based on the organization's mission. Spearheads the strategic/ business planning process. Annually reviews Not-for-profit's performance toward goals and objectives outlined in the business plan.

4. Succession planning, executive searches: Leads the search for a new President or delegates the responsibility to a task force. Conducts the research necessary to determine an appropriate salary for the President. Seeks approval from the full board before terminating an existing President or hiring a new President. Develops a succession plan for executive transition.
5. Urgent Issues. Resolves an emergency or organizational crisis (e.g., loss of funding or unexpected loss of President
6. Lobbying/ Advocacy: Reviews Not-for-profit's advocacy policy quarterly

Governance Committee deliverables template

The governance committee is responsible for ongoing review and recommendations to enhance the quality and future viability of the board. The focus of the committee revolves around the following six major areas:

1. Board Role and Responsibilities
    - Leads the board in regularly reviewing and updating the board's statement of its role and areas of responsibility, and the expectations of individual board members
    - Assists the board in periodically updating and clarifying the primary areas of focus for the board — the board's agenda for the next year or two, based on the strategic/ business plan

2. Board Building
    - Leads in assessing current and anticipated needs for board composition, determining the board's knowledge, attributes, skills, abilities, influence, and access the board will need to consider in order to accomplish future work of the board
    - Develops a profile of the board as it should evolve over time
    - Identifies and presents potential board member candidates and explores with each candidate his or her interest and availability in board service
    - Nominates individuals to be elected as directors of the board
    - In cooperation with the board chair, meets annually with each board member to assess his or her continuing interest in board membership and term of service. Works with each board member to identify the appropriate role he or she might assume on behalf of the organization.

3. Board Education
    - Designs and oversees a process of board orientation, including information prior to election as a board member and information needed during the first cycle of board activity for new board members
    - Designs and implements an ongoing program of board information and education for all board members

4. Board Effectiveness
- Conducts an annual assessment of the board's performance; proposes, as appropriate, changes in board structure, roles, and responsibilities
- Provides ongoing counsel to the board chair and other board leaders on steps they might take to enhance board effectiveness
- Annually reviews and updates the board's policies and practices regarding member participation, conflict of interest, confidentiality, etc., and suggests improvements as needed

5. Board Leadership
- Takes the lead in succession planning, taking steps to recruit and prepare for future board leadership
- Nominates board members for election as board officers

6. Organizational Governance
- Annually reviews the agency bylaws and articles of incorporation, suggests amendments as needed
- Annually reviews agency personnel policies and suggests amendments as needed
- Annually reviews other agency policies and suggests amendments as needed

AUDIT AND FINANCE COMMITTEES DELIVERABLES TEMPLATE
In the wake of Sarbanes-Oxley, best practices indicate the need for two separate and distinct financial committees-- a finance committee, and an audit committee-- for the following reasons:

· Segregation of financial duties adds accountability when finance and audit committee are detached

· This practice eliminates board members holding two roles, one of operations oversight and the other of accepting critique from auditors and implementing possible solutions

The audit committee's principal responsibilities are to hire an independent auditor, review the audit report with the auditor, and ensure that appropriate internal controls are present. This committee can also oversee the organization's ethical standards by serving as the point of contact for the staff Internal Audit Director.

No federal law currently addresses the role of audit committees for charitable organizations. However, states may move toward assigning audit committees. For example, a California law passed in 2004 requires that charitable organizations with revenues of over $2 million must appoint an audit committee which is separate from the finance committee. The chair of the audit committee cannot be on the finance committee, and members of the finance committee must constitute less than one-half of the membership of the audit committee. These standards, while not law in Pennsylvania, provide useful guidelines for creating an audit committee with the independence it needs to perform its job.

The board or its audit committee should not include paid staff as part of the audit review process. It is also suggested that the audit committee does not contain board members who serve on the finance committee. Three or five members on the audit committee are the optimal numbers to allow for ease of communication, and to rule out the possibility of a tie in voting.

If, due to number of board members, it is not possible to have a separate audit committee, at least, board members who oversee the audit should be objective, independent, with financial expertise.

Audit Committee/Risk Management Deliverables

The audit committee is responsible for assisting the board in oversight activities. The work of the committee revolves around the following three major areas:

1. Annual independent audit
    1. Ensures the audit is put out for bid every 3-5 years
    2. Recommends appointment (or reappointment) of the independent auditor
    3. Reviews the scope and approach of the audit proposed by the independent auditor
    4. Reviews the independent auditor's fee arrangements
    5. Serves as the liaison with the audit firm
    6. Conducts a post-audit review of the financial statements and audit findings, including any significant suggestions for improvements provided to management by the independent auditor
    7. Reviews the performance of the independent auditor

2. Financial statements

    8. Serves as check and balance to the finance committee by reviewing organization's annual financial statements and annual IRS Form 990

3. Fraud prevention

   9. Annually reviews the organization's code of conduct and conflict-of-interest policy, annually reviews staff and directors conflict-of-interest statements and follows through with any consequent investigations
   10. Provides an avenue for the receipt of anonymous and other complaints from employees and others regarding accounting, auditing internal control, or financial reporting matters.
   11. If necessary, institutes special investigations and, if appropriate, hires special counsel or experts to assist

FINANCE COMMITTEE DELIVERABLES TEMPLATE
The finance committee is responsible for assisting the board in ensuring the organization is in good fiscal health. The work of the committee revolves around the following seven major areas:

1. Organizational fiscal policies
- Annually reviews organizational fiscal policies (not staff operating policies) such as acceptable reserves for the organization, board's involvement in signing major purchases or financial commitments, appropriate use of board-designated funds and suggests amendments as needed

2. Financial records
- Ensures that accurate and complete financial records are maintained
- In regular meetings with management, monitors income and expenditures against projections

3. Financial reporting
- Chair of the committee presents quarterly or monthly financial statements to the board at each meeting, ensuring the reports are accurate and meaningful

4. Budget and financial planning
   - Proposes for board approval a budget that reflects the organization's goals, business plan, and board policies
   - Ensures that the budget accurately reflects the needs, expenses, and revenue of the organization

5. Organizational assets
   - Approves major transactions, such as purchase or sale of real estate and other major assets
   - Oversees investment of reserves/ endowment
   - Annually reviews the organization's risk management provisions in place, including appropriate insurance coverage for the organization and for the board

- Financial literacy of the board
- Establishes a training program to ensures the board understands the financial statements presented
- Ensures that the board as a whole is well-informed about the organization's finances
- Interprets general financial issues in the external environment in order to guide the organization

7. Regulatory requirements
    - Ensures compliance with federal, state, and other requirements related to the organization's finances
    - Ensure that the IRS Form 990 or any other forms required by government are filed completely, correctly, and on time
    - Reviews, with the organization's counsel, any legal matters that could have a significant effect on the organization's financial statements
    - Reviews the findings of any examinations by regulatory agencies
    - Reviews the policies and procedures in effect for executive compensation and benefits

DEVELOPMENT COMMITTEE DELIVERABLES TEMPLATE

The development committee of the Board of Directors works with the Chairperson of the Board, the President, and Not-for-profit development staff to ensure that Not-for-profit's total development program is in concert with Not-for-profit's strategic direction and needs. The committee engages the entire board in the fundraising process. The development committee's work revolves around the following three areas:

1. Quality Assurance and Accountability

    - Ensures that the organization has appropriate policies and guidelines for accepting gifts and donor solicitation which are compatible with Not-for-profit's mission, and in compliance with state and federal fundraising laws
    - Ensures that the case for support is strong, current, based on Not-for-profit's mission and goals, and in accordance with the organization's business plan

2. Fundraising Leadership

    - Develops expectations for financial contributions from the board, builds board members' capacities, and identifies suitable involvement opportunities
    - Involves and motivates other Directors and volunteers in cultivation and solicitation of gifts

- Serves as the board's central source of information about the fundraising climate in general, and about the status of the organization's fundraising activities in particular
- Solicits gifts at levels required for annual, special, and planned giving programs
- Participates actively in special events and provides leadership for capital campaigns
- Develops and signs solicitation and acknowledgment letters

3. Strategic Support for Cultivating and Soliciting Major Gifts

- Helps to develop strategies for cultivation and involvement of major gift prospects (i.e., individual, foundation, and corporate)
- Provides access for staff to new major gift prospects
- Helps to evaluate potential prospects for increased contributions

PROGRAM EVALUATION COMMITTEE DELIVERABLES TEMPLATE
Best practice is to have as few board committees as possible. When not-for-profit boards seek to streamline committees, those committees focused on program development and/or evaluation are most frequently eliminated. Current articles and books on board structure and governance do not consider program committees as viable entities, for several reasons outlined below:

- Program committees often duplicate the work of staff. The Board of Directors should be structured to help the Board do its job, not help the staff do theirs.
- Some not-for-profit organizations feel that the organization's program (its "products") should be overseen by the whole board, not an isolated committee.
- Eliminating the program evaluation committee allows the board function at a higher level, macro-governance rather than micro-management. Board members can spend valuable time making strategic decisions rather than worrying about operations.

In the absence of a Program Evaluation Committee, the Board can ensure the programs of the organization are working to fulfill the mission and contractual obligations through well-organized staff reports to the Board. Several options for reporting include brief written outcome measurement-oriented reports from each program department provided prior to each board meeting, or brief yearly presentations to the board from program staff. If the reports are tied to goals and outcomes determined in the Not-for-profit business plan, the Board can monitor progress toward those goals.

CORPORATE ADVISORY COUNCIL DELIVERABLES TEMPLATE

The mission of the Corporate Advisory Council (CAC) is to engage the resources of the corporate sector in collaboration with Not-for-profit to strengthen Latino communities. The CAC is made up of executives from the area's most respected corporations that have expressed support for advancing the mission and vision of Not-for-profit. The CAC meets bi-annually with Not-for-profit leadership to provide expert evaluation of Not-for-profit's strategies. With the collective insight, commitment, and financial support of Not-for-profit's corporate partners, Not-for-profit is able to provide high-quality, relevant and effective services.

- The CAC provides a unique forum in which corporate executives and Not-for-profit leadership work to achieve the following:
- Evaluate the challenges and opportunities facing Not-for-profit and adapt strategies which strengthen Latino communities
- Function as an independent, unbiased sounding board to evaluate Not-for-profit's progress toward its goals and outcomes
- Generate ideas for extending Not-for-profit's outreach and effectiveness with service delivery model
- Advise Not-for-profit leadership on corporate trends, providing a broader context for the organization's work
- ☐Champion Not-for-profit's mission in the corporate sector, building corporate support for the strategic initiatives of Not-for-profit and enhancing the relationship between Not-for-profit and the corporate sector

APPENDIX C
BUDGET PROJECTION TEMPLATE

APPENDIX D
INTERNAL CONTROL MANUAL TEMPLATE

TABLE OF CONTENT

1.   CASH MANAGEMENT
1.1   CHECK SIGNATURE
1.2   BANK RECONCILIATION – ONLINE ACCESS
1.3   PETTICASH
1.4   CREDIT CARDS
1.5   DEPOSITS
1.6   INVOICES
2.   EQUIPMENT AND INVENTORY
2.1   DEPRECIATION
3.   CASH DISBURSEMENT
3.1   PURCHASE ORDERS
3.2   PAYROLL
3.3   EXPENSE REIMBURSEMENT
3.4   TRAVEL REIMBURSEMENT
3.5   CONTRACTORS AND RECURRENT VENDORS
4.   IN-KIND TRANACCTIONS
5.   JOURNAL ENTRIES AND REPORTING
6.   BUDGETING AND FORECASTING
7.   COMPENACTION DETERMINATION

CASH MANAGEMENT

1.   CASH MANAGEMENT: Cash receipts are typically for revenue. Most cash receipts are received in check and deposited within two weeks to the bank. Exceptions sporadically occur with Fiscally Sponsored Programs. Some services require the staff to occasionally perform services paid in cash. In this case, a list of names is provided, along with date of service, and amount collected (specified if cash or check). Money is given to ED (Executive Director) who will deposit directly to bank account or send envelop to main office for deposit.

1.1   CHECK SIGNATURE: President, Board Secretary/Treasurer or liaison, and Executive Director are the only authorized personnel to sign checks. In addition, they, along with accounting, are authorized to communicate with the bank. It is policy of the organization that an authorized signer is not allowed to write a check to him/her self. The transaction has to be approved by another authorized signer and reviewed by accounting (AC). The accounting's responsible for ensuring check signatures, and support documentation is correct. If a vendor requires a payment over $5,000, accounting is responsible to collect at least two approved signatures on the check. When a check is reported lost, or hasn't been cashed within three months, accountant will contact program manager/vendor to inquire about the check. If determined that it was lost, accountant will call bank and put a stop for payment, void the check in the system, and consequentially generating a new check through the regular procedure.

1.2   BANK RECONCILIATION -- ONLINE ACCESS: At the end of every month accounting reconciles bank accounts and enters the reconciliation into the accounting software. The accounting verifies beginning balances and ending balances, as well as any un-cashed checks or payments made in the past, deposits and withdrawals. Bank Reconciliation will also contain PayPal transfers (described below in section 1.2), and ACH (see process under section 3.5), credit/cash card (section 1.4) transactions. The accounting can access the bank online to transfer funds between the savings and the checking accounts if necessary before every payroll. The online access is limited to these specific functions. Also, the President, Board Secretary/Treasurer, and ED have online access to review balances or any specific transaction. In addition, the President, Board Secretary/Treasurer or ED is responsible to review and approve the Monthly Financial Package (see description of Monthly Financial Package under section 5 – Journal Entries and Reporting).

In the case of fiscal sponsored projects regarding the option to receive donations via PayPal through: Each fiscal sponsored program director has a portal via the website. Grant writer/ED and AC will have access to PayPal login information. Grant writer/ED will use it to generate donation letters, accounting will use it to extract reports and transfer donated amount standing in PayPal account over to bank account.

Not for profit is responsible for:
A.   Ensure that each project is configured so when donors enter the site, they will be prompt to choose the program to donate.
B.   At the end of the month, accounting will reconcile each account, collect any support documentation from our fiscally sponsored programs, and record properly the revenue into our accounting system.
C.   At the end of the month, after reconciling, accounting will transfer money from PayPal account to EP bank's Savings accounts.
D.   With monthly reports, accounting will provide a report on transactions coming from PayPal reporting system.

Additional policies that apply only to certain sponsored programs based on their uniqueness in their operations will be detailed in each Sponsored Program Internal Control Manual.

1.3   PETTICASH: We do not have any petti cash policy and discourage it.

1.4   CREDIT CARDS: Fiscal office has one "Business Check Card." Management discourages the frequent use of it since its use doesn't allow the normal course of approval for purchase orders. When used, management understands the need to sometimes purchase things over the internet. In those instances, communication occurs via internet to obtain approval from accounting. Also, transactions over $1,000 (not purchased over the internet) are acceptable with the approval of President/Executive Director and accounting. Because the Business Check Card, when used as credit card, is charge directly into the bank account, its reconciliation occurs when monthly bank account reconciliations are done. It is responsibility of the user of the card to provide accounting appropriate support documentation of the transaction within the first fifteen days after its use.
We offer the use of the credit card to our Fiscal Sponsored program under limited exceptions. Fiscal department understands the need at times of purchasing items over the internet, in such cases, requests will need to be sent to accounting with at least two weeks; exceptions can be made by Executive Director/President in advance for approval, verification of funds, and execution of the transaction. In the event that Fiscal Sponsored programs need to pay vendors with credit card because no other option is available, details will have to be arranged and approved by accounting and President.
Additional policies that apply only to certain sponsored programs based on their uniqueness in their operations will be detailed in each Sponsored Program Internal Control Manual.

1.5   DEPOSITS: Central office discourages payments in cash. All invoices get paid with check. When a check comes on the mail, if mail comes under President or other employee name, the President/employee gives check and any documentation attached to the accounting. When they come under organizational name, accounting receives the correspondence and when a check is attached immediately enters it into the accounting software, files the support documentation, and goes within the next two days to the bank to deposit the check. If the check or the sum of the checks is above $5,000 the deposit will occur on the same day, in most cases. Deposits made directly into the PayPal account, will require notification to accounting and should have support documentation. Accounting will reconcile the PayPal account on a monthly basis and transfer any deposit to the savings account. Regarding moneys that are generated from crowdsourcing campaigns (i.e. GoFundMe): on a monthly basis accounting logs in and reviews deposits made in that account. Then, accounting transfers the money into savings account generating an Account Payable to the program. AC holds the money until further notification is made of transferring the money directly to the program.

1.6   INVOICES: According to contract or grant stipulation, accounting prepares invoices in the accounting software and sends them to the grantor or contractor. For those cases that don't have a contract or policy stipulation on payment, fiscal office encourages payment of invoices within 30 days. Additional policies that apply only to certain sponsored programs based on their uniqueness in their operations will be detailed in each Sponsored Program Internal Control Manual.

2.   EQUIPMENT AND INVENTORY

It is policy of the organization to capitalize equipment over $1,000. Additional policies that apply only to certain sponsored programs based on their uniqueness in their operations will be detailed in each Sponsored Program Internal Control Manual.

2.1   DEPRECIATION: It is policy of the organization to depreciate all its assets via the straight line method and based on the official life suggested by the IRS. AC on a monthly basis enters the depreciation of the organization's assets into the Accounting system as part of the month end activities.

3.   CASH DISBURSEMENT

3.1   PURCHASE ORDERS: Fiscal office has as a best practice policy, whenever possible, to pay within 30 days as a commitment to promoting and maintaining positive business relations. The office only pays in check and in limited cases by credit card when there is not the option to pay by check or when special agreements have been made with fiscal sponsored programs. Purchase orders (others than supported by a contract such as insurance, etc.) over $5,000 will require two signatures by an approve bank signer. AC enters Purchase Orders as they are incurred. All employees must provide all documentation to the AC not later than the first week of the following month to make sure they get included in the appropriate month.

3.2   PAYROLL: Organization subcontracts ADP to process and pay our employees and taxes on a biweekly payroll. The accounting reviews with Executive Director hours worked, requests for paid or unpaid time off one week before every payroll. Accounting updates Time-off schedule on the Working papers at every payroll. Three days before the pay date, AC logs in into the Payroll System (password protected) and enters/updates/confirms the amount of hours worked for hourly employees, and the salary amount for salaried based employees. The system provides a draft of the final payroll and if everything is correct accounting runs payroll. Then AC verifies amount to be deducted from the bank, goes to the bank electronically and verifies if there is enough balance in the checking account to process payroll. If there is not, the accounting transfers funds from the savings.

Organization encourages all employees to sign for automatic deposits. By the second day of payroll, the accounting receives ADP's report, reviews the information, and delivers to the employees their payroll stub generated by ADP. At the end of the month, accounting reconciles and records transactions into the accounting software. If any error goes into payroll, it is the accounting responsibility to contact ADP and request an amendment to the period with issues and record such corrections into the accounting software. Since ED and accounting meet biweekly before every payroll, a biweekly payroll report is no longer part of the Financial Package.

Simple IRA deductions will take place monthly with the last payroll of the month. ADP system contains the amount or percentage desired per employee to be deducted (entered by accounting when contribution started). Organization matches 3percent on IRA contribution. Accounting changes amount at payroll time if employee requests in writing to change deduction amount of percentage. Once ADP sends payroll report, and after month end reconciliation, accounting enters contributions into the system of the Financial Institution managing the Simple IRA funds (employee and employer, password protected), runs the roster, and prints a record of the transaction. Institution deducts funds directly from the bank on the third day of submission. Simple IRA policy is presented to all eligible employees at hiring, however, per EP policy, organization will only start matching funds after approbatory period.

3.3   EXPENSE REIMBURSEMENT: Expense reimbursements are due not later than the first week of the following month in which they were incurred. Expenses incurred by all employees will require supervisor's approval. For board members, the President/Treasurer will approve expenses, for the Executive Director or related parties working in the organization, the Board Secretary/Treasurer/ED/ Board Liaison will approve expenses. Home-office expenses will be ruled by the IRS 587 publication.

3.4   TRAVEL REIMBURSEMENT: Travel is recorded based on the different services provided and it includes parking expenses. There are cases in which contractors include travel reimbursement as an additional amount paid. In those cases, AC receives a report from President on travel incurred and invoices contractors for such expenses as well as records the expenses into accounting system under the appropriate contractor. Miles reimbursement is recorded per IRA Standard rate at $0.5750/mile

3.5   CONTRATORS AND RECURRENT VENDORS: Fiscal Sponsored programs will determine contractor's payment based on organization's contractual rates. In addition, organization offers recurrent vendors and contractors automatic transfer payments via the Bank System (password protected). Interested contractors and vendors will submit a "Bank Deposit Authorization" form containing bank information and approval for EP to proceed with direct deposit. If there is a contract in place, and available funds, as well as the need of recurrent payments; a general approval on fixed amounts may be generated to be approved by the President/ED. In case that amounts varied and prior to the payment date, accounting will fill out individual ACH Authorization forms per vendor/program consultants either by President or ED for approval. For the cases where a contract is stipulated, a second signature on automatic payment over $5,000 won't be necessary since stipulations on payments in the contract will already be acknowledged. President/ED will sign ACH Authorization form, funds available for Fiscal Agents will be discussed with accounting and once approved, payment will proceed. It is responsibility of the vendor/consultant to notify ED when bank account information changes. It is also responsibility of the vendor/contractor to provide proper invoice and support documentation prior to the payment schedule date.

4.   IN-KIND TRANACCTIONS: The organization captures on a yearly basis the amount of in-kind work that is provided by members. Accounting records the amount of hours at the expense level causing a zero impact in the financials but reflecting the amount donated.

5.   JOURNAL ENTRIES AND REPORTING: ED and accounting meet on a monthly basis to review and approve Financial Package, which contains: Bank Statements (both offices), transactions and cash disbursements generated by the President (approved by ED) and Executive Director reimbursements (approved by President & AC), payroll report from ADP, Financial Statements, and budget changes and projections for the month/year. In addition, the President and the accounting meet before board meetings to review Financials, allocations, and Budget projections. In addition, ED and accounting review on a bi-weekly basis payroll. At the end of the year ED, President reviews with AC Year End Financial Statement, draft of audited financial, Adjustment generated by auditors, and 990 draft and compare with Year End Financials provided by AC. Accounting receives from Director of ID office a detail report of all transactions occurred during the month, and copies of all support documentation. The accounting reconciles ID office bank accounts and enters into Accounting System all bank and other transactions detailed in the report. When the month is closed in the accounting system, accounting sends a report to program directors for their programs.

6. BUDGETING AND FORECASTING: Toward the end of every fiscal year accounting meets with President/ED and determines the budget for the next year. Once the Budget is ready, it gets approved by the board at the next board meeting. Accounting enters the approved budget into the accounting software. On a monthly basis, accounting compares actuals to approved budget and in monthly meeting with ED both review actuals, updates to clinic's budget, program updates, clinic's billing status, invoices before they are sent out to customers/contractors/grantors and analyze variance on budget. In addition, ED reports on grant applications or upcoming contracts. When meeting with the President before board meeting, projections on budget are discussed and analyzed. AC reviews cash flow projections sporadically and builds a report to ED when requested. Management and board members will get reports at board meetings with actuals, updated budget, and at end of fiscal year drafts of audited report for pre-approval and later a final audited financials.

7. COMPENSATION DETERMINATION: Organization's top management officials are accountable for ensuring that the organization's mission is carried out at the highest levels of quality, service, and stewardship within the communities the organization serves. The Board of Directors determines executive compensation. The Executive Director's salary was determined based on an independent analysis to help ensure that compensation levels are reasonable to attract and retain the highest caliber of professionals needed to carry out its mission. The executive compensation is also based upon the respective percentage of time working at organization and benchmarks itself against organizations of comparable mission across the region and the nation that are creating and scaling complex education and social sector programs and services. Market data are assembled for all elements of executive compensation (salary, benefits, and perquisites). Furthermore, the compensation levels reflect the scope of each top manager's responsibilities, educational background, experience, and industry standing, as well as individual and organization performance. Also, the top management officials' compensation cannot exceed amounts allowed by grants and contracts. Finally, it is the obligation of a compensation committee to assess the performance of Executive Director, determine his/her compensation, and report its finding in this regard to the Board. The committee is also responsible for reviewing and approving the performance assessments and compensation recommendations for the top management positions. When the compensation committee is not in place, ED performance is assessed at every board meeting when program updates are reported.

When there are related parties working within organization the Board of Directors determines compensation for the related party individual and is based upon market levels and percentage of time working at Education Plus, Inc. The Board of Directors is also responsible for reviewing and approving the performance assessments and compensation recommendations for any related party individuals.

APPENDIX E
FISCAL SPONSOR AGREEMENT TEMPLATE

Agreement Between

Not for Profit Organization
And
Organization/Program

This Agreement, made on the ---- day of Month, Year by and between Not-for-profit, a 501 c3 not-for-profit corporation, and Organization/Program.

WITNESSETH:

1. **SERVICES:** During the Terms of this Agreement, Not-for-Profit shall perform the services described in the attached letter marked as Attachment "A" hereto ("Work Statement"). Organization/Program hereby engages Not-for-Profit as an independent consultant to provide the specific services that Not-for-Profit will perform and the specific schedule for providing these services shall be in accordance with the provisions of Paragraph One (1) and consistent with Attachment "A".
2.
3. **OTHER SERVICES:** The parties may, at any time and from time to time by a written agreement or instrument executed by both parties, provide for additional services to be performed by Not-for-Profit for or relating to Organization/Program or add to or expand the scope of Service provided for in Attachment "A" for such additional consideration and under such other consideration or additional or terms as the parties deem appropriate. Except as otherwise provided in the agreement instrument signed by the parties, at such additional or expanded services shall be considered "Services" covered by and subject to all the terms of this Agreement. Notwithstanding the foregoing, no additional or expanded Services shall require PHMC to engage in any activities or to exercise any authority excluded from this Agreement by Paragraph 3, unless the applicable agreement or instrument specifically states the intention of the parties to proceed contrary to Paragraph 3 of this Agreement, by specific reference to that Paragraph.

4. **EXCLUSION of EXECUTIVE and MANAGEMENT AUTHORITY:** In Accordance with the terms in Attachment "A", the Services to be provided by Not-for-Profit involve serving as Organization/Program's fiscal agent, advice and technical assistance only and do not extend to executive or management decisions or prerogatives of any kind. In no event shall this Agreement be construed to grant Not-for-Profit any of the authority of the Board of Directors or corporate offices or management of Organization/Program for any matter. This Agreement and the Activities of Not-for-Profit hereunder are not intended and shall not be considered to relieve the Board, officers, or management of Organization/Program of any authority, duties or responsibilities.

5. **FEES:** Not-for-Profit will charge 4percent overhead as fiscal agent.

6. **PERFORMANCE:** Organization/Program shall use reasonable efforts to perform Services detailed in Attachment A. Organization/Program acknowledges that Not-for-Profit is not responsible for the success or failure of all or any portion of Organization/Program's business.

7. **WARRANTIES:** If relevant, Organization/Program represents and warrants to Not-for-Profit that (1) it has and will comply in all respects, with all requirements of the grants from any governmental agency; (2) it has and will maintain in full force all licenses, permits, and approvals required for the operation of its businesses and the conduct of the Programs; (3) it has conducted and will conduct the Programs in compliance with all applicable federal, state, and local laws, regulations, and ordinances.

8. **INSURANCE:** If relevant, Organization/Program shall, upon Not-for-Profit' reasonable request, cause Not-for-Profit to be named a co-insured under such insurance policies and cause the policies to provide that they may not be canceled or terminated without at least 10 days advance written notice of cancellation or termination to Not-for-Profit.

9. **TERM:** The term of this agreement shall begin on Month, Day, Year and continue until Month, Day, Year , provided that the parties may extend this Agreement for such a period and under such terms as they deem appropriate by a written agreement or instrument executed by both parties.

10. **TERMINATION:**
    A. Not-for-Profit may terminate this Agreement, effective immediately upon giving Organization/Program written notice of termination.

B. Either party may terminate this Agreement, effective immediately upon giving the other party written notice of termination, if the other party (i) breaches or fails to perform any provision of this Agreement in any material respect and fails to cure such breach or failure within 14 days after written notice thereof , or (ii) consents to the appointment of a receiver custodian trustee or liquidator for all or any portion of its property; files a voluntary proceeding under any federal or state law for the relief of debtors; has filed against it and not dismissed within 30 days any involuntary proceeding for the appointment of a receiver, custodian, trustee or liquidator for all or any portion of its property or any proceeding under any federal or state law for the relief of debtors; or ceases, or admits in writing its intentions cease, the conduct of its business in the ordinary course.
C. Upon termination of this Agreement for any reason, each party shall have and may exercise all remedies available to it under applicable law, with no remedy being exclusive and all remedies being cumulative.
D. Organization/Program shall give Not-for-Profit at least 60 days' notice of non-renewal of this agreement. Should not-for-profit decide not to renew this agreement and desire to receive certain services from not-for-profit, the rates on Attachment C shall apply.

11. **INDEPENDENT CONTRACTOR:** The relationship of Not-for-Profit and Organization/Program under this Agreement shall be one of independent contractors only. Neither party shall have the authority to bind or obligate the other party in any manner or to incur any indebtedness on behalf of the other party, and no such authority shall be implied.

12. **INDEMNIFICATION:** Organization/Program shall defend, indemnify, and hold harmless Not-for-Profit from and against any and a;; claims, demands, loses, costs, damages, suits, judgment, penalties, and expenses and liabilities of any kind and nature whatsoever, including reasonable attorneys' fees, incurred by not-for-profit arising out of or in connection with any aspect of the not-for-profit businesses and activities, including without limitation any aspects of the Programs, except to the extent actually caused by not-for-profit's negligence or intentional misconduct.

Not-for-Profit shall defend, indemnify, and hold harmless Organization/Program from and against any and a; claims, demands, loses, costs, damages, suits, judgment, penalties, and expenses and liabilities of any kind and nature whatsoever, including reasonable attorneys' fees, incurred by not-for-profit arising out of or in connection with any aspect of the not-for-profit businesses and activities, including without limitation, any aspects of the Programs, except to the extent actually caused by not-for-profit negligence or intentional misconduct.

13. **Applicable Law**. Pennsylvania law shall govern the validity, construction, interpretation and effect of this Agreement.

14. **FURTHER ASSURANCES:** Each party shall, upon the reasonable request of the other party, take such action and execute and deliver such documents as may be reasonably necessary or appropriate to effectuate the terms of this Agreement and by the transactions and relationship contemplated hereby.

15. **ASSIGNMENT:** Neither party may assign or transfer all or any portion of this Agreement, whether voluntarily, in voluntarily, by operation of law or otherwise, without the prior written consent of the other party, and any attempted assignment or transfer to the contrary shall be null and void and of no effect.

16. **HEADINGS:** The paragraph headings of this Agreement are for convenience of reference and do not form a part of the terms and conditions of this Agreement or give full notice thereof.

17. **ENTIRE AGREEMENT.** This Agreement contains the entire understanding between the parties, no other covenants or representations having induced either party to execute this Agreement. This Agreement may not be amended or modified, in any manner, except by a written agreement duly executed by the party to be charged.

18. **NOTICES**. All notices, statements and other communications required or permitted under this Agreement shall be in writing and shall be sufficiently given only if personally delivered, mailed by registered, certified or first class mail, transmitted by a reputable express courier service or transmitted by telecopier and confirmed by first class mail within 24 hours to the party to receive notice at the following addresses, or at such other addresses as party may, by notice, direct.

If to Not-for-Profit:INSERT ADDRESS

If to Organization/Program: INSERT ADDRESS

All notices shall be deemed as given when received, except that notice by first class mail shall be deemed as given on the second business day after the notice is mailed. IN WITNESS WHEREOF, the partied have executed this Agreement, under seal, the day and year first above written.

APPENDIX F
CASE STATEMENT TEMPLATE

Section 1. **Summary of the ASK** -- max. 100 words long. It explains the ASK theme

Section 2. **The introduction** --six paragraphs max. 300 words. It specifies the need and challenges you face if not funded, including the impact if challenge is not met; For example, $5 million for "a capital project."

Section 3. **The organization's history** -- max. 10 paragraphs totaling 500 words.

Section 4. **The organization's philosophy** -- max.150 words. It explains the organization's concept behind a wonderful service that needs a capital project fund. What makes your organization special?

Section 5. **The organization's mission**. Why your mission matters today (the who you are and what you do). It brings the reader up to date on who the organization is and what the organization is doing. The midsection: at max. 1,600 words, the longest, too.
Examples:
-How did your organization begin? What is its mission/vision? (Note: It may be important here to say something about the organizational structure and work philosophy of your group, particularly for businesses that want to see your "business model")
-What makes your organization unique?
-How large is your organization and how many does it serve?
-What are your primary programs, services, or areas of focus? In other words, how does your organization work to meet the challenge?
-What results has your organization achieved thus far?

Section 6. **The vision** -- in max. 500 words. What are your organization's future plans?

Section 7. **The call to action/The ASK**. The section devotes max. 1,200 words to what will be built with the $5 million.
Example:
-The Ask/Include Contact Information
-Why are you asking for money? What is the cost of doing your work?
-If this is a special campaign, how much do you hope to raise? How will the money be spent and what are the long-term impacts? How will the donor make a difference?

Section 8. **A closing thank-you**. A max. 250-word wrap-up that summarizes the ask and pleads, "Won't you give?"

APPENDIX G
MARKETING AND COMMUNICATION STRATEGIES

Free Range Thinking: Adapted from Goodman Media
(http://www.goodmanmedia.com/)
Many not-for-profits have a good cause but a lousy message. People relate to people and therefore stories about work/organizations must provide human protagonists to draw the audience in and lead them through the narrative.
1. Stories are about people
2. The people in your story have to want something
3. Stories need to be fixed in time and space
4. Let your characters speak for themselves
5. Audiences bore easily: You have to make them wonder, what happens next
6. Stories speak the audience's language
7. Stories stir up emotions: Need to make the audience feel vs. analyze data
8. Stories don't tell: they show
9. Stories have at least one "moment of truth"
10. Stories have clear meaning

Tips and Techniques' for Visionary Speeches: Adapted from Spitfire Strategies
(https://www.spitfirestrategies.com/)
- Remember that half an hour of speaking = 4,000 words.
- Use simpler words whenever possible
- Change language from passive to active
- Use shorter sentences -- no run-on
- Practice, Practice, Practice

Foresight and imagination are the two main qualities that distinguish visionary speeches -- and those who deliver them -- from the pack.
- Foresight presents the audience with a look into the future and persuades them to believe not in a change that should take place, but one that invariably will take place and that they must take action in order to change the current momentum.
- Maximizing on imagination offers the audience a more optimistic vision of what can and should be. In this speech, the speaker presents a vision that is different than both the current reality -- and the future outcome if left unchanged.

Rhetorical Techniques
- Contrasts: Using a contradiction of juxtaposing a positive with a negative can summarize your point in a pithy punchy way "one small step for man; one giant leap for mankind."

- Puzzles and Questions: Presenting a puzzle or asking a question forces the audience to listen -- and try to react -- to what you are saying. Puzzle: "Of all natures' gifts to the human race, what is sweeter to a man than his children?"
- Lists of Three: Three is a magic number -- people can remember small groupings of words or concepts, especially when they flow together because of similar letter sounds of rhyming.
- Paint a Picture: Use similes and other comparisons to enhance your speech when describing activities your organization pursues or people you work with or serve. "I'll be floating like a butterfly and stinging like a bee."
- Dramatic Pause: Taking the time to pause before beginning a speech, in mid-sentence, or prior to responding to a question can help you collect your thoughts – and make you seem more authoritative and deliberate as you continue. Making eye contact with audience members as you pause is also a good trick to center the attention on you and your speech. "Yesterday, December 7, is a day that will live in (pause) infamy, Pearl Harbor was suddenly and deliberately attacked…"
- Anecdote: Using a brief but compelling anecdote can be a great way to make a point in a speech. It can change up the tone during your speech and refocus your audience on you.
- Include the Audience: Referring to the audience -- by asking a direct question or making an inclusive statement -- puts the pressure of them to pay attention to you "You and I have a rendezvous with destiny."

Avoiding the Messaging Trap -- Tips from Guide Star (https://www.guidestar.org/Home.aspx)
Messaging is how we use words to move people to take action. The increased sophistication and power of tools at our fingertips has created a dangerous trap, however. A novice can now create a fairly sophisticated website or e-mail campaign. A glossy, professional look is necessary but not sufficient in moving a target audience to the desired actions. Similarly, clear, concise, and grammatically correct text is not enough. An excellent and inexpensive guide to how to craft and tune your message is *Writing Copy for Dummies*.

Key points on how you communicate who your organization is include:
- ✓ Emphasize the benefits! (should relate to your mission)
- ✓ Highlight your key difference
- ✓ Be consistent (about who you are)
- ✓ Be credible
- ✓ Keep it simple

Emphasize the Benefits

People are lazy readers. Always connect the dots between what you do and what it does for them. If you run a soup kitchen in a suburban area, you could say that you feed the hungry, but that may not resonate as well as saying that your support helps neighbors through such crises as loss of jobs until they get back on their feet. Think about how what you do is most relevant to those you are reaching out to.

In the not-for-profit world, organizations get in trouble with messaging when their mission is really a program description. If your mission is to educate teenagers about the legal system, you may need to reach beyond your mission. Why are you teaching kids this? Is it to encourage more to be lawyers or to reduce a sense of alienation from the justice system? Your potential donors are not nearly as interested in the means as the ends. Touch upon what will matter to them.

Highlight Your Key Difference
Your communications will include a description of who you are that should reflect your positioning -- i.e., what services your organization provides, who you provide them to, and how your organization is different from related organizations. Don't say simply that you feed the hungry. Why should someone give to your organization rather than another that feeds the hungry? Maybe it's your geographic focus. Maybe you teach recipients cheaper, more nutritious ways of preparing food. Whatever your key difference is, flaunt it.

Be Consistent
Be consistent in how you portray your organization. If you are experienced at e-mail marketing, the reference to consistency may seem counter to what you learned about splitting a campaign into two or more variations to test different approaches. Testing tweaks in the call to action is not the same, however, as changing how you describe who you are.

You might wonder, "Aren't I supposed to highlight different things based on the audience receiving my message?" Absolutely, but you can't pretend to be a completely different animal to each audience. Nor can you change who you say you are in each communication to a specific audience. A conservation organization should have one key message to highlight for potential members -- perhaps, enjoy our properties as much as you'd like without paying admission fees -- and another for large donors -- perhaps, we're the most efficient organization in Massachusetts for conserving land and educating the public. Highlight the aspect most relevant to the audience but include a consistent blurb about your organization in each communication. If you are revising the description of your organization repeatedly, you probably have not agreed on your positioning yet.

Be Credible

Being credible means providing evidence. Numbers make great evidence. Let's say that you have found that donors are interested in funding the most efficient provider of shelter for the homeless. You could highlight the number of homeless people you helped or how your overhead decreased as a percentage of costs last year. Your readers probably won't remember the evidence you cite, but if it is credible, it will help glue your positioning into their memories.

Keep It Simple
Finally, keep it simple. Regardless of how acute our mental facilities are, we know that the more items we are given to remember, the lower the probability of remembering any. The less you ask donors and members to remember about you, the better they will remember it. Conservation organizations may occasionally do things outside of conserving land for species protection. They might conduct a native plant sale annually, for example. They don't, however, need to list every activity they undertake when they are explaining who they are on their Web site or in their brochure.

Making Your Organization's Presentations Great: Adapted from Spitfire Strategies
- Design Guidelines (title slides, logo placement, minimize font (preferably one) and color options
- Content:
    1. One story, strong opening, and closing. Never read the slides, end with Q&A...
    2. Your presentation is not a speech and a series of slides; it is the sum of the parts. Your audience doesn't separate what you say from the slides when they are watching your presentation. **An effective presentation requires that you decide what you are going to say before you decide what you are going to show.**
    3. Great presentation design is achieved not when there is nothing more to add, but when there is nothing left to be taken away.
    4. Often visuals that complement and reinforce the story associated with the content, rather than serve as literal visual representations of the text, are most compelling

Fundamentals for Transforming Your Slides
1. Change the background color
2. Add a picture
3. Resize, crop, and recolor a picture
4. Add a rectangle and make it transparent
5. Animate and dim text

10 Ways You May Be Sabotaging Your Communications: Adapted from www.RichardMale.com

It was George Bernard Shaw who observed that "the greatest problem in communication is the illusion that it has occurred." You're busy, you work long hours, and you're passionate about your not-for-profit mission. Unfortunately, it's entirely possible that you are less effective in your communications than you think.

Consider whether your organization has made the following missteps:

1. Failure to define the problem. You may have the most innovative, most effective programs in the state, but if we don't understand why your not-for-profit exists in the first place, it's hard to appreciate the great work you're doing. Without a problem to solve, it's also difficult to make a convincing argument that you need volunteers, donations or grants. Don't assume people understand the magnitude of your issue or that they "connect the dots."
2. Using verbs that are vague. It's a lovely sentiment but watch your reliance on the word "help." We're all part of what is called the helping sector, after all. Think about the clarity of using more precise verbs, i.e., "We pay for," "We meet weekly with," "We provide transportation," etc. If a not-for-profit says, "We help keep seniors in their homes," does this mean they're putting padlocks on the doors? Watch out for the verb "serve" for the same reason. Did you spend an hour with this person . . . or a year?
3. Omitting an essential fact. It's only for people over age 65. It's free. It's by referral only. We operate in two counties. It's a 24-hour program. It's for Catholic schools. It lasts six months. Half of our funding is federal. And so on. Have a stranger listen to your best elevator speech and then ask them who, what, when, where, how, and why.
4. Failure to explain what makes you unique. This is what is called your "only-ness." Remember that there are thousands of not-for-profits in your region. "We are the only not-for-profit in our neighborhood/county/state/ region that _____." A related pitfall could be that your message fails to connect with people on a visceral, personal, or emotional level.
5. Overwhelming new audiences with too much information. Tell us what the problem is, and precisely how you address it. Then let us breathe and ask questions, refill coffee, or click on a link. Use short sentences and break up long paragraphs. Let the power of your information speak for itself. Beware of any PowerPoint or video that is longer than a few minutes. Ask for questions. Break up mind-numbing data with storytelling.
6. Use of jargon or acronyms. This seems to be an especially prevalent problem in health care and public-sector offices. A related consideration is whether the audience you're communicating to is likely to be confused, bored, intimidated, or offended by the vocabulary you're using. What generation are they? What technology do they prefer? What is their level of education or understanding? What is their direct connection to your cause or your industry?
7. Providing no data, old data, or bad data. Good data may still be meaningless if there is no context, i.e., "We provided housing for 200 families last month." Is that a lot? What is the gap -- the unmet need? Or should we be celebrating? How does this number compare to your work one year ago?

8. Lack of a target. "Project Ozma" was an experimental broadcast in 1960 of interstellar radio waves into outer space, just in case someone was out there to receive it. Do not do this. Think before you write/speak/blog/blast: Who is most interested in your cause? Who donated to you last year? Who is likely to need you this year? Who has what you seek? Which reporter covers your region/issue? Your communications budget of dollars and hours is limited, so make it count by using a laser-sharp focus.

9. You are too ambitious. If you cannot seem to maintain your 20-page website, then focus on five good (current, clean, engaging) pages. You also need to find the right frequency for your outbound communications: too infrequent, and your target audience will forget about you; too often, and they will find you annoying and shrill.

10. Your message changes too often. There is a natural assumption that our own taglines, creative, and campaign slogans must be stale (not because of any actual research, but simply that we ourselves are sick of hearing it and seeing it). Enough with the changing, the altering, the noodling. Find the right message and stick to it, repeat it, spread it, blast it, weave it in.

Using Evidence to Prove Your Point

"Evidence" describes the supporting material in persuasive writing. Evidence gives an objective foundation to your arguments and makes your writing more than a mere collection of personal opinions or prejudices.

Facts and figures, examples, narratives, testimony, and definition all are used to convince readers to accept the arguments and recommendations the writer is presenting. Because you are asking your readers to take a risk when you attempt to persuade them, audiences will demand support for your assertions. Search for evidence that is relevant and timely and that comes from sources your audience will respect and accept.

A few notes about evidence
- Emphasize factual examples.
- When appropriate, use powerful examples.
- Use narratives to create identification -- to draw your audience into your subject and reinforce their stake in the outcome.
- Emphasize expert testimony. It carries more weight than prestige or lay testimony. Be prepared to document the qualifications of the experts you use, if they are unfamiliar to your audience.
- Use multiple sources of evidence.
- Proofs are interpretations drawn from evidence that provide readers with good reasons for changing an attitude or following a course of conduct or action. Good reasons are concerned with showing an audience that something is admirable, desirable, or obligatory.

Most importantly, audiences evaluate good reasons in terms of their:
- Relevance (do they really apply to the situation or issue at hand?);

- Consequences (what will be the result of accepting or rejecting them?); and
- Consistency (do they fit together, and do they fit with our other prior beliefs/policies?).

Aristotle suggested that there are three types of proof: logos -- proof that emphasizes rational evidence; pathos -- proof based on motives and emotions; and ethos -- proof based on the personality, character, and reputation of the writer. More recent scholars have added one other form of proof: mythos -- proof based on the traditions, identity, and values of a group. The mythos of an organization can be an important element in persuasive business writing.

In most ethical and effective persuasive efforts, particularly in a business setting, logos usually predominate. Ethos and pathos can be important supporting players; pathos is the least used in business.

Adapted from Herbert Shapiro, Empire State College:
http://www7.esc.edu/hshapiro/writing_program/students/reference/main/evidence.htm

APPENDIX H
ORGANIZATIONAL HEALTH ASSESSMENT

Culture	Yes	No	Partial
1. What is our desired culture?	☐	☐	☐
2. Is our culture aligned with our strategy?	☐	☐	☐
3. What do we stand for?	☐	☐	☐
4. What do we not stand for?	☐	☐	☐
5. How do we measure our organization's impact?	☐	☐	☐
6. What are we willing to fund?	☐	☐	☐
7. What will we not fund?	☐	☐	☐

Leadership	Yes	No	Partial
8. Do we have strong leadership teams in place in all levels of our organization?	☐	☐	☐
9. Do we have a plan in place to support teams that are not cohesive?	☐	☐	☐
10. Are senior leaders in my organization effective at building trusted relationships?	☐	☐	☐
11. Do senior leaders follow-through on decisions?	☐	☐	☐
12. Do senior leaders hold each other accountable?	☐	☐	☐

Total Rewards	Yes	No	Partial
13. Do we regularly review our benefits offerings and assess whether they meet the needs of our employees? Do we survey our employees annually? Adjust accordingly?	☐	☐	☐
14. Do we have good participation in our retirement plan?	☐	☐	☐
15. Do we review our salaries against market benchmarks at least every 2 years?	☐	☐	☐
16. Do we offer workplace flexibility?	☐	☐	☐
17. Do we offer development opportunities for all levels of the organization?	☐	☐	☐

Human Capital	Yes	No	Partial
18. Does our website reflect our desired employer BRAND?	☐	☐	☐
19. Does our retirement process reflect our BRAND?	☐	☐	☐
20. How effective is our onboarding and orientation process? Does it reflect our BRAND?	☐	☐	☐

21. Do other HR processes reflect our desired employer BRAND? (Think performance management, total rewards, off-boarding, etc.) ❏ ❏ ❏
22. Have we identified metrics that matter for tracking purposes? ❏ ❏ ❏

Risk Mitigation   Yes   No   Partial

23. Do we know what our employees think about their experience with our organization? Do we do pulse or annual surveys? ❏ ❏ ❏
24. Are we compliance with our HR processes (retirement and selection through to termination and off-boarding) ❏ ❏ ❏
25. Are we in compliance with regularly agencies that govern our industry? ❏ ❏ ❏
26. Do we offer required training to mitigate risk such as: safety, anti-harassment, interviewing skills? ❏ ❏ ❏
27. Do we review our insurance policies annually to ensure we have appropriate coverage? ❏ ❏ ❏
28. Do we take proactive steps to prevent risk? (Safety committee, succession plans, engagement surveys, etc.) ❏ ❏ ❏

APPENDIX I
HUMAN RESOURCES: EMPLOYEE MANUAL CATEGORIES

TABLE OF CONTENTS
1. Acknowledgment of Receipt Form

2. ORGANIZATION OVERVIEW
   - Welcome and Introduction
   - Mission and Vision
   - Employee Manual Notice
   - Ethical Standards
   - Confidentiality and Confidential Information
   - Conflict of Interest
   - Family Education Rights and Privacy Act (FERPA)
   - Sensitive Information and Identity Theft
   - Board of Trustees Employee Grievance Procedure

3. COMPENSATION AND PAYROLL
   - Overtime Pay for Non-Exempt Employees
   - Pay for Full-time 10-Month Employees
   - Payday and Pay Cycle
   - Payroll Workday
   - Payroll Workweek and Pay Period
   - Recording of Time
   - Time Off – Compensatory Tim
   - Time Records for Non-Exempt Employees
   - Workweek Payments and Deductions
   - Non-Exempt Employee
   - Exempt Employee
   - Communicating Concerns or Questions About Pay

4. EMPLOYMENT AND BENEFITS
   - Anniversary Date
   - Break-In-Service
   - Continuing Education
   - Employment Classifications
   - Non-Exempt Employee
   - Exempt Employee
   - 10-Month Employee
   - 12-Month Employee
   - Certified
   - Non-Certified

- Full-Time Employee
- Part-Time Variable Hour Employee
- Part-Time Fixed Hour Employee (<35 Hours Per Week)
- Regular Employee
- Temporary Employee
- Per Diem/On-Call Employee
- Contractual Worker
- Volunteer
- Funeral/Bereavement Leave
- Holidays
- Insurance and Other Coverage
- Introductory Period
- Jury/Witness Duty
- Jury Duty
- Witness Duty
- Paid Time Off (PTO)
- Paternity and Adoption Pay
- Personal Days
- Retirement 403(b) Savings Plan
- Sick Days
- Social Security and Medicare Tax
- Unemployment Compensation
- Unpaid Leave of Absence (LOA)
- General LOA Guidelines
- Disability (Including Pregnancy)
- Military, Reserves, and National Guard
- Personal
- Workers' Compensation
- Voting
- Workers' Compensation

5. FEEDBACK ON PERFORMANCE, BEHAVIOR, ETC.

6. OTHER POLICIES
    - Attendance, Absence, and Lateness
    - Background, Reference, and Other Checks
    - Borrowing of Organization-Owned Equipment
    - Business Travel Expenses
    - Child Abuse, Neglect, and Sexual Misconduct
    - Computers, Computer Network, Internet-Enabled Devices, and Internet Access

- Computer Network, Computers, and Internet-Enabled Devices Use Limitations
- Duty Not to Waste or Damage Computer Resources
- Permitted Use of Internet, Computer Network, Computers, and Internet-Enabled Devices
- Dress Code and Personal Appearance
- Driving License and Driving Record
- Drug and Alcohol-Free Workplace
- Drug and Alcohol Screening
- Emergencies and Inclement Weather
- Employee Information
- Change of Personal Information
- Personnel Files
- Employment of Relatives
- Ending of Employment
- Gifts
- Health Examinations
- Outside Employment
- Personal Property and Personal Identity Information
- Pets and Children at Work
- Phones: Personal Cell and Other Personal Devices
- Phone System and Business Cell Phone
- Privacy
- References – Post-Employment and Current-Employment
- Smoking
- Social Media
- Solicitation and Distribution
- Staff and Student Interaction
- Use of Vehicles
- Weapons
- Workplace Bullying
- Workplace and School Violence
- Workplace Safety
- STATUTES
- Americans with Disabilities Act (ADA)
- Consolidated Omnibus Budget Reconciliation Act (COBRA)
- Employment: At-Will
- Equal Employment Opportunity
- Diversity
- Family and Medical Leave Act (FMLA)
- GINA
- Harassment and Sexual Harassment

- Sexual Harassment
- Reporting Harassment, Sexual Harassment, and Retaliation
- HIPAA Privacy
- Immigration Law Compliance
- Non-Retaliation Policy and Whistleblower Protection

APPENDIX J
POLICY BRIEF AND PUBIC TESTIMONY INSTRUCTIONS

Policy Brief Instructions

Follow CIRAC (Conclusion; Issue; Rule; Application; Conclusion) that is writing the Conclusion; defining the Issue; outlining the Rule(s); outlining the Application; and finishing with the Conclusion. Public Policy Paper Outline:

1) TITLE OF POLICY STATEMENT with names and credentials
Example: "Advocating for Nurse Practitioners to be reimbursed at 100 percent of the Medicare Rate"

2) SUMMARY (1 Page Max)
Summarize the problem statement and recommendations contained in the policy paper (Note: This section should NOT contain any references). You should always write this summary last, but you want to hit the reader from the get-go as to what the issue is you are advocating for. Example: Congress should change its rule to allow CMS to change its Medicare reimbursement policy where Nurse Practitioners are only paid 85 percent of a physician fee schedule.

3) PROBLEM STATEMENT/ISSUE **(35 percent of text)**
This section should describe the policy issue framed within research and data. Describe the extent of the problem, including the health and economic burden to the society, using the best available science and evidence.
If relevant, describe any disproportionate impact on underserved populations, and ethical, equitable, economic, and political issues.
Example: Description on how the Nurse Practitioners (NP) reimbursement came about historically and how that has a negative impact on service delivery and inequities in reimbursement given NPs often take care of the most vulnerable people in primary care.

4) CURRENT POLICY/LAW **(25 percent of text)**
Describe the current policy environment and/or law with regard to your policy issue, including any negative impact this law has on the people it impacts. This section should be well researched and look at federal and state law.

5) POLICY SOLUTION **(20 percent of text)**
Describe your policy solution to the problem/issue. What interventions and strategy(ies) is/are you proposing to address the problem. What is the scientific evidence that the strategy is likely to have an impact on reducing the problem or is effective and efficient? How big of an impact is it likely to have? Give at least one reference to scientific or other authoritative evidence for the effectiveness of the strategy.

Example: With regard to NPs and reimbursement, the following evidence (documented research) enhances access to care and enables them to serve more vulnerable people.

Research and write about the opposition, their viewpoint and evidence. Identify opposing evidence or alternative points of view to the proposed policy issue -- existence and extent of the problem; the validity of the evidence and ethical, equitable and legal issues when appropriate. Writing a balanced view and acknowledging what your opponents say are key to your argument.

Example: With regard to NPs we acknowledge that when Congress passed the law to allow CMS to only reimburse NPs 85 percent, it was because their argument was that NPs are paid less than physicians, which is true, and they have fewer loans. However, after you acknowledge the opposition, you should still conclude why you believe the policy you are advocating for is better than the opposition's argument.

6) ACTION STEPS/SUMMARY (1-2 Pages)
Summarize your policy paper, your position and what your advocacy position. Be clear that the action steps you propose are feasible, ethical and equitable to undertake and are culturally and linguistically appropriate to any affected populations. Authors should also consider any unintended consequences of the action steps.

7) REFERENCES
Authors should provide appropriate references to scientific or other authoritative evidence regarding the size/scope of the problem. Include the best available references that support the text --relevant peer review or evidence-based or official documents.
Do NOT use automatic referencing (i.e. endnotes). Each reference should be individually numbered and manually entered. Number each new reference the first time it appears; use that number to refer to the reference every time it is cited in the proposed policy statement.
Use APA format

Presenting Public Testimony Instructions
Following the writing of a policy, brief is often the ability to testify to key actors in public hearings. The purpose of these hearings is to allow the public to officially participate in government decisions; to gather facts and hear arguments through testimony; to help legislators make decisions in the public interest, and to air both sides of an issue before a decision is made. At the very participating in a public hearing helps you take a hard look at your issue; provides you with an opportunity to develop your arguments, broaden your base of support, and learn about the opposition.

Keep in mind that even though a policy or system strategy change might be self-evident, a committee chair may wish to demonstrate to his/her colleagues that there is a widespread support for a favored piece of legislation. In addition, a well-attended hearing demonstrates broad public involvement and concern on a controversial matter will not only send a strong message, it will also attract media coverage.

Steps:
1) Research testimony opportunities and register (as early as possible as you want to testify when members are fresh) to orally testify as oral testimony is the most powerful way to influence key actors.

2) Written testimony is accepted for inclusion in the record of a hearing. Offering oral testimony is the most powerful way to present testimony.

3) Prepare your written testimony (bring enough copies for all committee members, before the hearing so that they can distribute it to the committee. Your written testimony can make the points that you did not have time to make in your presentation. In the event of a highly controversial issue, you may wish to distribute them copies the press.

Written Testimony Guidelines
Identify your organization, the Bill name and number or issue, the committee or governmental body and your position.

Example:
  i. Flying Fish Conservancy3221 Shoreline Drive Bayside, MD 21110 (410) 555-1234
  ii. Testimony of the Flying Fish ConservancyIN SUPPORT OF HB 2110, THE FLYING FISH CONSERVATION BILL Before the House Environmental CommitteeFebruary 3, 2003

State your opinion on the issue in a summary paragraph at the top of the testimony. Explain what the legislation or policy would do and why you oppose or support it. Offer other solutions or alternatives if there are any.
Ask the body to support your position: "Therefore, I urge the committees to support HB 2110."
Easing yourself into public speaking by attending one or more hearings to familiarize yourself with the workings of a hearing.

Prepare your oral testimony. Oral testimony should only include highlights or your written testimony. Try out different styles of testimony such as "my personal experience" or "what this issue means to me" and keep in mind that effective testimony is sincere testimony that is straightforward and easy to understand and should be the easiest to prepare because you are expressing your own feelings and relating your experiences.

Oral Testimony Framework (3 Minutes or Less)
- Introduce yourself, state whether you support or oppose the issue, and give a reason why. Thank the hearing body.
- Make eye contact with legislators during your testimony.
- Explain the issue using facts, figures, background materials, quotes from experts and other references that will substantiate your opinion.
- Be professional, assertive, and reasonably brief.
- Try to use personal experiences.
- Don't read but use notes for guidance; a relaxed conversational style is more effective.
- Dress for success. Business attire is appropriate to demonstrate respect for the committee.
- Bring supporters. It can be very effective to bring a large group of people to a hearing as a show of support. Appoint one spokesperson to talk to the committee or media.
- Visual Aides. Consider the possibility of visual aids for effect. Check with committee staff in advance for approval.

Wait briefly after you finish for questions from committee members. If you do not know the answer, offer to get them an answer later.

APPENDIX K
POLICY BRIEF EXAMPLES

The following section offers some examples of different policy brief formats. The first two were sent to someone close to President Trump's transition team at a time when the new administration was considering reforms to the Affordable Care Act. Their purpose is to present the administration with a number of strategies they could implement to improve care and reduce costs through nurse-led care. NNCC and CCA's executive director met with the person who would present them to the transition team before they were written to get a feel for the administration's priorities and the types of things they would be open to. The briefs emphasize ideas important to the administration, like free market competition and reducing regulatory bureaucracy, while staying true to NNCC and CCA's mission.

The third brief summarizes the findings of a federally funded study evaluating the effectiveness of nurse-managed managed health clinics. Its purpose is to bring publicity to the study findings by presenting them in a format that is easy for policy makers to digest and understand. Even though the brief is lengthy, it makes use of bulleting and bold type to drive the key points that NNCC wanted to communicate. Examples four and five are intended to provide members of congress with background on a particular issue and/or information to support a specific policy position. The fifth brief, for example was written to provide a republican congressman with statistics and information he could draw upon to support his decision not to vote for the repeal of the Affordable Care Act. Background briefs, like examples four and five are generally used in conjunction with a factsheet, or some other short summary document the congress person can consult prior to digging into the longer brief for the details.

The last two policy brief examples are specifically designed to influence state policy makers. The first is a short brief intended to quickly introduce a state policy maker to an issue inhibiting access to care and present a possible solution. In this case, the issue has to do with delays in the Medicaid credentialing process for health care providers. It is a good example of how to write a clear, succinct brief. The last example is a more detailed brief that lays out the pros and cons of the systems several keys are using to credential and enroll Medicaid providers. It is unique in that it attempts to give policy makers an example of what is, and what is NOT working well.

Example 1: General Brief for Executive Office to Spark Conversation

STRATEGIES TO EXPAND ACCESS TO AFFORDABLE, QUALITY, CONSUMER-DRIVEN HEALTHCARE IN THE TRUMP ADMINISTRATION

INTRODUCTION:

Access to high-quality, affordable primary healthcare is in crisis. In response, President Trump has said that he envisions a healthcare system that emphasizes free market principles and personal economic freedom, while also broadening healthcare access, making care more affordable and improving care quality. The nation's looming primary care physician shortage and increasing demand for care present a major obstacle to accomplishing this vision. *According to the American Association of Medical Colleges, the country faces a projected shortfall of 14,900 to 35,600 physicians by 2025.[12] Simultaneously, primary care office visits are expected to increase by 3.8 percent nationally, coupled with a 2.2 percent increase in emergency room visits.[13] More than 83 percent of the country's 220,000 licensed nurse practitioners are certified in primary care, but the potential of well-educated nurses with advanced degrees to fill gaps in care, improve outcomes, and reduce costs has not been fully realized due to a variety of regulatory restrictions at the federal and state levels.*

Providing care to all Americans requires an expansion of systems already in place, as well as the implementation of new definitions, and roles; as well as simplifying and streamlining processes focused on special populations and consumer-driven healthcare models. Nurse-led health clinics, retail clinics and innovative consumer-driven health insurance models are prepared to lead the charge of ensuring healthcare access for all.

This memorandum provides a national strategy for expanding access to high-quality affordable market-driven healthcare through **consumer-driven healthcare** models that further the Trump administration's healthcare priorities.

BACKGROUND EXAMPLES OF EMERGING INNOVATIVE CONSUMER-DRIVEN MODELS OF PRIMARY CARE:

---

[12] Association of American Healthcare Colleges. The Complexities of Physician Supply and Demand: Projections from 2014 to 2025. https://www.aamc.org/download/458082/data/2016_complexities_of_supply_and_demand_projections.pdf. [Accessed 2016].

[13] The Commonwealth Fund. How Will the Affordable Care Act Affect the Use of Health Care Services? http://www.commonwealthfund.org/publications/issue-briefs/2015/feb/how-will-aca-affect-use-health-services.

Retail Clinics -- Retail clinics are primarily for-profit healthcare facilities located inside retail locations, such as pharmacies and grocery stores. Today, there are about 2,300 retail clinics in 43 states and DC, serving 30 million people and growing. The majority of retail clinics are led by nurse practitioners, with a smaller number staffed by physician assistants. The care encompasses basic primary care, preventive and wellness services, as well as some chronic disease monitoring and treatment. The clinics make care convenient and accessible by offering extended evening and weekend hours, visits that last 15-20 minutes, a transparent price structure, and costs that are 40 percent to 80 percent lower than other health care settings and no federal subsidies are provided.[14]

Nurse-Managed Health Clinics (NMHCs) -- NMHCs are not-for-profit community-based health centers primarily led by nurse practitioners. They offer affordable, accessible, high quality primary care, health promotion, and disease prevention services to underserved populations, regardless of their ability to pay. Currently, there are approximately 500 of these clinics in operation across the country, serving five million. About 60 percent of NMHCs are affiliated with schools of nursing and serve as low cost, community-based clinical training sites for a range of health professions.

School-Based Health Centers (SBHCs) -- SBHCs provide convenient, accessible, and comprehensive health care services where children and adolescents spend the majority of their time: in school. There are over 2,300 SBHCs in 49 states and DC; most are run by nurse practitioners or physician assistants serving millions of students. Services are comprehensive, encompassing basic primary care, well-child visits, preventive screenings, immunizations, and behavioral health and oral health services, among others. More than 55 percent of SBHCs extend care beyond the school by serving patients from the surrounding community. Studies have found that SBHCs reduce inappropriate emergency room use and hospitalizations for children with asthma.

Return on Investment: Cost savings are supported by the following findings:
- The average cost per visit at a retail clinic is about $60 compared to $356 for the emergency room, $124 for an urgent care center, and $127 for a traditional primary care physician visit.[15]
- Evaluation and management costs for nurse practitioner patients in Medicare were 11 to 29 percent lower compared to the evaluation and management costs for primary care physicians in Medicare.[16]

[14] Mehrotra, Ateev, Llu Hangsheng, John L. Adams, et al. Comparing Costs and Quality of Care at Retail Clinics with that of Other Medical Settings for 3 Common Illnesses. *Annals of Internal Medicine.151 no. 5*. Pages:321-328. [Accessed 2009].

[15] Mehrotra, Ateev, Llu Hangsheng, John L. Adams, et al. "Comparing Costs and Quality of Care at Retail Clinics with that of Other Medical Settings for 3 Common Illnesses." *Annals of Internal Medicine.151 no. 5*. Pages:321-328. [Accessed 2009].

- A 2015 review examining quality of care research conducted since 1980 concluded that "there is high-quality evidence that nurse practitioners in alternative provider ambulatory primary care roles are cost-effective with patient outcomes that are equivalent to or better than usual care and with lower costs.[17]

High quality is supported by the following findings:
- In 2012, a literature review conducted by the National Governor's Association concluded, "nurse practitioners can perform many primary care services as well as physicians do, and achieve equal or higher patient satisfaction rates among their patients."[18]
- Data from 37 articles published from 1990 to 2009 indicated that the care provided by nurse practitioners was comparable or better than the care provided by other providers across 11 outcome measures. The data also shows that outcomes related to health status, functional status, number of emergency department visits and hospitalizations, blood glucose, blood pressure, and mortality are similar for nurse practitioners and physicians.[19]
- Quality scores and rates of preventive care offered at retail clinics are similar to other delivery settings.[20]
- According to the Robert Wood Johnson Foundation, nurse practitioners are the primary care providers most likely to be working in rural or remote areas.

MARKET-DRIVEN CONSUMER-DRIVEN HEALTHCARE MODEL OPPORTUNITIES AND RECOMMEDATIONS:

---

[16] Perloff, J., DesRoches, C., and Buerhaus, P. (2015)." Comparing the Cost of Care Provided to Medicare Beneficiaries Assigned to Primary Care Nurse Practitioners and Physicians." *Health Services Research.* EPub.

[17] Martin-Misner, R., Harbman, P., Donald, F., Reid, K., Kilpatrick, K. et al. (2015). "Cost-effectiveness of nurse practitioners in primary and specialised ambulatory care: systematic review." BMJ Open, 5:e007167 doi:10.1136/bmjopen-2014-007167.

[18] Maria, Schiff et al. The Role of Nurse Practitioners in Meeting Increasing Demand for Primary Care. National Governors Association. [Accessed 2012].

[19] Stanik-Hutt, J., Newhouse, R., White, K., Johantgen, M., Bass, E., et al (2013). The Quality and Effectiveness of Care Provided by Nurse Practitioners. *The Journal for Nurse Practitioners.* Pages: 9(8), 492-500.

[20] Mehrotra, Ateev, Llu Hangsheng, John L. Adams, et al. Comparing Costs and Quality of Care at Retail Clinics with that of Other Medical Settings for 3 Common Illnesses. *Annals of Internal Medicine.151 no. 5.* Pages: 321-328. [Accessed 2009].

Return on Investment for Retail Clinics
The national presence and growing popularity of retail clinics places them in an ideal position to further the Trump administration's healthcare agenda.

Retail clinics and Access to Care
- **Consumer-driven and patient–centered:** Retail clinics emphasize consumer-driven principles of care that promote personal economic freedom. Because of their flexible schedules and easily accessible locations, retail clinics allow patients to receive care at the time and place that is most convenient to them. They also offer transparent pricing, so patients know exactly how much services cost.
- **Conveniently located and easily accessible:** 30 to 40 percent of the American population now lives within a 10-minute drive of a retail clinic.[21] This national penetration means that retail clinics can offer people additional healthcare options as the administration considers plans to repeal and replace the Affordable Care Act (ACA).
- **Addressing the provider shortage:** Retail clinics relieve the strain on the primary care physician workforce by utilizing non-physician providers, like nurse practitioners and physician assistants, who are able to offer the same quality of care at a reduced cost.
- **A critical healthcare entry point for value-based care:** Approximately 60 percent of retail clinic patients report not having a primary care provider.[22] The clinics serve as critical health care access points for these patients. Additionally, because retail clinics are often the first point of contact for patients accessing the healthcare system, they can serve as a central hub in any value-based care structure.

Retail Clinics and Cost
- **The lowest cost option for care:** The average cost per visit at a retail clinic is about $60 compared to $356 for the emergency room, $124 for an urgent care center, and $127 for a traditional primary care physician visit.[23]
- **Retail clinics lower costs by diverting patients from more costly healthcare access points:** 12 to 14 percent of all ED visits can be seen at convenient care clinics.[24]

---

[21] Rudavsky, R, Craig Evan Pollock, Ateev Mehrotra. "The Geographic Distribution, Ownership, Prices, and Scope of Practice at Retail Clinics." *Annals of Internal Medicine, 151, No. 5*. Pages: 321-328. [Accessed 2009].
[22] Mehrotra, Ateev, and Judith R. Lave. "Visits to Retail Clinics Grew Fourfold From 2007 To 2009, Although Their Share of Overall Outpatient Visits Remain Low." *Health Affairs, 31, No. 9*. [Accessed 2012].
[23] Mehrotra, Ateev, Llu Hangsheng, John L. Adams, et al. "Comparing Costs and Quality of Care at Retail Clinics with that of Other Medical Settings for 3 Common Illnesses." *Annals of Internal Medicine.151 no. 5*. Pages: 321-328. [Accessed 2009].
[24] Weinick, Robin M., Rachel M. Burns, Ateev Mehrotra. "Many Emergency Department Visits Could be Handled at Urgent Care Centers and Retail Clinics." *Health Affairs, 29, No.*

Retail Clinics and Quality
- **Retail clinics have a record of success in meeting care quality benchmarks:** Quality scores and rates of preventive care offered at retail clinics are similar to other delivery settings.[25]

POLICY RECOMMENDATIONS:
The three key policy recommendations detailed below would assist the Trump administration in emphasizing free market principles and personal economic freedom, while also broadening healthcare access, making care more affordable and improving care quality.

✓ **Establish a unified system of credentialing for retail clinic providers.**

Delays in the credentialing of retail clinic providers could be reduced and access to care expanded by establishing a centralized credentialing clearinghouse for all retail clinic providers. A 2012 article published in the New England Journal of Medicine states, "Credentialing and other systems that are used to establish contracts between providers and health plans are riddled with redundancy, with many organizations collecting virtually identical information from providers...a coordinated, nationwide credentialing system that is employed across the public and private sectors could save nearly $1 billion per year for providers."[26]

Retail clinics are, with a few exceptions, operated by national organizations, like CVS Health, Walgreens, and Walmart. The fact that retail clinic operators have national reach means that they could more easily adapt to and implement a uniform system of national credentialing for retail clinic providers. Establishing such a system would decrease the administrative burden on state and federal agencies, retail clinic operators and providers, while increasing access for patients and lowering costs.

✓ **Support a demonstration project evaluating a system of national contracting for retail health clinics.**

---

9. Pages: 1630-1636. [Accessed 2010].

[25] Mehrotra, Ateev, Llu Hangsheng, John L. Adams, et al. Comparing Costs and Quality of Care at Retail Clinics with that of Other Medical Settings for 3 Common Illnesses. *Annals of Internal Medicine.151 no. 5*. Pages: 321-328. [Accessed 2009].

[26] Cutler, D., Wikler, E., and Basch, P. Reducing Administrative Costs and Improving the Health Care System. *New England Journal of Medicine*. Pages: 367:1875-1878. Available at: http://www.nejm.org/doi/full/10.1056/NEJMp1209711. [Accessed 2012].

The national reach of retail clinics also makes them ideal for evaluating the benefits of a national contracting policy and uniform reimbursement rate for retail clinics. Just as with credentialing, a system of national contracting would reduce administrative burdens on providers and administrative staff, as well as costs. It would also lower the cost of services. Under Medicare, non-physician providers, like nurse practitioners, are reimbursed at 85 percent of the physician rate for most services. Since retail clinics use nurse practitioners and other non-physician providers, carrying this rate over to other health care programs would standardize contacting and lower costs.

✓ Support the expansion of the advance practice pharmacist (APP) role.

Pharmacists are the nation's third largest health profession. Most states currently relegate these providers to dispensing medications, providing health promotion and disease prevention education, and assisting in the navigation of health systems as it pertains to medications. However, four states -- California, Montana, New Mexico, and North Carolina -- have established an APP designation that empowers pharmacists to do more, such as provide limited primary care, exercise narrow prescriptive authority pursuant to a collaborative agreement, order tests, administer immunizations, and provide chronic care education. Initial research on the APP role has shown its potential to produce positive outcomes. An analysis of North Carolina pharmacists found that expanding the role of pharmacists within the healthcare team lowered risks linked to various health issues, such as low-density lipoprotein cholesterol, blood pressure, and adverse drug events.[27] Research from North Carolina also showed that APPs lowered costs by reducing both emergency room utilization and inpatient visits.[28]

The Trump administration could lower costs and expand access to care by supporting the establishment of a demonstration project testing the effectiveness of the APP role. Such a demonstration project would provide evidence evaluating the benefits of directly reimbursing pharmacists, as well as the capacity of APPs to decrease the cost of care (e.g., through lower emergency room usage and hospitalizations) and enhance access. The fact that retail clinics are often located in pharmacies and operate in close proximity to pharmacists makes them an ideal location to host a potential demonstration project.

---

[27] National Governors Association (NGA). "The expanding role of pharmacists in a transformed health care system." www.nga.org/files/live/sites/NGA/files/pdf/2015/1501TheExpandingRoleOfPharmacists.pdf.

[28] Kislan, M., Bernstein, A., Fearrington, L., and Ives, T. (2016). "Advanced Practice Pharmacists: a retrospective evaluation of the efficacy and cost of Clinical Pharmacist Practitioners managing ambulatory Medicare patients in North Carolina (APPLE-NC)." BMC Health Services Research: Available at: https://bmchealthservres.biomedcentral.com/articles/10.1186/s12913-016-1851-2.

CONSUMER-FRIENDLY HEALTH INSURANCE PLANS -- REFERENCE-BASED PRICING (RBP PLANS):

Currently, there are major variations in cost for some medical services from one provider to the next. Worse, most often patients don't know how much a service will cost even when they are at the doctor's office -- they find out only when they receive an explanation of benefits (EOB) in the mail weeks after the care was provided. Consumer-friendly Reference-based Pricing (RBP) Plans are designed to change this.

So how does RBP work? Simply put, the idea is that a healthcare provider's billed price for a certain service does not represent the cost of care or the market value. Therefore, the RBP plan will pay the reasonable value for the service, factoring in the full range of fees (private and public) that comes into a health system. RBPs provide an incentive for the consumer to review pricing information in advance and to select a provider accordingly. Employers typically start off with a short list of services/procedures included in RBP plans that expands as members gain experience with the approach and learn to use the decision-making support tools. Services where we see great cost variation without much variation in quality -- like an MRI -- are often a major focus of the RBP strategy. Also, once an RBP plan has been introduced in a community, you often see the highest-cost providers lowering their prices so they don't lose business.

RBP is all about transparency. As out-of-pocket costs rise, both employers and employees are more interested in information on the cost of services. Transparency is not just about the price. Many of the transparency tools also include access information, (such as wait time) and some type of quality indicator. A best practice would be to pair pricing transparency with medical decision support coaching, to convey the message to employees that now that they know how much the treatment costs, they might be interested in knowing more about alternatives to consider.

It is estimated that RBP will drive down healthcare costs by 40 percent based on the current insurance market.[29] While it traditionally works best for self-insured employees, it will also work well for small employers who join larger employee benefit networks.

Below is a list of actions Congress could take to support RBP

- Require each provider's charge master (list price) to be referenced in Medicare (for transparency across providers and fairness)

---

[29] AmWins Group Benefits. "Four Reasons Why Reference-based Pricing Could Become the Norm for Self-insured Employer Groups." Factsheet Available at: http://www.amwins.com/docs/default-source/Insights/client-advisory_referencepricing_1-15.pdf.

- Some providers charge as much as 10 to 20 percent of the current Medicare reimbursement rate for services to the uninsured. This could be changed by requiring that providers charge uninsured persons no more than the reasonable and customary amount for services. This cost could be determined by comparing the amount of rolling weighted reimbursement actually received by the provider over the preceding four quarters to what Medicare would have reimbursed during that same period. (For example, if the average received by the provider over the last four quarters was $1,500 and Medicare would have paid $1,000, the provider would be able to collect 150 percent of the Medicare reimbursement rate)
- Permit medical underwriting, which lowers costs for those who are healthy
- Provide tax incentives that encourage the adoption of RBP plans
- Revise the Fair Debt Collection Practices Act to make it clearly illegal to collect a debt from a consumer in excess of the reasonable and customary cost for services
- The ACA includes a provision under Section 501(r) of the Internal Revenue Code that is designed to prevent providers from billing insured individuals for additional costs once the provider has been paid a reasonable and customary amount for the services, but the IRS has not enforced this provision. Enforcing this provision could control cost and support RBP

Note: All of these changes could be introduced as part of legislation allowing states to opt-out, so as not to create a federal mandate.

Establish a Federally Qualified Health Center (FQHC) Special Populations Reimbursement Rate for Nurse-Led Practices and Super Utilizers of Services:

Even though nurse-managed health centers (NMHCs) and school based health centers (SBHCs) serve a high percentage of uninsured and vulnerable patients with complex, costly conditions, a large percentage of these centers do not qualify for federally qualified health center funding. For example, only about 40 percent of SBHCs partner with FQHCs. Section 330 of the Public Health Service Act provides health centers caring for special populations, such as migrants and the homeless, an enhanced reimbursement rate designed to cover the cost of caring for the uninsured and super utilizers. Establishing an enhanced special population reimbursement rate for nurse-led practices caring for vulnerable populations would position them on equal footing with other safety-net providers, extend primary care to more patients, lower costs, and improve care quality. It would also enhance competition among safety-net providers, since nurse-led practices use lower cost non-physician providers, whereas most traditional FQHCs are physician directed.

A special populations rate could be established through the creation of a demonstration project involving Medicare and Medicaid patients. Statistics from the Commonwealth Fund show that a demonstration project expanding the number of patients with access to a healthcare home could reduce hospital admission costs by 18 percent and total healthcare costs by 7 percent, while increasing the number of patients receiving proper care coordination by 20 percent.[30]

Additionally, providers are often unwilling or unable to handle the complex needs accompanying patients with intellectual and developmental disabilities (I/DD). As a result, children and adults with I/DD often go without care. This lack of access exacerbates existing health problems, making them more serious and more costly when they are finally treated. In fact, state Medicaid programs spend close to $60 billion annually serving children and adults with I/DD. These costs could be lowered by the establishment of a Medicaid demonstration project granting a special reimbursement rate to NMHCs caring for I/DD patients as part of a specialized primary care model. Under the integrated initiative, I/DD patients would receive primary care, home health, and dental care from nurses and other providers at a bundled rate of $225 per visit. The bundled rate will ensure that patients with I/DD have access to more consistent and comprehensive preventative care that leads to fewer emergency room visits and reduces the probability that more serious conditions will develop.

POLICY RECOMMENDATIONS:

- ✓ Offer and support health insurance alternatives, including tax incentives and other incentives for companies and government plans to use Reference Based Pricing Plans (RBP), also known as consumer-friendly health plans (recommendations listed above).
- ✓ Support the establishment of a special population's reimbursement rate that will put nurse-led practices on equal footing with FQHCs and enhances competition.
- ✓ Support the establishment of a special population's reimbursement rate for NMHCs offering care to I/DD patients as part of an integrated care bundled payment model.

About the Convenient Care Association

The Convenient Care Association (CCA) is the national trade association for the over 2,300 retail-based convenient care clinics that provide consumers with accessible, affordable, quality healthcare in retail-based locations. CCA works primarily to enhance and sustain the growth of the convenient care industry through sharing resources, best practices and common standards of operation.

---

[30] The Commonwealth Fund. Primary Care: Our First Line of Defense. http://www.commonwealthfund.org/publications/health-reform-and-you/primary-care-our-first-line-of-defense.

CCA's membership encompasses more than 97 percent of the more than 2,300 retail-based clinics in operation providing basic primary and chronic disease care in the clinics. Retail-based clinics provide a convenient access point into the healthcare system and play an increasingly important role in population health. The clinics are an integral part of community networks and serve as healthcare hubs for millions by providing care and linkage to additional services. CCA has partnerships with national organizations and engages in scaling and replication of high-impact models, consulting and technical assistance to other organizations and the promotion of promising practices within education and health through the dissemination of articles and publications in national journals.

Example 2: Nurse-Led Care: A Market-Driven Health Care Solution

I. Introduction -- President-elect Trump has said he envisions a health care system that emphasizes free market principles and personal economic freedom, while also broadening healthcare access, making care more affordable, and improving care quality. The nation's looming primary care physician shortage and increasing demand for care presents a major obstacle to accomplishing this vision. According to the American Association of Medical Colleges, the country faces a projected shortfall of 14,900 to 35,600 physicians by 2025. Simultaneously, primary care office visits are expected to increase by 3.8 percent nationally, coupled with a 2.2 percent increase in emergency room visits. More than 83 percent of the country's 220,000 licensed nurse practitioners are certified in primary care, but the potential of well-educated nurses with advanced degrees to fill gaps in care, improve outcomes, and reduce costs has not been fully realized due to a variety of regulatory restrictions at the federal and state levels. Taking full advantage of nurse-led care will further the Trump administration's health care priorities by giving consumers more options for accessible, affordable, quality care, enhancing market-driven competition in healthcare, and lowering costs.

The National Nurse-Led Care Consortium (NNCC), a 501(c) (3) not-for-profit that advocates for nurses as leaders in healthcare delivery, has prepared this memorandum, which presents an introduction to models of nurse-led care, an overview of the return on investment in nurse-led care, and a description of four key policy recommendations the administration should consider in order to immediately begin extending the benefits of nurse-led care to consumers. In short, the key policy recommendations are:
(1) Support a demonstration project establishing a special populations' reimbursement rate for nurse-led clinics caring for vulnerable populations, like nurse-managed clinics (NMHCs) and school-based health centers;
(2) Enforce existing laws preventing discrimination against Advanced Practice Registered Nurse (APRN) providers by managed care organizations and health insurance vendors. APRNs include: Nurse Practitioners, as well as Certified Nurse Midwives, Certified Registered Nurse Anesthetists, and Clinical Nurse Specialists;
(3) Support a dual provider credentialing process for Medicare and Medicaid; and,

(4) Support a demonstration project that provides a special reimbursement rate for NMHCs caring for adults and children with intellectual and developmental disabilities (I/DD).

II. Models of Nurse-led Care -- Please find below a brief description of four prominent models of nurse-led care.

Nurse-Managed Health Clinics (NMHCs) -- NMHCs are not-for-profit community-based health centers primarily led by nurse practitioners. They offer affordable, accessible, high quality primary care, health promotion, and disease prevention services to underserved populations, regardless of their ability to pay. Currently, there are approximately 250 of these clinics in operation across the country. About 60 percent of NMHCs are affiliated with schools of nursing and serve as low cost, community-based clinical training sites for a range of health professions.

Retail Clinics -- Retail clinics are primarily for-profit healthcare facilities located inside retail locations, such as pharmacies and grocery stores. Today, there are about 2,300 retail clinics in 43 states and DC. The majority of retail clinics are led by nurse practitioners, with a smaller number staffed by physician assistants. The care encompasses basic primary care, preventive and wellness services, as well as some chronic disease monitoring and treatment. The clinics make care convenient and accessible by offering extended evening and weekend hours, visits that last 15-20 minutes, a transparent price structure, and costs that are 40 to 80 percent lower than other health care settings.

School-Based Health Centers (SBHCs) -- SBHCs provide convenient, accessible, and comprehensive health care services where children and adolescents spend the majority of their time: in school. There are more than 2,300 SBHCs in 49 states and DC; most are run by nurse practitioners or physician assistants. Services are comprehensive, encompassing basic primary care, well-child visits, preventive screenings, immunizations, and behavioral health and oral health services, among others. More than 55 percent of SBHCs extend care beyond the school by serving patients from the surrounding community. Studies have found that SBHCs reduce inappropriate emergency room use and hospitalizations for children with asthma.

Nurse-led Private Practices – More than 20,000 nurse practitioners certified in primary care operate their own private practices or are part of nurse-led group practices. Primary care nurse practitioners are significantly more likely than other primary care providers to practice in urban and rural areas. They are also more likely to provide care in a wider range of community settings and serve a high proportion of uninsured or vulnerable patients. Evidence shows that outcomes for patients of nurse practitioners in primary care are equivalent or better than outcomes for patients of other primary care providers. These include outcomes related to disease-specific physiologic measures, improvement in pathological condition, reduction of symptoms, mortality, hospitalizations and other utilization measures, as well as patient satisfaction.

III. Return on Investment -- Nurse-led care, while being equivalent in quality, lowers costs throughout the healthcare system. Cost savings are supported by the following findings:

The average cost per visit at a nurse-led retail clinic is about $60 compared to $356 for the emergency room, $124 for an urgent care center, and $127 for a traditional primary care physician visit.

Between 1990 and 2000, one NMHC was able to reduce emergency room visits by uninsured patients by 25 percent. This led to an estimated cost savings of $13.9 million.

Evaluation and management costs for nurse practitioner patients in Medicare were 11 to 29 percent lower compared to the evaluation and management costs for primary care physicians in Medicare.

A 2015 review examining quality of care research conducted since 1980 concluded that "there is high-quality evidence that nurse practitioners in alternative provider ambulatory primary care roles are cost-effective with patient outcomes that are equivalent to or better than usual care and with lower costs.

The freedom to choose nurse-led models of care increases access to high quality care, as demonstrated by the following:

In 2012, a literature review conducted by the National Governor's Association concluded, "nurse practitioners can perform many primary care services as well as physicians do, and achieve equal or higher patient satisfaction rates among their patients."

Data from 37 articles published from 1990 to 2009 indicated that the care provided by nurse practitioners was comparable or better than the care provided by other providers across 11 outcome measures. The data also shows that outcomes related to health status, functional status, number of emergency department visits and hospitalizations, blood glucose, blood pressure, and mortality are similar for nurse practitioners and physicians.

Quality scores and rates of preventive care offered at retail clinics are similar to other delivery settings. According to the Robert Wood Johnson Foundation, NPs are the primary care providers most likely to be working in rural or remote areas.

IV. Policy Recommendations -- The four key policy recommendations detailed below would assist the Trump administration in supporting a consumer-driven healthcare environment by leveraging nurse-led models of care.

Support a demonstration project establishing a special populations' reimbursement rate for nurse-led clinics caring for vulnerable populations -- Even though nurse-managed health centers (NHHCs) and school-based health centers (SBHCs) serve a high percentage of uninsured and vulnerable patients with complex, costly conditions, a large percentage of these centers do not qualify for federally qualified health center funding. For example, only about 40 percent of SBHCs partner with Federally Qualified Health Centers (FQHCs). Section 330 of the Public Health Service Act provides health centers caring for special populations, such as migrants and the homeless, an enhanced reimbursement rate designed to cover the cost of caring for the uninsured and super utilizers. Establishing an enhanced special population reimbursement rate for nurse-led practices caring for vulnerable populations would position them on equal footing with other safety-net providers, extend primary care to more patients, lower costs, and improve care quality.

A special populations rate could be established through the creation of a demonstration project involving Medicare and Medicaid patients. Statistics from the Commonwealth Fund show that a demonstration project expanding the number of patients with access to a healthcare home could reduce hospital admission costs by 18 percent and total healthcare costs by 7 percent, while increasing the number of patients receiving proper care coordination by 20 percent.

Enforce existing laws preventing discrimination against APRN providers in managed care organizations -- Recent research shows that 25 percent of the nation's managed care organizations (MCOs) will not contract with nurse practitioners as primary care providers. There is no justifiable reason for this type of arbitrary discrimination, especially considering nurse practitioners are less costly and deliver care that is equal or better than other types of providers. The refusal of MCOs to contract with nurse practitioner primary care providers only serves to restrict competition and inhibit consumer choice. In 1997, a Republican-led Congress passed the Balanced Budget Act of 1997 (PL 105-33). Section 1932(b)(7) of the Act contains language intended to stop arbitrary discrimination by MCOs against non-physician providers, like nurse practitioners. The language reads: "A group health plan and a health insurance issuer offering group or individual health insurance coverage shall not discriminate with respect to participation under the plan or coverage against any health care provider who is acting within the scope of that provider's license or certification under applicable State law. "

Similar language exists in the regulations for the Medicare and Medicaid programs. When commenting on the intent of the Balanced Budget Act language, the Department of Health and Human Services under President Bush emphasized the need to prevent anti-competitive provider discrimination, stating,

"We believe that in section 1932(b)(7) of the Act the Congress intended only to ensure that MCOs do not adopt arbitrary policies concerning non-physician providers who, in the past, may have been discriminated against because they do not hold the same licenses and certifications as practicing physicians. Any discriminatory actions may have provided beneficiaries with fewer choices and may have reduced beneficiaries' overall access to quality health care."

Despite the existence of this language, the Obama administration has not taken any action to ensure nurse practitioners are not discriminated against by MCOs. Enforcing the provider non-discrimination regulations in Medicare and Medicaid will immediately bring greater competition to MCO networks and promote greater consumer choice.

Support a dual provider credentialing process for Medicare and Medicaid -- Nurse practitioners and other providers who apply to be credentialed in state Medicaid programs often wait six to eight months before they receive provider numbers and can begin billing for care provided to enrollees. These long delays in the credentialing process impact access to care, because providers are not reimbursed for the care offered to Medicaid recipients during the waiting period. The main cause of these delays appears to be bureaucratic inefficiency. Many states require providers to meet extensive regulatory requirements to complete the provider enrollment application, yet the agencies charged with processing the applications cannot keep up with the demand.

The Trump administration could streamline the credentialing process by instituting a dual provider credentialing process for Medicare and Medicaid. Most of the documentation providers submit to enroll in Medicare is the same documentation required by state Medicaid programs. Therefore, instituting a dual credentialing process for the two programs would eliminate duplicate regulatory requirements. The system could simply transfer documents already submitted during the Medicare credentialing process to state Medicaid programs, or providers that complete the Medicare credentialing process could be automatically enrolled in Medicaid.

Support a demonstration project that provides a special reimbursement rate for NMHCs caring for adults and children with intellectual and developmental disabilities (I/DD) -- Children and adults with I/DD tend to have more complex healthcare needs than those without. For example, those with Down syndrome are more likely than the general population to develop heart disease and early onset dementia, and patients with muscular dystrophy experience earlier rates of mortality. The problems faced by this population are further complicated by their lack of access. Providers are often unwilling or unable to handle the complex needs accompanying patients with I/DD. As a result, children and adults with I/DD often go without care. This lack of access exacerbates existing health problems, making them more serious and more costly when they are finally treated. In fact, state Medicaid programs spend close to $60 billion annually serving children and adults with I/DD.

The research highlighted above illustrates that nurse-led models of care, like NMHCs, are more cost effective than traditional models of care. The fact that NMHCs also operate in more convenient, easily accessible community-based locations places them in an ideal position to serve patients with I/DD. The Trump administration could decrease Medicare and Medicaid costs while increasing the availability of care to this population by supporting the establishment of a Medicare demonstration project granting a special reimbursement rate to NMHCs caring for I/DD patients as part of a specialized primary care model. Under the integrated initiative, I/DD patients would receive primary care, home health, and dental care from nurses and other providers at a bundled rate of $225 per visit. The bundled rate will ensure that patients with I/DD have access to more consistent and comprehensive preventative care that leads to fewer emergency room visits and reduces the probability that more serious conditions will develop. Additionally, the project will offer evidence of the model's effectiveness in caring for I/DD patients, which could be used to expand the demonstration if the return on investment is positive.

Example 3: General Policy Brief designed to meet with Congress person to discuss areas where he or she might help.

PROPOSAL FOR SPECIALIZED MEDICAL HOME SKILLED NURSING AND PRIMARY CARE MODEL FOR CHILDREN AND ADULTS WITH INTELLECTUAL AND DEVELOPMENTAL DISABILITIES AND MEDICAL COMORBIDITIES

Introduction:
Woods Services is a 501(c)(3) Pennsylvania nonprofit, health and human services corporation that serves 650 vulnerable children and adults with intellectual and developmental disabilities (I/DD) in community-based educational and residential settings in Pennsylvania. Children and adults with I/DD, need accessible, affordable, quality primary and preventive healthcare along with dental and behavioral health services. Serving the I/DD population often requires highly skilled and specialized primary medical and dental care for a population which may have medical and behavioral complications resulting from genetic or other types of conditions.

<u>Unlike the cursory physical exams most of us are accustomed to, primary care visits for people with I/DD take an average of 45 minutes to an hour, given the medical and emotional complexities of the I/DD population with medical and behavioral co-morbidities.</u> Additionally, direct access to highly skilled care in close proximity to where the I/DD population reside is critical to prevent unnecessary emergency room visits and hospitalizations for this very vulnerable and medically compromised population.

Woods proposes three recommendations, which will improve primary care services for the I/DD population with medical and behavioral comorbidities. These are 1) establishing a definition of a special population of people with I/DD and significant medical and behavioral comorbidities; 2) establishing a special population reimbursement rate for primary care for this population, and 3) establishing a demonstration skilled nursing facility that tests a model of care that will improve outcomes for this population.

Background:
According to the Centers for Disease Control, there are 4.5 million people in the U.S. with intellectual/developmental disabilities (I/DD). While many people with I/DD live independently and with few or no supports, a subset of people with I/DD have multiple severe conditions that require highly specialized supports, increased access to primary care and careful care coordination. Some of these conditions include such diverse genetic or neurologic conditions as traumatic brain injury, autism spectrum disorder, muscular dystrophy, cerebral palsy, epilepsy, in addition to mental illness, emotional, and behavioral challenges. It is a challenge the meet the complex medical and behavioral health needs of this population in traditional settings. **Despite the trend in the disability advocacy community to push for the closure of all residential facilities and to provide all services in a community-based setting, the medically compromised population of people with I/DD that Woods serves to its main campus would not be well-served in community settings.** Woods maintains the belief that the residents of its main campus programs are so medically fragile that they would be at great risk of harm if they were not able to receive the comprehensive health services of its residential model.

Woods and its affiliates provides innovative and integrated health, behavioral, education, workforce, and care management services to 4,000 children and adults in the I/DD, child welfare, behavioral, and acquired brain injury public health sectors. Of these, 650 children and adults with I/DD and complex medical and genetic disorders are served in residential treatment on its main campus. The mission of Woods is to advance the quality of life and standard of care for individuals with exceptional needs. Woods provides the appropriate level of care that ranges from personal care assistance to highly skilled nursing and complex medical care that can only be delivered by disability-trained professionals, doctors and specialists. Woods and its affiliates primarily serve individuals with residential, education and vocational services from Pennsylvania, New Jersey, and New York, but has a national reach given its expertise in serving people who are medically and behaviorally frail and vulnerable.

Definition of Intellectual and Developmental Disabilities

Intellectual disability is a disability that occurs before age 18. People with this disability experience significant limitations in two main areas: 1) intellectual functioning and 2) adaptive behavior. These limitations are expressed in the person's conceptual, social, and practical everyday living skills. Typically, people with an IQ below 70 are considered to have an intellectual disability. People with an IQ below 25 are considered to have profound intellectual disability; many people with profound intellectual disability also have genetic conditions which may have caused the disability, and which may further complicate the person's health status. Adaptive behavior is the collection of conceptual, social and practical skills that people have learned in order to function in their everyday lives.

According to the Developmental Disabilities Act (Pub. L. 106-402), the term developmental disability means a severe, chronic disability that:
- is attributable to a mental or physical impairment or a combination of those impairments;
- occurs before the individual reaches age 22;
- is likely to continue indefinitely;
- results in substantial functional limitations in three or more of the following areas of major life activity: (i) self-care, (ii) receptive and expressive language, (iii) learning, (iv) mobility, (v) self-direction, (vi) capacity for independent living, and (vii) economic self-sufficiency; and
- reflects the individual's need for a combination and sequence of special, interdisciplinary, or generic services, individualized supports, or other forms of assistance that are of lifelong or extended duration and are individually planned and coordinated.
- Before the age of ten, an infant or child with developmental delays may be considered to have an intellectual or developmental disability if his or her disabilities are likely to meet the above criteria without intervention.

Many individuals with intellectual disability also meet the definition of developmental disability. However, it is estimated that at least half of individuals with intellectual disability will not meet the functional limitation requirement in the DD definition. The DD definition requires substantial functional limitations in three or more areas of major life activity. The intellectual disability definition requires significant limitations in one area of adaptive behavior (The Arc, 2016)

In order to address the complex needs of the medically fragile I/DD population, Woods has moved towards a specialized primary and dental care practice coupled with a home health model in which centralized and integrated medical, dental, and behavioral health services are provided in a close and accessible location to the campus- and community-based I/DD population Woods serves. The success of this health program thus far is evident in the fact that participants typically exceed predicted mortality rates and the negative progression of syndromes, such as Rett Syndrome (a genetic mutation on X chromosome, which causes a neurological disorder with slowed head growth, severe scoliosis, eventually compromising the respiratory system) is slowed or halted. In addition, this model has been able to ensure the provision of dental and psychiatric services, two of the greatest areas of need for this population.

Issue 1: It is undisputed that many children and adults with I/DD tend to have multiple health issues and more complex medical issues than those without, including medical and behavioral co-morbidities and frailties such as chronic disease and behavioral health issue. Given the special needs of this group, and the history of not being well-served by the traditional medical and behavioral health community, we propose assigning a special population definition to this group in order to ensure that comprehensive services can continue to be provided in a way that meets their high level of need.

Woods provides comprehensive services to individuals with I/DD with the *most* complex medical and behavioral issues. When intellectual or developmental disabilities are linked to a variety of genetic disorders, the medical challenges may significantly exceed those of persons without such genetic anomalies. Consider the association of heart disease and early onset dementia in persons who have Down syndrome, or the early mortality experienced by persons with Rett Syndrome or Duchene's muscular dystrophy, or weight-induced medical problems experienced by persons with Prader-Willi Syndrome.

Recommendation: Create an *I/DD Medical and Behavioral Frail* definition for this special population that includes having an I/DD diagnosis, coupled with medical, genetic and/or behavioral co-morbidities and frailties.

Issue 2: The special population of people with I/DD who are medically compromised as a result of a combination of genetic disorders, chronic disease and behavioral health issues requires much more time in primary care visits, an increased need for care coordination, as well as greater skills and experience with this population.

Section 330 of the Public Health Service Act provides health centers caring for special populations, such as migrants and the homeless, an enhanced reimbursement rate designed to cover the cost of caring for the uninsured and "super-utilizers" of health care services. Establishing an enhanced special population reimbursement rate for practices caring for vulnerable populations positions them on equal footing with other safety-net providers, extends primary care to more patients, lowers costs, and improves care quality.

According to the American Association on Intellectual and Developmental Disabilities there is a marked health disparity between persons with I/DD and those without I/DD. *Evidence-based studies demonstrate that the medical needs of persons with I/DD are greater than the general population, and as a result, are more costly.* In fact, close to $60 billion is spent annually in Medicaid funding by government to serve children and adults with I/DD. Currently, Woods provides primary health and dental care, skilled nursing, as well as other comprehensive services Woods' frail clients require. Visits by clients of Woods now account for more than **$2.5 million in costs for emergency room visits and hospitalizations a year.**

Furthermore, many people with I/DD may have conditions overlooked, especially chronic diseases that are common in the general population (diabetes, asthma, obesity, dental issues, cardiovascular disease), because health care providers may be exclusively focused during a health care visit on conditions that only relate to the person's disability (Anderson et al, 2013). With this population, rules, regulations and services must be sufficiently person-centered to accommodate both consumer choice and consumer need. A one size fits all model is not satisfactory. A special population rate would allow for the extended time needed for primary care visits during which multiple issues are likely to need to be addressed. In addition, a special population rate could help alleviate health disparities among people with I/DD by potentially increasing the number of providers and access to services. With this proposed model, Woods would be able to create a true medical home for Woods clients and community members, expand access to primary and dental care and reduce the cost of care for its population by at least one-third.

Recommendation: A Special Population portable adjustable reimbursement rate for the *I/DD Medical and Behavioral Frail* of at least $220 per visit for primary care should be established under Health Resources and Services Administration and CMS. Expanding the health services that Woods provides will result in increased access to primary care, improved care coordination, and a reduction in ER visits and hospitalizations among its residential and community patient resulting in significant overall savings.

Issue 3: Over the past two decades, the disability community, advocates and others have advocated tirelessly to promote the rights of persons with disabilities to live and receive services in home and community settings and to close residential facilities. In fact, the Americans with Disabilities Act (ADA) website uses as its motto, "Community Integration for Everyone." However, the special I/DD Medical and Behavioral Frail population described above requires multiple levels of care -- care which must be individually-tailored, and which may need to change throughout the lifespan and people grow, learn and change. Woods must also advocate for the special population of people with I/DD who also often have genetic disorders, and multiple medical and behavioral issues which make it extremely difficult for appropriate services to be found in community-based settings. Woods' comprehensive residential services provide a solution to this challenge and ensure that medically compromised people with I/DD can receive the services they need, including skilled nursing. Woods believes that without the skilled nursing facility option, its clients would be at extreme risk of harm.

Woods and other major providers of services for people with I/DD, in alignment with this philosophy, have also advocated tirelessly to improve services, to design and promote services to support community integration wherever possible, in terms of living arrangements, in the employment arena, in health care and in other settings. Woods has provided specialized services, including on-site skilled nursing care, for more than 600 residents on its campus, who have not been able to have their needs met in community-based and home settings. Modeled after traditional skilled nursing facilities, Woods provides private and semi-private rooms, meals, nursing care, physical and occupational therapy, speech-language pathology services, medical social services, medications, medical supplies, transportation and dietary counseling, and services though health and occupational professionals who have the skills and expertise to meet the many complicated health and social needs of the most medically frail people with I/DD who would otherwise not be able to access such services on their own in the community. Through the experience of serving hundreds of residents ages 4 - 94 who have a wide range of complex medical, behavioral and emotional needs, Woods has gained tremendous expertise in the provision of comprehensive health and other services to this very vulnerable population. Woods has designed an adaptable model of skilled nursing to carry out this high level of care by compassionate and knowledgeable professionals.

Recommendation: A special skilled nursing facility (SNF) demonstration should be established through CMS at select existing residential I/DD facilities who already serve the complex needs of the I/DD population with medical and behavioral co-morbidities who require 24/7 medical support, like Woods at its Langhorne campus. Specifically, a SNF for the I/DD medical and behavioral frail population should be established at an adjustable rate of at least $400 a day. The skilled nursing facility will include skilled nursing by health care professionals highly experienced with the medically fragile I/DD population and physician and specialty support, which will ensure the continued health, wellness and safety of this vulnerable population, and which will reduce ER visits and hospitalizations.

About Woods

Woods Services is a 501(c)(3) not-for-profit organization that provides a continuum of highly individualized supports and services for 4,000 individuals with the most complex and intensive medical and behavioral healthcare needs through a network of four not-for-profit organizations in Pennsylvania and New Jersey (described below). Woods supports people with the most severe intellectual/developmental disabilities in residential treatment and community settings that best meet their social, emotional and medical needs. Woods applies evidenced-based treatments and a public health approach to develop innovative and individualized supports that empower people with disabilities and challenges to reach their highest potential. Woods Services is headquartered in Langhorne, Bucks County, Pennsylvania and its on-site programs provide supports for 675 children and adults ages 4 - 89 with intellectual disabilities, autism, and other developmental disabilities, brain-injury, neurological disorders, behavioral health challenges, and co-occurring medical conditions. Programs include Beechwood NeuroRehab brain -- injury post-acute rehabilitation, residential services, health and dental care, education, day habilitation, vocational services that include three social enterprises, work center supported employment, clinical services, therapies such as speech, physical therapy, and occupational therapy and assistive technology.

Woods employs more than 3,500 people throughout their network -- roughly 2,200 people in Pennsylvania and 1,300 people in New Jersey. 68 percent of Woods employees are minorities and 69 percent are women.

Woods provides services to consumers from a number of states; with a vast majority of individuals coming from New Jersey (2,044) and Pennsylvania (1,970). In addition to New Jersey and Pennsylvania, client home states include, but are not limited to, New York, Maryland, Delaware, District of Columbia, Virginia, West Virginia, South Carolina, Ohio, Kentucky, Tennessee, Florida, and California. More than 90 percent of consumers and their families served by Woods fall within the low to moderate income bracket, come from diverse backgrounds, and more than 95 percent of Woods clients are under the age of 21.

Woods Services Affiliate Not-for-profit Partners:

Allies
Allies provides community housing and supports for **350 people** with special needs in the communities of their choice throughout New Jersey. They operate Greensleeves Boutiques, which are social enterprises that employ individuals with and without disabilities to manage and staff its stores. They also provide day habilitation, community inclusion services, intensive residential services for children and vocational supports.

Archway Programs
Archway programs serve **1,600 people** with physical, cognitive, emotional, and neurological disabilities in southern New Jersey. Offered programs include education in two schools for youth struggling with behavior disorders and/or multiple disabilities, before and after school programs in **26 schools** in **nine school districts**, career training, early intervention for infants and toddlers, residential and community programs, intensive in-home services for youth with autism, and partial care services for adults with severe mental illness; 12-18 year olds with psychiatric diagnosis; and 5-12 year olds with emotional and/or learning disabilities.

Brian's House
Brian's House provides supports for **210 individuals** with intellectual disability and/or autism, brain-injury, neurological disorders and other developmental disabilities located in Chester County, Pennsylvania. Programs at Brian's House include community homes, vocational training, work center supported employment, transitional employment, supportive employment and day habilitation.

Tabor Services
Tabor meets the needs of **1,406 at-risk children, young adults and families** in Bucks County, Lehigh Valley, and Philadelphia. Tabor provides a wide variety of child welfare services including traditional, emergent, and therapeutic foster care, supportive independent living and mentoring, and it operates one of 10 Community Umbrella Agencies (CUA) in Philadelphia. The CUA provide case management services for **405 families** at risk. Tabor programs include foster care, special needs adoption, in-home protective services, intensive family support, youth mentoring, family reunification and treatment foster care for children who have experienced trauma.

APPENDIX L
POLICY FACT SHEET EXAMPLES

Example 1
Letter to Speaker in the PA State House

Dear Speaker Turzai,

On behalf of the Convenient Care Association (CCA), I am writing to request that you bring HB 100 sponsored by Representative Jesse Topper (R-78) to the House floor for a vote before the end of this legislative session. The CCA was founded in 2006 to provide a unified voice for the retail-based convenient care industry. Convenient care clinics, often referred to as "retail clinics," are healthcare facilities located inside retail locations, such as pharmacies and grocery stores. The industry is currently made up of more than 2,300 retail clinics across the country. Our members have collectively provided more than 35 million patient visits, and over 90 percent of patients are satisfied with clinic services. Retail clinics offer high-quality, low-cost, and accessible healthcare. The care is provided by nurse practitioners and physician assistants, and encompasses basic primary care, preventive and wellness services, and some chronic disease monitoring and treatment. Retail clinic services, which are convenient and affordable, help increase access to care and prevent complications that often result in costly emergency room admissions. A major study sponsored by the RAND Corporation and published in the Annals of Internal Medicine found that care at convenient care clinics was equivalent in quality to other settings and 40 to 80 percent less costly.[31]

There are approximately 97 retail clinics serving thousands of patients throughout Pennsylvania. These clinics are affiliated with CVS MinuteClinic, Walmart, Walgreens, FastCare, Geisinger CareWorks, and RiteAid RediClinics. Five retail clinics are located in Allegheny County, each of these records approximately 20-40 patient encounters per day, including weekends and holidays.

HB 100 eliminates the physician collaboration requirement for nurse practitioners who have practiced in collaboration with a physician for at least three years and 3,600 hours. Removing this unnecessary regulation would help increase access to care for Allegheny County residents by lowering the cost of care and increasing consumer choice and competition in healthcare. In recognition of the bill's potential to lower costs and increase business competition, the Federal Trade Commission (FTC) urged the Pennsylvania House of Representatives to pass HB 100 in a January 2018 letter to Rep. Topper. The FTC remarked,

"Removing existing supervision requirements to permit independent APRN-CNP prescribing and practice has the potential to <u>benefit Pennsylvania consumers by increasing competition among health care providers, which likely would improve access to care, contain costs and expand innovation in health care delivery</u>."

---

[31] "Comparing Costs and Quality of Care at Retail Clinics with that of Other Medical Settings for Three Common Illnesses." *Annals of Internal Medicine* [Accessed August 2009].

Maintaining collaborative agreements with physicians can cost each retail clinic as much as $30,000. Without this requirement in place, retail clinics and other providers would be able to pass potential cost savings on to consumers while strengthening the overall business model. In fact, a recent study estimates that HB 100 could save Pennsylvanians $6 billion over the next 10 years.[32]

Organizations like the Pennsylvania Hospital and Healthsystem Association, Commonwealth Foundation, AARP and Americans for Prosperity have voiced their support for HB 100. Given the bill's bipartisan appeal, I again urge you to bring HB 100 to a vote. Please do not hesitate to contact me at (215) 219-8857 or tine@ccaclinics.org with any questions.

Example 2
Convenient Care Clinics:
High Quality Care
QUESTION: How good is the care at convenient care clinics (CCCs)?

ANSWER:
The quality of care provided at CCCs is high. Clinic providers usually include licensed, highly-trained nurse practitioners and sometimes physician assistants who are qualified to diagnose, treat, and prescribe to a scope well beyond the typical scope of services in a convenient care clinic. They are supported by an electronic health record, including established evidence-based protocols, and are supervised by local physicians according to state law. CCCs have provided more than 35 million patient visits to date.

THE FACTS:
• The nurse practitioners (NPs) who generally staff CCCs are registered nurses with master's degrees or doctorates in nursing practice. They are licensed and certified to diagnose, treat and prescribe medications for common medical conditions, as well as administer preventive care.
• Research consistently shows that NPs provide care that is comparable in quality to physician care.[35]
• CCC healthcare professionals use evidence-based protocols that adhere to established clinical practice guidelines and regulations.[36]
• Quality scores and rates of preventive care offered are similar for convenient care clinics as for other delivery settings.[37,39]

---

[32] "The Value of Full Practice Authority for Pennsylvania's Nurse Practitioners." Duke University School of Law. Available at:
https://law.duke.edu/news/pdf/nurse_practitioners_report-PA-TechnicalAppendix.pdf. [Accessed July 2015].

- Convenient care clinics had a 92.72 percent compliance with quality measure for appropriate testing of children with pharyngitis vs HEDIS average of 74.7 percent; they also had an 88.35 percent compliance score for appropriate testing of children with URI vs HEDIS average of 83.5 percent.[36]
- Retail clinics have a return visit rate comparable with standard medical offices -- care is high quality and does not generate additional follow up utilization.[38]
- CCCs use electronic health records, and at the patient's request, these can be shared with a patient's primary care provider in order to facilitate continuity of care. Additionally, the use of EHRs in the clinics monitor evidence-based practice performance.
- CCA's Quality and Safety Standards were developed with input from leading medical, nursing and quality organizations and are more stringent than those recommended by the American Medical Association, American Academy of Family Practitioners and American Academy of Pediatrics. CCA members follow OSHA, CLIA, HIPAA, ADA and CDC requirements and guidelines.
- CCA members are committed to monitoring quality and safety on an ongoing basis, including:

—Peer review and collaborating physician review;
—Aggregating, collecting and reporting data on quality and safety outcomes; and
—Monitoring patient satisfaction, which generally exceeds 90 percent.

[35]Mundinger, Mary. "Primary Care Outcomes in Patients Treated by Nurse Practitioners or Physicians." JAMA. 2000.

[36]Jacoby, Richard, Albert G. Crawford, et al. "Quality of Care for 2 Com-mon Pediatric Conditions Treated by Convenient Care Providers." *American Journal of Medical Quality*. [Accessed 2010].

[37]Mehrotra, Ateev, Llu Hangsheng, John L. Adams, et al. "Comparing Costs and Quality of Care at Retail Clinics with that of Other Medical Settings for 3 Common Illnesses." *Annals of Internal Medicine.151 no. 5*. Pages: 321-328. {Accessed 2009].

[38]Rohner, James E. Kurt B. Angstman, et al. "Early Return Visits by Primary Care Patients: A Retail Nurse Practitioner Visit Versus Standard Medical Office Care." *Population Health Management, 15, No. 4*. Pages: 216-219. [Accessed 2012].

[39]Shrank, William H., Krumme, Alexis A., et al. "Quality of Care at Retail Clinics for 3 Common Conditions." *American Journal of Managed Care. 20, No. 10. Pages*: 793-801. [Accessed 2004].

APPENDIX M
Sample Legislation

Below are two pieces of sample legislation. The first is a piece of federal legislation that deals with the credentialing and enrollment of healthcare providers in Medicare and Medicaid. The first section labeled rationale is not normally included in legislation. It was included here in order to give the potential sponsor and congressional staffers an idea of the legislation's purpose and the need for the bill. The second bill is an example of state legislation that deals with the expansion of scope of practice for pharmacists.

Example 1
Demonstration Project to Study the Cost Saving Potential of Establishing a Joint Credentialing Process for Medicare/Medicaid Providers.

(a) RATIONALE. -- Health care providers seeking to enroll in state Medicaid programs can experience delays of up to six to eight months. These long delays have a detrimental effect on access to care for the nation's most vulnerable patients and drive up the cost of care. Studies show that administrative costs, like those associated with credentialing, can add as much as 30percent to the cost of direct care. These costs are absorbed by all aspects of the healthcare system, including: federal, state, and local governments, hospitals, small physician practices, nurse practitioner-led practices, and residential facilities serving patients with intellectual and developmental disabilities, that depend on Medicaid payments. A 2012 article published in the New England Journal of Medicine states, "Credentialing and other systems that are used to establish contracts between providers and health plans are riddled with redundancy, with many organizations collecting virtually identical information from providers…a coordinated, nationwide credentialing system that is employed across the public and private sectors could save nearly $1 billion per year for providers." A nationwide system of credentialing already exists under the Medicare program. The demonstration described herein would decrease credentialing delays, eliminate unnecessary redundancy in the credentialing process, lower costs and improve access to care by extending Medicare's national credentialing process to the Medicaid program. This goal will be accomplished by creating a joint system of credentialing for the Medicare and Medicaid programs, under which providers who have already met the Medicare program's credentialing requirements would be automatically enrolled in the Medicaid program. Under this demonstration, participating states would waive state Medicaid program credentialing requirements for eligible providers who demonstrate compliance with the Medicare program's credentialing requirements. The purpose of the demonstration is to offer evidence of (1) the cost savings potential associated with establishing a joint provider credentialing process for the Medicare and Medicaid programs; and (2) the effect of the joint Medicare and Medicaid credentialing process on access to care for patients. Although, credentialing delays place administrative burdens on all aspects of the healthcare system, this demonstration focuses on safety-net providers most likely to serve high percentages of Medicaid patients.

(1) ESTABLISHMENT. --
(A) IN GENERAL. --The Secretary shall establish the joint Medicare and Medicaid provider credentialing demonstration under title XVIII of the Social Security Act (42 U.S.C. 1395 et seq.), under which five participating states shall voluntarily agree to waive the credentialing requirements of their state Medicaid programs for eligible providers who have met the requirements for participation in the Medicare program.
(B) NUMBER. --The demonstration shall include up to five states and all the eligible providers within those states who agree to participate in the demonstration.
(C) WRITTEN AGREEMENTS. -- States participating in the demonstration shall enter into written agreements with eligible providers in order to issue of waivers of state Medicaid program credentialing requirements to those eligible providers who have met the requirements for participation in the Medicare program.
(3) WAIVER AUTHORITY. -- The Secretary may waive such requirements of titles XI and XVIII of the Social Security Act as may be necessary to carry out the demonstration.
(D) EVALUATION. -- No later than July 1, 2020, the Secretary shall submit to Congress a report on the demonstration. Such report shall include an analysis of the following:
(1) The reduction in the average time needed for eligible providers participating in the demonstration to complete the Medicare and Medicaid credentialing process. Each year of the demonstration, participating states and the U.S. Department of Health and Human Services shall report the average time needed to credential eligible providers in the Medicare and Medicaid programs, in relation to a base processing time established prior to the initiation of the demonstration.
(2) The reduction in administrative costs to the participating states as a result of the establishment of the joint Medicare and Medicaid credentialing process. Each year of the demonstration, participating states shall report the average administrative cost of processing applications from providers applying to be credentialed and enrolled in a participating state's Medicaid program, in relation to the base yearly cost of processing Medicaid credentialing applications prior to the establishment of the demonstration.
(3) The increase in access reported in the participating states as a result of the establishment of the joint Medicare and Medicaid credentialing process. Each year of the demonstration, participating states shall report the number of visits per month recorded by eligible providers newly enrolled in state Medicaid programs. This number shall be compared to the estimated number of patient visits missed due to delays in the credentialing process prior to the establishment of the joint credentialing process.
(4) Other items the Secretary determines appropriate and relevant.
(E) DEFINITIONS. -- In this section:
(1) DEMONSTRATION. -- The term "demonstration" means the joint Medicare and Medicaid provider credentialing demonstration established under subsection (a).
(2) SECRETARY. -- The term "Secretary" means the Secretary of Health and Human Services.

(3) ELIGIBLE PROVIDER -- The term "eligible provider" includes those providers practicing in retail clinics, nurse-managed health clinics, specialty clinics for people intellectual and physical disabilities, urgent care clinics, federally qualified health centers, federally qualified health centers look-alikes, rural health clinics and school-based health centers within the participating states that: (1) meet all the credentialing requirements for the Medicare program; and (2) apply for a waiver of the credentialing requirements for their state's Medicaid program. Eligible providers who demonstrate completion of all the Medicare credentialing requirements will be granted waivers and automatically enrolled in their participating state's Medicaid program.

(4) RETAIL CLINIC -- The term "retail clinic" is defined as a health care facility located in or adjacent to a retail business location, such as a pharmacy, grocery store, or other retail location open to the public, that offers same day, walk in appointments for services that include, but are not limited to, acute care, some aspects of primary care, wellness, or patient education, and chronic disease management services.

(5) NURSE MANAGED HEALTH CLINIC -- The term "nurse-managed health clinic" is defined in 42 U.S.C.A. § 254c-1a.

(6) URGENT CARE CLINIC -- The term "urgent care clinic" is defined as a stand-alone health care facility that offers same day, walk in appointments for services that include, but are not limited to, acute care, some aspects of primary care, wellness, or patient education, and chronic disease management services, as well as other services that may include, but is not limited to laboratory testing and X-rays.

(7) FEDERALLY QUALIFIED HEALTH CENTER -- The term "federally qualified health center" is defined in 42 U.S.C.A. § 1396d.

(8) FEDERALLY QUALIFIED HEALTH CENTERS LOOK-ALIKE -- The term "federally qualified health center look-alike" is defined in 42 U.S.C.A. § 1396d.

(9) RURAL HEALTH CLINIC - The term "rural health clinic" is defined in 42 U.S.C.A. § 1395x(aa).

(10) SCHOOL-BASED HEALTH CENTER -- The term "school-based health center" is defined in 42 U.S.C.A. § 42 U.S.C.A. § 1397jj.

(11) SPECIALTY CLINICS -- the term "specialty clinics" refers to clinics serving intellectual and physical disabled persons, supported by Medicaid and Medicare.

Example 2

ASSEMBLY, No.
STATE OF NEW JERSEY
218th LEGISLATURE

INTRODUCED

Sponsored by:

An Act expanding access to care through greater use of pharmacists and amending P.L.2003, c.280.

Be It Enacted *by the Senate and General Assembly of the State of New Jersey:*

Section 24 of P.L.2003, c.280 (C.45:14-41) is amended to read as follows:

Definitions relative to pharmacists.
1. "Pharmacist in collaborative practice" means a pharmacist engaged in the collaborative drug therapy management of a patient's drug, biological and device-related health care needs, or other services listed in C.45:14-63 pursuant to a written protocol, in collaboration with a licensed physician, nurse practitioner, or physician assistant and in accordance with the regulations jointly promulgated by the board and the State Board of Medical Examiners and the State Board of Nursing.

"Practice of pharmacy" means a health care service by a pharmacist that includes: compounding, dispensing and labeling of drugs, biologicals, radio pharmaceuticals or devices; overseeing automated medication systems; interpreting and evaluating prescriptions; administering and distributing drugs, biologicals and devices; maintaining prescription drug records; advising and consulting on the therapeutic values, content, hazards and uses of drugs, biologicals and devices; managing and monitoring drug therapy; collecting, analyzing and monitoring patient data; performing drug utilization reviews; storing prescription drugs and devices; supervising technicians, interns and externs; and such other acts, services, operations or transactions necessary, or incidental to, providing pharmaceutical care and education. In accordance with written guidelines or protocols established with a licensed physician, nurse practitioner, or physician assistant, the "practice of pharmacy" also includes collaborative drug therapy management and other services including initiating, modifying, continuing or discontinuing drug or device therapy; ordering or performing of laboratory tests under collaborative drug therapy management; and ordering clinical tests, and laboratory tests.

2. Section 24 of P.L.2003, c.280 (C.45:14-63) is amended to read as follows:
a. No pharmacist shall administer a prescription medication directly to a patient without appropriate education or certification, as determined by the board in accordance with the requirements set forth in the rules jointly promulgated by the board and the State Board of Medical Examiners or Board of Nursing. Such medication shall only be for the treatment of a disease for which a nationally certified program is in effect, or as determined by the board, and only if utilized for the treatment of that disease for which the medication is prescribed or indicated or for which the collaborative drug therapy management permits or is related to a serviced listed in this section and administered pursuant to a written protocol, in collaboration with a physician or nurse practitioner or physician assistant.

b. (1) Notwithstanding any law, rule, or regulation to the contrary, a pharmacist may administer drugs to a patient 18 years of age or older, provided the pharmacist is appropriately educated and qualified, as determined by the board in accordance with the requirements set forth in the rules jointly promulgated by the board and the State Board of Medical Examiners and <u>State Board of Nursing,</u> and provided the drugs are administered under any one of the following conditions:

(a) pursuant to a prescription by an authorized prescriber for a vaccine and related emergency medications;

(b) in immunization programs implemented pursuant to an authorized prescriber's standing order for the vaccine and related emergency medications; or

(c) in immunization programs and programs sponsored by governmental agencies that are not patient specific.

<u>(d) pursuant to a written protocol, in collaboration with an authorized prescriber.</u>

(2) A pharmacist may administer an influenza vaccine to a patient who is seven years of age or older. For a patient who is under 18 years of age, a pharmacist shall not administer a vaccine except with the permission of the patient's parent or legal guardian. For a patient who is under 12 years of age, a pharmacist shall not administer a vaccine unless pursuant to a prescription by an authorized prescriber. Nothing in this subsection shall be construed to require a patient 12-years of age or older to obtain a prescription for an influenza vaccine.

3. <u>A pharmacist may administer tobacco cessation medications (limited to nicotine replacement products) to patients 18 years of age or older pursuant to a written protocol, in collaboration with an authorized prescriber and in accordance with rules adopted by the board.</u>

4. The New Jersey State Board of Pharmacy, the State Board of Medical Examiners, <u>and the State Board of Nursing</u> may, pursuant to the "Administrative Procedure Act," P.L.1968, c.410 (C.52:14B-1 et seq.), adopt rules and regulations as may be necessary to implement the provisions of this act.

5. This act shall take effect on the first day of the fourth month next following the date of enactment.

---

[i] https://www.prb.org/poverty-and-inequality-us-counties/
[ii] https://ssir.org/articles/entry/ten_nonprofit_funding_models
[iii] William Foster & Gail Fine (2007). How Nonprofits Get Really Big. Stanford Social Innovation Review. https://ssir.org/articles/entry/how_nonprofits_get_really_big
[iv] Foster, Kim, & Christiansen (2009). Ten Nonprofit Funding Models. Stanford Social Innovation Review. https://ssir.org/articles/entry/ten_nonprofit_funding_models
https://prositions.com/relationship-strategies-assessment/
[v] Performance Management Revolution. Harvard Business Review (October, 2016)

ENDNOTES

AmWins Group Benefits. "Four Reasons Why Reference-based Pricing Could Become the Norm for Self-insured Employer Groups." Available at: http://www.amwins.com/docs/default-source/Insights/client-advisory_referencepricing_1-15.pdf.

Association of American Healthcare Colleges. "The Complexities of Physician Supply and Demand: Projections from 2014 to 2025." Available at: https://www.aamc.org/download/458082/data/2016_complexities_of_supply_and_demand_projections.pdf. [Accessed 2016].

BMC Health Services Research. Available at: https://bmchealthservres.biomedcentral.com/articles/10.1186/s12913-016-1851-2.

Bennis W, Nanus B. *Leaders: The Strategies for Taking Charge*. New York: Harper and Row Publishers Inc. 1985.

The Commonwealth Fund. "How Will the Affordable Care Act Affect the Use of Health Care Services?" Available at: http://www.commonwealthfund.org/publications/issue-briefs/2015/feb/how-will-aca-affect-use-health-services.

The Commonwealth Fund. "Primary Care: Our First Line of Defense." Available at: http://www.commonwealthfund.org/publications/health-reform-and-you/primary-care-our-first-line-of-defense

"Comparing Costs and Quality of Care at Retail Clinics with that of Other Medical Settings for Three Common Illnesses." *Annals of Internal Medicine*. 2009.

Dan Amira. "By President Obama's Own Standard, This is a Bad Compromise." *N.Y. Maga*zine. Available at: https://perma.cc/C8L5-4TP9. [Accessed 1 August 2011].

Federal Trade Commission. "Policy Perspectives Competition and the Regulation of Advanced Practice Nurses." Available at: https://www.ftc.gov/system/files/documents/reports/policy-perspectives-competition-regulation-advanced-practice-nurses/140307aprnpolicypaper.pdf. [Accessed 2014].

"The Future of Nursing: Leading Change, Advancing Health." *Institute of Medicine*. Page: H-18 (2010). Available at: https://www.nationalacademies.org/hmd/~/media/Files/Report%20Files/2010/The-Future-of-Nursing/Future%20of%20Nursing%202010%20Recommendations.pdf. [Accessed 12 November 2016].

Geedey, NM. "Following a New Roadmap to Leadership Success. Nursing Management. 2004. Pages: 35(8): 49-51.

Hughes, F., Bamford, A., Porter-O'Grady. "Interface Between Global Health Care and Nursing Leadership." *Nurse Leader*. 2006.

Hughes, F.A., Duke, J., Bamford, A., Moss, C. "The Centrality of Policy Entrepreneurship and Strategic Alliances to Professional Leadership Within Key Nursing Roles," *Nurse Leader*. Vol 4, Issue 2, pp 24-27. 2006.

Hughes, F.A. RN, D Nurs. "In Search of a Place at the Table." *Nursing Review*. Pages: 11-12. 2008.

Hughes, F. Policy, "A Practical Tool for Nurses and Nursing." *Journal of Advanced Nursing*, 49(4):331.

Jacoby, Richard, Albert G. Crawford, et al. "Quality of Care for 2 Common Pediatric Conditions. Treated by Convenient Care Providers." *American Journal of Medical Quality*. 2010.

Kislan, M., Bernstein, A., Fearrington, L., and Ives, T. (2016). "Advanced Practice Pharmacists: A retrospective Evaluation of the Efficacy and Cost of Clinical Pharmacist Practitioners Managing Ambulatory Medicare Patients in North Carolina (APPLE-NC)."

Martin-Misner, R., Harbman, P., Donald, F., Reid, K., Kilpatrick, K. et al. (2015). "Cost-effectiveness of Nurse Practitioners in Primary and Specialised Ambulatory Care: Systematic Review." BMJ Open, 5:e007167 doi:10.1136/bmjopen-2014-007167.

Mass, H. "Nursing Leadership." Nursing BC; 2005. Available at: www.findarticles.com. [Accessed June 2008].

Matthew A. Davis, Rebecca Anthopolos, Joshua Tootoo, Marita Titler, Julie P. W. Bynum and Scott A. Shipman. "Supply of Healthcare Providers in Relation to County Socioeconomic and Health Status." *Journal of General Internal Medicine*. 2018.

Mather, M. (2016). "Poverty and Inequality Pervasive in Two-Fifths of U.S. Counties.*" Population Reference Bureau*. [online] Prb.org. Available at: https://www.prb.org/poverty-and-inequality-us-counties/.

Mehrotra, Ateev, and Judith R. Lave. "Visits to Retail Clinics Grew Fourfold From 2007 To 2009, Although Their Share of Overall Outpatient Visits Remain Low." *Health Affairs, 31, No. 9*. 2012.

Mehrotra, Ateev, Llu Hangsheng, John L. Adams, et al. "Comparing Costs and Quality of Care at Retail Clinics with that of Other Medical Settings for 3 Common Illnesses." *Annals of Internal Medicine.151 no. 5*. Pages: 321-328. 2009.

Mundinger, Mary. "Primary Care Outcomes in Patients Treated by Nurse Practitioners or Physicians." JAMA. 2000.

National Governors Association (NGA). The Expanding Role of Pharmacists in a Transformed Health Care System." Available at: www.nga.org/files/live/sites/NGA/files/pdf/2015/1501TheExpandingRoleOfPharmacists.pdf.

"Nursing Leadership in a Changing World.*"* Canadian Nurses Association. *Nursing Now*

No. 18. January 2005.

O'Neil E. "Nursing Leadership: Challenges and Opportunities." Policy, Politics and Nursing
Practice: 2003. Pages: 4(3):173-9. Available at: http://www.ppn.sagepub.com [Accessed June 2008].

Jennifer Perloff, Catherine M. DesRoches and Peter Buerhaus. "Comparing the Cost of Care Provided to Medicare Beneficiaries Assigned to Primary Care Nurse Practitioners and Physicians." Health Services Research. 2016.

Richard Male and Associates. "Helping Nonprofits and NGOs Around the World Thrive in Challenging Times." Available at: http://richardmale.com/. [Accessed 2018].

Rohner, James E. Kurt B. Angstman, et al. "Early Return Visits by Primary Care Patients: A Retail Nurse Practitioner Visit Versus Standard Medical Office Care." *Population Health Management, 15, No. 4*. Pages: 216-219. 2012.

Rudavsky, R, Craig Evan Pollock, Ateev Mehrotra. "The Geographic Distribution, Ownership, Prices, and Scope of Practice at Retail Clinics." *Annals of Internal Medicine, 151, No. 5*. Pages: 321-328. 2009.

Schiff, Maria, et al. "The Role of Nurse Practitioners in Meeting Increasing Demand for Primary Care." National Governors Association. 2012.

Shrank, William H., Krumme, Alexis A., et al. "Quality of Care at Retail Clinics for 3 Common Conditions." *American Journal of Managed Care. 20, No. 10. Pages*: 793-801. 2004.

Stanik-Hutt, J., Newhouse, R., White, K., Johantgen, M., Bass, E., et al. "The Quality and Effectiveness of Care Provided by Nurse Practitioners." *The Journal for Nurse Practitioners*. Pages: 9(8), 492-500. 2013.

Te Pou o Te Whakaaro Nui. The National Centre of Mental Health Research, Information and Workforce Development. Available at: www.tepou.co.nz.

Te Kaunihera Tapuhi O Aotearoa. "Competencies for Nurse Practitioners." Nursing Council of New Zealand. 2008.

Thomas.loc.gov. *Congress.gov | Library of Congress*. Available at: http://thomas.loc.gov. UN Special Rapporteur on the Right to Health (2017)."The Value of Full Practice Authority for Pennsylvania's Nurse Practitioners." Duke University School of Law. Available at: https://law.duke.edu/news/pdf/nurse_practitioners_report-PA-TechnicalAppendix.pdf. [Accessed July 2015].

Vote Smart. "The Voter's Self Defense System." Available at: https://votesmart.org/. [Accessed 2018].

Weinick, Robin M., Rachel M. Burns, Ateev Mehrotra. "Many Emergency Department

Visits Could be Handled at Urgent Care Centers and Retail Clinics." *Health Affairs, 29, No. 9*. Pages: 1630-1636. 2010.

World Health Organisation. "Mental Health Gap Action Programme: Scaling up Care for Mental, Neurological and Substance Abuse Disorders." *World Health Organisation Press, Geneva*. 2010.

Dan Amira. "By President Obama's Own Standard, This is a Bad Compromise." *N.Y. Mag*. Available at: http://nymag.com/daily/intelligencer/2011/08/debt_ceiling_compromise_barack_obama.html [https://perma.cc/C8L5-4TP9]. [Accessed 1, August 2011].

Made in the USA
Middletown, DE
18 February 2023